Plant a Tree

Also by Michael Weiner

Earth Medicine–Earth Foods

Man's Useful Plants

Plant·a·Tree

*A Working Guide to
Regreening America*

by Michael Weiner

Macmillan Publishing Co., Inc.
New York

Collier Macmillan Publishers
London

In his travels from Maine, Massachusetts, and Rhode Island to Korea, China, and Japan between 1907 and 1927, E. H. Wilson took the photographs that appear on the following pages: 114, 118, 126, 129, 132, 134, 136, 139, 142, 147, 149, 151, 153, 154, 163, 165, 167, 169, 171, 172, 175, 191, 201, 203, 207, 211, 213, 227, 238, 244, 255, 257, 258, 260, 273.

Macmillan Publishing Co., Inc.
866 Third Avenue, New York, N.Y. 10022
Collier-Macmillan Canada Ltd.

Library of Congress Cataloging in Publication Data

Weiner, Michael A.
    Plant a tree.

    1. Trees. 2. Tree planting. I. Title.
SB435.W36   635.9'77'0973   73-19048
ISBN 0-02-625660-6

First Printing 1975

Printed in the United States of America

For Janet,
Who Helped Slay the Wolf
That I Might Write in Peace

Acknowledgments

This book largely owes its inspiration to Benton Arnovitz, who first suggested the idea.

To the many municipal arborists and foresters throughout the United States and Canada who so kindly aided me I am grateful. To the staff of the Arnold Arboretum of Harvard University and to the institution itself I am extremely indebted.

I am especially indebted to Beverly S. Nakano for the majority of line drawings, to Maile Yawata for some, and Robley W. Nash, Maine State Entomologist for permission to use several excellent line drawings. The collection of tree photographs was kindly provided by courtesy of the Arnold Arboretum.

Other people who have contributed significantly to the present state of the book are: Henry M. Cathey, Loring E. Clark, Brian Fewer, H. E. Heggestad, Milton Jacoby, Lani Lofgren, Theodore Mastroianni, James T. Oates, William Olkowski, P. P. Pirone, Donald B. Pritchard, Gary O. Robinette, and Donald P. Watson.

The International Shade Tree Conference (ISTC) kindly permitted inclusion of their regional tree lists and deserve special thanks.

Contents

Intro-
duction

We will not . . . shut our eyes to the fact which no observer of men will dispute, that in every age and country are born some persons who belong rather to the past than the present—men to whom memory is dearer than hope—the by-gone ages fuller of meaning than those in the future. These are the natural conservatives whom Providence has wisely distributed, even in the most democratic governments, to steady the otherwise too impetuous and unsteady onward movements of those who, in their love for progress, would obliterate the past, even in its hold on the feelings and imaginations of our race.*

———————

In the extremes life is hard put to survive. In the cold regions on earth (and we do *all* inhabit this planet, no matter our differences) human life can only be maintained by bringing in artificial warmth, and food from more temperate climates is an absolute necessity in the coldest of the cold (seals and other sea animals may be available but vegetable life is certainly scarce).

In the hottest regions, such as the deserts, human life survives only through great ingenuity in transporting water and food from more temperate climates.

At the equator, and within 45 degrees north or south, human and other life forms are most diverse. In this region life is easily maintained.

Similarly, the human mind is most easily stabilized by dwelling in an equatorial reality. While men should not fear the knowledge of their extremes, and even make contact with these regions on occasion (sometimes once is enough), it is in the center that peace resides. Man may travel far in his thinking but must come home to his center for sustenance. The center consists of the basics that have sustained man on earth since his beginnings: abundant food and beverage; companionship; family; and respect for all plants and animals, stones and shadows, ponds and streams, winds and odors; in short, respect for his world.

Trees are very much a part of man's center.

While more species are to be found about the equatorial regions than any other places on earth there are thousands of species, both native and exogenous, that will grow in the United States. Hopefully, this guide will stimulate an increase in the numbers and types of trees beneath which man may seek rest while at the same time the many benefits to air, soil, and water are gained.

In the near past many people worked in some part for the testament they would leave behind. How one would be thought of after one's death was a fairly dominant theme in the minds of many constructive people, except the slaves.

This resounding thought expressed itself in the activities of those who carried it most strongly within themselves: through a work of art (Rodin telling Rilke that "one must work all the time . . . for one's salvation"), a creative act of science, an honest day's work, or a simple tree planted in a patch of earth. When man first began to cultivate plants he did so to provide himself with a constant supply of food. So too were medicinal plants eventually set to grow in little plots about the village. Through time man learned to propagate and maintain other essential plants that gave him, in addition to food and medicine, an abundant supply of shelter-making material, beverages such as tea, coffee, and chocolate, fiber for his clothing, arrow poisons, dyes, perfumes, and eventually highly specialized products such as paper, rubber, and plastics.

Emerging from the forests and other protected surroundings some of our ancestors felt a certain nakedness or exposure. Yet the open fields or burned-over forests were often the easiest habitats in which to cultivate useful plants, and settlements were developed in these areas. These locales also eliminated the need to travel back and forth from the "plantation" to the dwelling.

To re-create some of the soothing protective qualities of the forest while providing themselves with certain useful products, our early agricultural ancestors transplanted familiar useful trees into their settlements.

After tending his gardens, or hunting, man once again rested beneath the canopy of great trees.

As these settlements were expanded into villages and then into towns and cities trees were often omitted from the growing communities. It was only where truly "civilized" communities were established (i.e., regions where the basic necessities were easily produced and where man had time to create works of art and design his living environment with thoughts devoted to aesthetic as well as practical considerations) that trees were set in any great number. The greater the degree of civilization the more numerous were the trees.

———————

* *Andrew Jackson Downing in* The Architecture of Country Houses, *1850, reprinted by Dover Publications, Inc., 1969, p. 265.*   —*Andrew Jackson Downing*

Looking about ourselves today we can see that the same rule still applies. America's oldest, most civilized cities and towns still show grand avenues and common streets filled with great trees. The common, modern communities may have equal (or even greater) *numbers* of trees per square mile, but these are not *great trees*, giants that dwarf man, restoring him to his proper place in nature. Of course, a tree also shields man from the sun and cools and moisturizes the air, while eliminating unpleasant background noises, and these too are dramatic aesthetic sensations. However, I am one of those who believes that most sane people need to be reminded of their relative size in the universe in order to have a sense of orderliness and belonging in their lives.

The Purpose of This Guidebook

By disseminating this little book I hope to restore respect for great trees. Trees that will grow with people, through several human generations, carrying a continuity that is unavailable from modified little hybrids. The peculiar "modern" trees may have characteristics that make them *initially* desirable, such as rapid growth, uniformity, and controlability, but through time they fail to attain the grandeur available to us only from tall, growing species. It should also be remembered that if trees do in fact purify the air (they do), provide us with oxygen (they do), add moisture (yes), and baffle noise (certainly), then the larger the tree the greater its contribution to these desirable qualities in our lives.

Trees must again be planted that eventually dwarf not only man but his machines and even his buildings! (Will giant sequoias grow in cities?) We must get away from those maniacal architects and knee-jerk landscape architects who go along with them who see trees as small daubs of rubber on cardboard mock-ups of their buildings.

In a recent article for the trade (*Landscape Architecture*, July 1973, p. 360) one innovative writer asked and answered the following question: "What's wrong with plastic trees? My guess is that there is very little wrong with them. Much more can be done with plastic trees and the like to give most people the feeling that they are experiencing nature." The same writer went on to say that people will respond to nature the way they are *taught* to respond and that "responsible interventions" may be useful means of programming such response.

Note the word "feeling" in the above quotation. To the author of this article nature is not a real phenomenon. Trees *are* mere daubs of rubber to them and it is suggested that people be taught to see trees the same way.

It is, in part, to counter this maniacal attitude that this guidebook to very *real* trees is written!

The individual property holders, leasers, or occupants of America must take responsibility for their foliar environments; both for the immediate future and a future beyond our own life spans. We must plant for our children's children as the wisest of our grandfathers did for us.

Information and Illustrations from Antique Texts on Trees

To compose this guidebook several older books about tree-planting were utilized. Here were found sound, basic principles developed in ages when men did things by *themselves*, keeping to a minimum their reliance on man-made resources. One result of this research into the "antique" is the inclusion here of many natural, or organic, fertilizers that are easily available but at present in little use. Scant space is given to the overly prescribed commercial fertilizers. The "modern" fertilizers may act more quickly, yielding quicker initial growth, but the manures and other "old fashioned" fertilizers give longer-lasting benefits to the tree while they add humus to the soil.

It is important to note that, while traditional ideas about the selection and growth of trees are incorporated, current research has not altogether been overlooked. Newly devised biological methods of pest control and problems of pollution and trees are included.

Not only were antique books gleaned for useful, productive planting and maintenance procedures as well as for parameters of species selection, but most of the illustrations, as well, were borrowed from another time.

Here, the photographic competence of two of the great men of the plant world are featured together in quantity for the first time. The tree photographs of E. H. Wilson and Alfred Rehder are included not only for their excellent technical qualities but also because they transmit a sense of grandeur while projecting ageless windows into the future. They are, in a sense, timeless.

During expeditions to China, Korea, and Japan E. H. Wilson brought back to America some very hardy and beautiful species that have since been planted in profusion. Throughout this century (man being a tinkerer of nature) some of these species have been "modified" through cloning or hybridization. Once again these early tree portraits should prove useful, as representative images of the tree prototypes once abundant in America. With enough interest some of the most desirable of these species will once again dominate the gray cities and picturesque towns of our country.

Trees and Pollution

In addition to the important aesthetic gains provided by an abundance of trees we are all generally aware of the role our plant allies play in the struggle to avoid choking in our technological waste.

It is a well-known fact that trees and other green plants produce oxygen and consume carbon dioxide, and this point will not be expanded here. However, it is worth remembering that *most* atmospheric oxygen is produced by plankton and other *ocean* plants as well as by photolysis in the ionosphere. Although terrestrial vegetation provides only about 10–15 percent of atmospheric oxygen, this is still a critical quantity for an earth growing in oxygen-consuming creatures and inventions. It may be handy to remember that each acre of a growing forest produces about four tons of oxygen each year; the oxygen requirements of eighteen people. Therefore, trees are now and will continue to be essential oxygen-producers.

Dr. H. E. Heggestad writes about "Plants that Withstand Pollution and Reduce It" in the 1972 *Yearbook of Agriculture*:

Plants . . . reduce pollutants in water and soil. They also remove significant amounts of gaseous pollutants and particles from the air. The microscopic plants in soil also reduce air pollutants and degrade many toxic chemicals that enter the soil.

Plants hold topsoil in place. Thus, they reduce sediment and excess nutrients which pollute water. Plants also make effective sound barriers, and so reduce noise pollution.

In the United States, ozone is the major pollutant that affects vegetation.

Other air pollutants of concern . . . are peroxyacetyl nitrate (PAN), sulfur dioxide, and fluorides. Nitrogen dioxide and ethylene are not as likely to cause acute injury, but they may stunt the growth of plants and cause their premature old age.

Ozone and PAN are photochemical oxidants formed by sunlight acting on products of fuel combustion, par-

ticularly the nitrogen dioxide and hydrocarbons that come from motor vehicle exhausts.

Ethylene is also a product of fuel combustion, and to a very minor extent it is produced by vegetation.

Sulfur dioxide results from smelting ores and from burning fuels containing sulfur—such as coal and crude oil.

Fluorides are emitted in the production of aluminum, steel, ceramics, and phosphorous fertilizers.

Plants are good air pollution detectives . . . West Germany requires planting of forest species around certain industries as a check on emission of toxicants. Sensitive plants may show visible effects of pollution long before their effects can be observed on animals or materials.

Certain relationships between species have been established. For instance, European linden is more tolerant of ozone than is white ash. On the other hand, linden is more susceptible to salt in the soil.

Salts occur naturally in soils and waters and may be considered pollutants only when man introduces extraneous salts. This obviously occurs when salt is used to de-ice city streets and highways.

Salts supply plants with mineral nutrients essential for their growth. When present in excess, however, salts are injurious.

In humid regions, rain readily leaches salts out of the soil, and salinity is not normally a problem. In sub-humid and arid regions, plants must be watered, and salts present in irrigation waters are the main source of salt accumulation in the soil. Many irrigated areas in modern as well as in ancient times have been "salted out" or severely damaged as a result of salt accumulation.

When you water your plants they absorb water, but leave behind in the soil most of the salts that were in the water. The only way to remove these salts is to use more water than that which evaporates and is used by the plants. If the excess water can drain away below the roots, it will carry with it the excess, unwanted salts. This is called leaching.

Leaching with a 6-inch depth of water, for example, will reduce the salinity of the top foot of soil by 50 percent, and a 12-inch depth of water will reduce it by 80 percent. Chemical amendments, such as gypsum, are needed to reclaim sodium-affected soils. Subsoil drainage must be provided if it is not naturally adequate.

Trees from normally saline habitats, like the tamarisks and mangroves, are highly tolerant {of salt}. Other tolerant species include the black locust and honey locust. Coniferous trees, such as the blue spruce, white pine, and Douglas fir, are relatively sensitive, but ponderosa pine and eastern red cedar are moderately tolerant as are also white oak, red oak, spreading juniper and arborvitae.

Plants normally absorb salts through their roots, but

many will take up salts directly through their leaves if the foliage is wetted by sprinkling. Fruit trees, such as plum and other stone fruits, and citrus absorb salts so readily through their leaves that sprinkler systems usually must be designed to avoid wetting the foliage of these trees.

The extensive salt damage to trees, shrubs, and grass along streets and highways de-iced by salt is harder to control by plant selection. Salt concentrations in water draining off the highway can be so high that no plant adapted to northern conditions may be able to survive. Further, the loss of magnificent roadside trees may not be acceptable, even if some humble salt-tolerant replacement species is available.

It would be better to install drains to carry the brine solutions away from the highway without damaging roadside trees. Design of new highways and roadside plantings should take into account the effects and de-icing by salt.

Salinity, like air pollution, cannot be completely eliminated. However, if adequately salt-tolerant plant species are readily available, the salinity may not be damaging.

Trees as "Air Conditioners"

Dr. Garry Robinette, executive director of the American Society of Landscape Architects, has described in the March 1968 issue of *Horticulture* some other important mechanisms whereby trees purify our environment:

At a time when there is much talk about air pollution, it appears that one of the greatest sources of natural air conditioning is being overlooked. Plant materials are among the most effective air conditioners in existence. In this age of great public and governmental concern over the pollution of our air supply, it seems appropriate to point out that plants help condition and cleanse our air more than we realize.

Basic to an understanding of this function of plants is familiarity with both human and plant respiratory cycles. Every high school biology student knows that human beings and animals inhale oxygen and exhale carbon dioxide among other gases. Since plants need and absorb carbon dioxide from the atmosphere for use in their photosynthetic process and since they also give off oxygen as a waste product, there is obviously a strong interdependence between plants and man. The plants function primarily to purify our air by absorbing harmful excess carbon dioxide and by giving off oxygen vital to man's survival. Without vegetation and animals the life-cycle on earth would be broken.

Actually, there are other ways in which plants condition our air. The functions of commercial interior air conditioners include heating or cooling, humidifying or dehumidifying, cleaning and circulation of air, as well as

How Plants Condition the Air: The human-plant respiratory cycle.

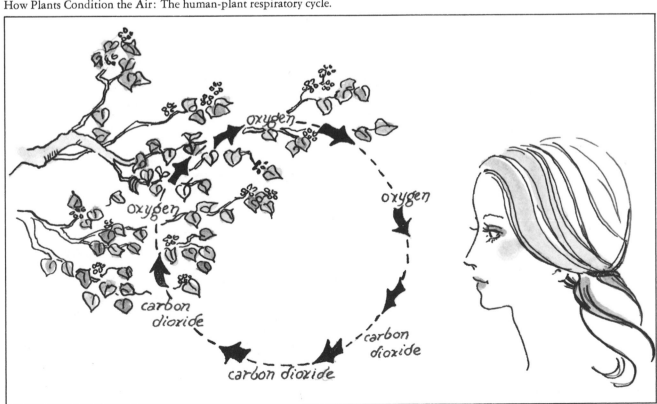

Dilution

ventilation. Plants, as air conditioners, also control temperature, air flow, and moisture content. Their efficiency in these aspects may be demonstrated in a discussion of climate control with plants. For the purpose of this discussion, however, we are concerned with air conditioning as an engineering function of plant materials. This involves primarily contaminant collection and control.

Plants do remove from the air impurities such as airborne dirt and sand, fly ash, dust, pollen, smoke odors and fumes. It has been said correctly that "plants eat dust." There are at least six basic ways in which they do this. These methods or techniques are: (1) dilution, (2) precipitation or filtration, (3) narcosis, (4) oxidation, (5) air washing, (6) reodorization or masking.

Dilution refers simply to the mixing of good or clean air with polluted air. The commercial air conditioner does this by forcing good air into a area containing stale

impure air. Plants also mix good and bad air but, rather than forcing one kind into another, filtration and dilution takes place. The uncontaminated, oxygen-enriched air is present in, around and under vegetation. As the bad air flows through the good air, it is mixed with it and diluted.

The method of electrical precipitation in air conditioning involves the electrical charging of dust particles (which also carry odor) and the collection of these particles on a grid having a strong force field. Plants work on the same basis but, instead of an iron grid, the plants use leaves, branches and stems and, instead of an electrical charge, the pubescence (hairiness) and moisture on the leaves trap the dust particles and hold them until they are washed away by the rain.

Narcosis is a temporary state of depression and when used in regard to air conditioning it means an area rela-

Reodorization

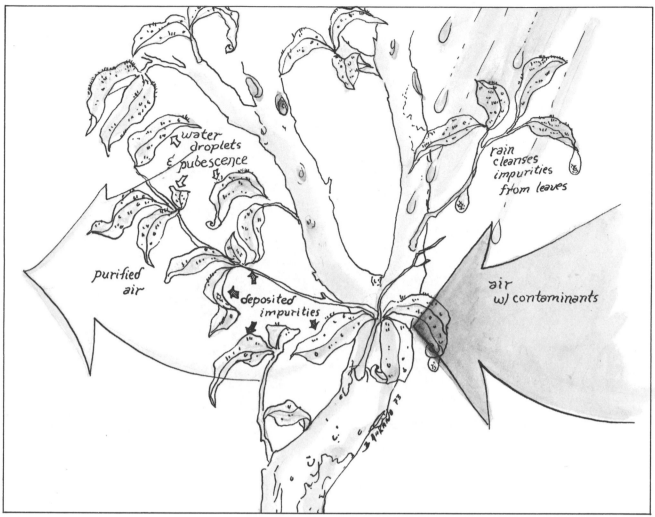

Precipitation

tively free of turbulence as opposed to the surrounding areas. In this semi-void particles are allowed to settle out of the contaminant laden air. A wooded area or a forest thus provides such a calm settling chamber for air pollutants.

Oxidation is the introduction of excess oxygen into polluted air. An acceptable ration of "good" to "bad" air is 1 part of bad air to 3,000 parts of relatively pure air. Along many of our nation's highways the ratio may be as low as 1 to 1,000. It has been proposed that, where possible, a half mile wide green belt be planted on either side of the freeways and expressways. These green belts could be converted into park lands and would readjust the air balance in two ways: 1. The unpolluted fresh air would dilute and diminish the smog built up over the expressways; 2. The green vegetation would actually remove pollutants and restore oxygen to the atmosphere.

The amount of water transpired by a growing plant is, likewise, considerable. A birch tree, for instance, standing alone in the open loses 75 to 100 gallons per day in the summer. Mature apple trees transpire as much as 600 tons of water per day. The fact that plants hold in suspension around themselves and on their leaves large amounts of water enables them to act as air cleaners in another way. In commercial air conditioning air washers are designed to produce intimate contact between air and water for the purpose of obtaining the transfer of heat and moisture between the two and removing impurities from the air. Thus, the moisture held in suspension on and around a plant serves as an air washer for the polluted, windborne air passing around or over a plant and its leaves.

Commercially, fumes and odors are controlled by masking. This is accomplished by replacing the obnoxious odor with a stronger, more powerful, bearable or pleasing smell. This reodorization, accomplished by air conditioners or aerosal atomizers, is also performed by many plants. There are many with particularly fragrant blossoms, for instance—Korean spice viburnum, honeysuckle, jasmine, mock-orange—which may be effectively planted between the source and the recipient of a disagreeable odor.

Clean, pure air of the proper temperature and humidity is absolutely essential to man. For this reason he has devised air conditioners to perform this function for his

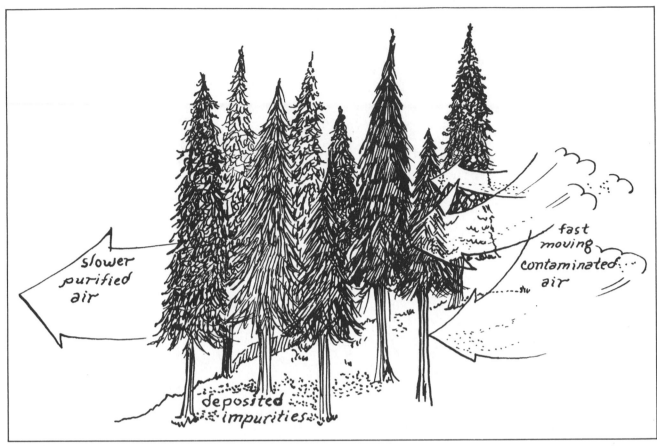

Narcosis

interior environment. It would be foolish, indeed, to neglect to take fullest advantage of the capabilities of the great natural air conditioners which can effectively perform the same function for his exterior environment.

Oxidation

Trees and Soil

While plastic or zero trees in urban areas would diminish both the quality of life and the atmosphere, laying waste the forest trees would encourage the loss of topsoil over wide areas, while diminishing the quan-

tity of available drinking water throughout the region.

The most startling example of the results of massive forest destruction was first recorded over 4,000 years ago in China. "The Revenge of the Trees"* as told by Joseph Gaer might wisely be incorporated into every child's package of bedtime stories. America, too, must be prepared for another "Emperor Shun"; should he appear in the form of colorful magazine ads which depict the joys of a "managed forest," a friendly lumberman who informs us of our "growing needs" for toilet and other paper, or a helpful government official who reminds us that the national forests are for "mixed use."

EMPEROR SHUN'S ORDER

In another land, a great distance from our own, and in other times, going back to the dim past, there flowed a mighty river through long and twisting valleys and vast plains.

That land was China, the time was more than four thousand years ago, and the river, not unlike our own Mississippi, was the Hwang Ho—the Yellow River, the River of Destiny.

In those far-off days all the land along the Yellow River, and deep inland both north and south, was covered with trees. From the Kunlun Mountains in the far west, through Kansu and Shawan, Shansi and Shensi, across Honan, and all the way to the Gulf of Pohai in the

Air washer

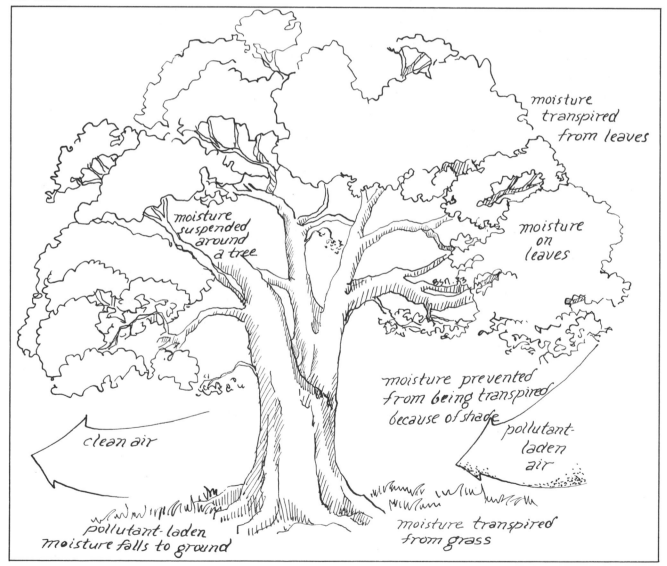

* *Reprinted by permission of Brandt & Brandt, 101 Park Avenue, New York. Copyright 1939 by Joseph Gaer.*

Yellow Sea, the banks of the Yellow River were bordered with trees. The forests were full of singing birds and wild animals; nuts and berries grew in abundance; and in the spring wildflowers covered the ground.

For many centuries the people on either side of the Yellow River had little to complain about to their ancestors, whom they worshiped. They sang songs, played strange lutes, and offered up little sacrifices to the Great Spirits of Nature. Life flowed happily in the part of the Flowery Kingdom that lay along the wooded banks of the Yellow River.

Then, about four thousand years ago, the land came under the rule of an emperor of the Hsia dynasty, named Shun. Emperor Shun carefully observed the rich forests on either side of the twenty-five-hundred-mile river, and decided that the soil was good for cultivation.

If the trees were cleared from the land, he reasoned, crops could be grown upon it. If the soil cultivated produced good crops, the farmers would be rich. If the farmers grew rich, the emperor would be able to levy new taxes upon them.

New sources of income were always welcomed by the royal head. And so it happened that Shun, after the manner of emperors, issued an order. It was dated nearly two thousand years before the days of the philosopher Kung. This order stated that the land along the Yellow River must be cleared for farming, and the Emperor appointed a forester by the name of Yih to destroy by fire all the forests along that section.

What Forester Yih thought about the emperor's order no one has ever recorded. But that he carried out the royal command thoroughly there can be no doubt, for soon after receiving his commission Forester Yih started many fires. Long stretches of forest were turned into ashes. Most of the wild life was destroyed with the trees; some escaped into the southern provinces of China.

For a while there was rejoicing over the land plowed and seeded. For the land, rich in humus, grew crops plentiful beyond all expectation. Emperor Shun's name entered into grateful prayers.

But this happy state of affairs did not last. The topsoil of the cleared land, in rapidly melting snows and heavy rains, began to slide down into the Yellow River. Erosion crept across the farms. Hot winds of summer dried the fine soil; more hot winds that followed carried the rich topsoil away in storms of dust. The streams emptying into the rivers swelled with silt. Higher and higher rose the Yellow River. It broke through the barrier of banks and dikes. Water flooded the land.

When this happened the first time, people said it was unheard of, that it had not happened in ten generations or more. And when the flood subsided they returned

to their farms, hoping it would not happen again for another ten generations or more.

But the Yellow River, which resembles our own Mississippi, began to show its power of destruction when no longer restrained by forests, until finally, each year during the heavy rainfalls, people began to dread the invasion of their homes by the waters of the river.

With the passing of time the floods became more frequent, the land grew poorer, and the misery of the people became greater.

Close to two thousand years passed from the days of Emperor Shun to the days of Emperor Chin Shih Huang Ti. Emperor Chin gave much thought to the impoverished land. The suffering of the people along the Yellow River, he realized, was due to their poverty. And their poverty was due to the land's having been denuded of its forests.

The happiness and security of a people is the responsibility of its government, thought Chin. He therefore issued an order that the mistakes of Emperor Shun should be rectified, and the land along the Yellow River again be restored to the forests. "He who fails to grow a tree," the order read, "shall go coffinless to the grave."

The people were willing enough to follow the Emperor's order. But they were helpless. The land did not belong to them. The land was owned by the feudal lords.

When the order became public, the feudal lords assembled in great secrecy. They indignantly decided that the Emperor had no right to interfere with their manner of handling their own property. The governors of the provinces agreed with the feudal lords. They all shook their sage heads: the sovereign rights of the provinces must be upheld.

Many men went to their graves without coffins. But the land was not reforested.

In the four thousand years following Emperor Shun's decree the Yellow River has destroyed millions of lives and caused untold misery. Each time the poor people rebuild their homes from the ruins left by the flood and bravely start out anew, the waters of the Yellow River sweep over them and wipe them out again.

The Yellow River has become known as the Unconquerable, the Scourge of the Sons of Han, China's Sorrow.

"The Spirits of the Forest are taking revenge," the people of China said. For the people believed that the tree gods were aroused and would not relent until they were restored.

The people of China believed that trees have souls and spirits like human beings. They believed that when tree spirits are driven out they wait for new trees to grow, in which they can again reside in peace.

Successful Tree-Planting Programs
Cities, Towns, and Special Programs

Many cities and towns in America are committed to "beautifying" with foliage but San Francisco stands apart in having designed a program that is motivating much tree planting by *citizens*. Other cities may have greater numbers and older trees, but these were planted in an earlier time and are unfortunately not the result of contemporary planning concepts. Some cities have outplanted San Francisco with regard to the number of new trees, but no other major American city has been as successful in eliciting support from its inhabitants.

Aside from the fact that San Francisco is one of America's most charming cities and has often attracted thousands of dynamic altruistic individuals, there is another factor that has enabled their "Plant a Tree" program to gain such success. The key factor is a city government honestly committed to a retreeing of the streets and roadways without regard to which department gets the credit. In other words, the San Francisco Department of Public Works *does not insist* on planting all trees with department crews.

Somewhere along the line the decision was made to have as many trees planted as possible and most of the "red tape" was eliminated for those who wished to do it themselves. (However, even with the streamlining of bureaucratic problems and the involvement of so many individuals in the planting program, many barren San Francisco streets still await the touch of life.)

In some American cities it is actually *illegal* to plant trees in the inner city on public property. Individuals who inquire about permission to cut open concrete sidewalks are warned to consult the city building codes or are told to visit the local botanical garden to see trees in the city.

The success of San Francisco's street tree program may be duplicated elsewhere by following the methods used to encourage and coordinate private efforts by the San Francisco Department of Public Works.

Anyone interested in planting one or several trees on his own or city property receives the following printed material on inquiry. Perhaps this material will be a useful guide for community groups in other places, as well as in San Francisco.

* * * * * * *

For additional information please contact the Street Planting Division, Department of Public Works, 558-4057.

* * * * * * *

SUGGESTED PROCEDURES FOR NEIGHBORHOOD STREET TREE PLANTING PROJECTS

ENLIST several neighbors to help activate a project in your block in the section of the block where you live.

* * * * * * *

GIVE the application blank and the information sheet from the City to your neighbors. Carry the fact sheet with you; your neighbors will have many questions about the project.

* * * * * * *

MAKE a personal recheck to see if the homeowner has made up his mind. This may be done by telephone; choose the method which fits the situation.

* * * * * * *

CONTACT VOLUNTEERS and helpers; pick up applications and get them to the Department of Public Works, Street Planting Division, 2323 Army Street. Permits will be mailed back to individual homeowners or to the group leader if desired.

* * * * * * *

FOLLOWING receipt of permits, contact homeowners to learn if they'll have the trees put in by a contractor, or whether it will be a do-it-yourself job. The homeowner has permission to do his own work.

* * * * * * *

MAKE a list of homeowners who wish work done by a contractor. The project leader can contact several contractors and get comparative bids for the work.

* * * * * * *

CALL people to notify them when work will be done by contractor.

* * * * * * *

PAYMENT is a matter to be settled between the homeowner and the contractor. The homeowner will be billed individually, not as a member of a group.

* * * * * * *

(It's suggested the issue not be forced if the homeowner does not wish to plant, or have planted, an individual tree. At all times, all concerned should be made to know that this project is all on a voluntary basis.)

A RECOMMENDED PROCEDURE FOR YOUR STREET TREE PLANTING PROJECT

Fill out the application (yellow form) and mail it to the Street Planting Division office. (If in doubt of the kind of tree to plant put on your application "As Recommended.") Refer to the enclosed brochure of the Street Tree Exhibit and the booklet "Recommended Trees for San Francisco."

In a short time after receiving the application a repre-

(Sample Note, Useful for Starting a Block Project)

Dear Neighbor:

Within the next few days I will call on you to ask that you join
with the rest of the block in planting a tree on the sidewalk in
front of your property.

By planting a tree in front of your property our block will
look more attractive. The value of your property will be
raised without raising your tax assessment. Trees reduce
smog and also act as a baffle for street noises.

Your neighbors will submit requests for tree planting permits
as a unit. I will contact you and ask that you sign a permit
request. A representative from the Department of Public
Works will advise us on the best locations and kinds of trees
for our block.

If you are not the property owner, would you contact the owner
and let him know you support the tree planting project
in our block?

                                        Sincerely yours,

                                        Block Captain
                                        Tree Planting Program

(A form used by the Richmond District Community Council)

sentative of the Division will visit the site, mark the sidewalk for the desired number of trees, and if you are home, will discuss and suggest a number of trees that would thrive and be compatible in your area. If you are not home at the time of call the representative will leave a note or call you.

If a group of neighbors are planting ten or more trees on the block the City will schedule the cutting and the opening of the sidewalk at no cost to the project. In most cases it may take two to three months for this service. We recommend that all of the signed applications be mailed in together indicating the project leader by name. When our representative goes to your area he will contact the leader.

During the waiting period you could make preparations in advance of starting your tree planting project.

If you desire to have a contractor to do the job completely this would be the time to shop for the best price for the best job. We suggest that you follow the Street Planting Division's recommendations for planting. Let the contractor know how you want the job installed and hold him to it. Also, you might ask to see a sample of the trees that he is going to install for you and inquire what guarantee he makes.

If your group intends to plant the trees themselves, sharing the work or doing it individually, we suggest: Locate the desired trees, making partial payment with the agreement that the nursery will hold the trees for you until you ask for them.

Arrange for a debris box or other method for the disposal of the subsoil and other materials.

Arrange for the delivery of a well mixed top soil. A representative of the Planting Division will be glad to discuss this subject with you and make recommendations as to quantity, how to mix with the native soil, etc.

If supporting posts and straps are available, the Planting Division will supply them at no cost. Also we will gladly demonstrate how the preparation of the planting should be handled.

CARING FOR TREES IS INVESTMENT PROTECTION

In the short span of eight or nine years the homeowners and the businessmen of San Francisco have planted some 75,000 street trees. No one can deny that our beautiful City looks more attractive with this new tree population.

The initial monetary value of these young trees is over $2.5 million, and with proper care their value will increase each year. The aesthetic value to a neighborhood as well as the value to health should not be overlooked.

The Department of Public Works Planting Division offers a few suggestions in regard to the proper care of one's tree.

Watering is most important. Irrigate so that the water penetrates deep and as often as is necessary.

Examine the tree ties. Do not allow them to bind or to cut into the bark of the tree.

Make the post supports secure and straight for as long as the tree requires support.

Weed the area around the tree and apply frequent light applications of fertilizer.

Protect your investment, do not neglect your tree.

For free tree planting information write Planting Division, Department of Public Works, 2323 Army Street, or call 558-4057.

In addition to these helpful guidelines, the interested individual also receives two general motivating brochures which are illustrated with photographs showing the difference between treed and barren streets; a diagrammatic picture of the Funston Avenue Street Tree Exhibit, helpful because it gives the common names of trees growing on this avenue, with coded identification numbers, making tree selection more alive than available from a book; a list of nurseries, planter box suppliers, and concrete saw-cutting services; a simple application for a permit to plant sidewalk trees (which does *not* have to be notarized); a diagram that shows how to plant, both in containers and in sidewalk cuts, as well as a step-by-step instruction sheet for planting and maintenance (see later chapters in this book for the details); and a well-organized booklet of all recommended trees that includes the common and scientific name, description, soil and moisture requirements, and miscellaneous comments about each tree.

This is an excellent program for any city to adopt, and further details can be received by writing to: Supervisor, Street Planting Division, Bureau of Street Cleaning, City and County of San Francisco, Department of Public Works, 2323 Army Street, San Francisco, California.

The city of St. Louis, in cooperation with their Division of Forestry, has a unique idea for encouraging the planting of trees. The following card is sent out with the homeowner's water bill. It is notable for the streamlined organization that yields a planted tree or trees for the individual who mails just one card.

We may ask why the Water Department involved itself with street tree planting in St. Louis. Did the directors realize that trees would be the most productive method for holding rainwater in the water table?

The city of Toledo, Ohio, has one of the most productive street tree-planting programs in the United States, having planted approximately 75,000 trees in the past ten years. The impetus for this activity and

How you can have street trees planted in front of Your Home or Business Property

The Department of Parks, Recreation And Forestry will be happy to plant street trees in front of your home or business property in an area between the sidewalk and curb. City ordinance requires that a fee of $10 be charged for each tree planted. To order, indicate your choice (according to planting space available) and return this completed card with your check or money order. The Forestry Department will inspect and approve the planting site. Trees are planted in spring and late fall.

TREES AVAILABLE — Please indicate your choice

For less than 4 ft. planting areas with limited limb spread
- ☐ European Linden
- ☐ Bradford Callery Pear
- ☐ Emerald Queen Maple
- ☐ Redbud

For 4 to 6 ft. planting areas and up to 30 ft. limb spread
- ☐ Red Maple
- ☐ Sweet Gum
- ☐ Marshal Seedless Ash
- ☐ Green Ash

For greater than 6 ft. planting areas and unlimited limb spread
- ☐ Pin Oak
- ☐ American Linden
- ☐ Norway Maple
- ☐ White Ash

For planting areas under overhead wires
- ☐ Rosebud
- ☐ Purple Leaf Plum
- ☐ Radiant Flowering Crabapple
- ☐ Bradford Callery Pear

Enclosed is $_____ for _____ trees which I request (check box) be planted in front of my home or business property.

ADDRESS WHERE TREES ARE TO BE PLANTED

PROPERTY OWNER'S NAME

PROPERTY OWNER'S ADDRESS IF NOT SAME AS PLANTING ADDRESS

SEND CHECK OR MONEY ORDER MADE PAYABLE TO:

DIVISION OF FORESTRY
Department Of Parks, Recreation And Forestry
5600 Clayton Road (In Forest Park)
St. Louis, Missouri 63110

commitment to a green city was initiated by a crisis. More than 25,000 majestic elm trees were destroyed over a period of time by the Dutch elm disease before the Toledo city fathers recognized the severity of the disease and its eventual ramifications. Since then a commitment has been made to replace the lost elms and to protect the remaining trees from pests, injury, and neglect.

One key lesson from the Toledo tragedy has been to avoid planting just *one* species in an entire neighborhood. While individual streets generally show a single species in uniform row, neighborhoods are now planted with *many* varieties to avoid the possibility of losing all trees in one area as a result of a single invading organism.

The Toledo Forestry Department now plants more species and varieties than any other city in America. As a result of the severe Dutch-elm-disease trauma as many as 24 different varieties of a single species (maple) have been planted throughout the city. Each year newly introduced varieties are added, while varieties that have proven unsatisfactory are discarded.

The city of New York is seldom thought of as being particularly green with trees, yet the Department of Parks plants about 11,000 trees each year. Of this number approximately 9,000 are set out in street plantings while 2,000 trees go into the city parks.

Despite the great losses that occur as a result of mechanical injury, vandalism, and dog urine, which injures the bark and exposes the tree to insect and fungal attack, New York City has a tree population of over 2.5 million trees. Under the conditions in which these poor creatures must survive, New York's tree program must be listed as a mild success. Tough city conditions now limit the list of "highly recommended street trees" to about one dozen species and includes Callery pear, Christine Buisman elm, dawn redwood, flowering Japanese cherry, ginkgo, honey locust, London plane, seedless ash, red oak, Regent sophora, silver linden, willow oak, and zelkova "Village Green."

The courage shown by this city Parks Department might be emulated in other cities that have fewer problems in the extreme but that still fail to plant any trees in downtown areas on the premise that "nothing will grow there."

The city of Boston, once resplendent with trees, and still spotted with many majestic specimens, is now undertaking a "Plantree" project, which, it is hoped, will result in a much restored foliar appearance.

This project, the idea of Joseph E. Curtis, commis-

sioner of the Department of Parks and Recreation, basically simplifies the bureaucratic problems involved for individuals who wish to plant trees by eliminating the need to obtain permits. Also, donations through a memorial program are solicited to enable the department to regreen the barren streets. For a fixed sum, trees are planted in a park or street and named for the donor. Those who contribute ten or more trees are allowed to choose the site for those trees.

"We urge you to plant, plant trees—wherever you find suitable space and reasonable chance for survival" (Plantree, Boston).

While this program is to be commended it is hoped that some of the funds committed for the bicentennial program in Boston (and other American cities) will be diverted for a truly lasting and useful monument—trees.

In Philadelphia the Pennsylvania Horticultural Society is hoping to plant as many as 10,000 new trees in 33 city parks by 1976. Funds for trees are contributed by individuals whose names are entered on an honor roll. While 10,000 trees may seem a large number it is quite small in relation to the 3 to 5 *million* tree population in the city's parks. By comparison, the city of Glasgow, Scotland plants 25,000 trees each *year!*

The Horticultural Society is attempting to tie the plantings in with the nation's bicentennial celebration. A spokeswoman, Mrs. Ernesta Ballard, estimates "the average life span of a tree in an urban environment is about 100 years." Further, ". . . many trees that were planted about the time of the 1876 centennial will be dying."

Here then is the nucleus of an idea for America's bicentennial celebrations. Instead of wasting millions of dollars on parades (with legacies of litter) or on more buildings, perhaps the national commission will suggest that state commissions and private groups invest instead in massive tree plantings. Mrs. Linda Parrish, a schoolteacher from Universal City, Texas, recently wrote the following in a letter to the *Arborist's News*: "If every American planted one tree in memory of the Declaration of Independence and the Constitution of the United States, then, long after the speeches and parades, the trees would stand as living memorials dedicated to life, liberty, and the pursuit of happiness guided by law and order."

Marblehead, Massachusetts, is a coastal New England town that best typifies what parts of America can once again become. Except for an ugly, untreed, business district that runs for three or four blocks on Atlantic Avenue, this town is one of the most densely green inhabited areas in America.

In walking through "Old Town," a magnificently maintained link with America's origins, one is impressed with sensations of tranquillity long since gone in most of our towns. Through the half-drawn window shades one sees people reading quietly, playing the piano, or romping with their children on hand-loomed carpets. Fireplaces burn, copper hardware glows, and everywhere trees seem to protect these domestic cameos.

Of course, the trees of this town have not come all this way by themselves. As in other Massachusetts towns, Marblehead has a tree warden, whose job it is to look after the existing trees and plant new ones wherever possible. Loring E. Clark is not an average town employee. He works harder at his job than most people (for the past thirty years) because he feels "he wants to leave something for the future."

Since Clark's tree program is more than typical of most American towns it is included here verbatim as it appeared in the town report for 1972. While it is hoped this program may serve as an example for those in the business of caring for trees elsewhere in America it is suggested that fewer pesticides be employed and some of the biological controls outlined in the chapter on maintenance be attempted.

TREE WARDEN

To the Citizens of Marblehead:

I respectfully submit my report for the year ending December 31, 1972.

January to March we have the pruning, trimming and lifting up of all elms, lindens, oaks, etc., throughout the town. In March or April, as soon as the soil is workable, we start tree planting. The town is still accepting so many new streets and the demand for new trees is far greater than the supply; therefore I plant by request. Each tree is wrapped to stop the bark from drying out during the summer and is also watered through the dry periods. When the foliage starts to come on all trees throughout the town, the tree planting program must be stopped and the trees are planted in the town nursery and planted again in the fall. A total of 407 trees was planted this year. Auto accidents, storms and vandalism necessitated the replacement of 62 trees this year. This is an increase over last year. Trees planted were Lavallei and Paul's scarlet hawthorn, Japanese flowering cherry (Kwanzan), Mt. Fuji cherry, Idaho, globe flowering locust, five varieties of malus flowering crab trees, and ruby flowering chestnut. The regular trees planted on older streets to keep them uniform with variety

and size are: oaks, Norway, sugar, Crimson King maples, linden, elm and Shademaster locust.

From March to the middle of September, at intervals between the tree planting program, we carry on the spraying of all trees, shrubs and roadside brush in town when needed. The mist sprayer makes it possible to spray the business districts, main streets and lower parts of town with heavy traffic, which we never have been able to do before except at an early hour in the morning. A systemic insecticide called Meta-Systox-R2 was used again this year for the control of "honeydew" aphids and the control was outstanding. An insect called oak leaf skeletonizer was a major pest this year with small green worms hanging down on tiny webs from the oak trees. The worms then form small white-ribbed cocoons beneath the trees. It takes two sprayings a year because of two hatchings, one about June 20th and another about October 8th. Dylox was used on all of our oak trees and the control was successful. The infestation was not as great this year because a good control was achieved on the late hatching of last year. We continued to have trouble with the birch leaf miner. It takes two sprays, one in May and another in July, to control two cycles of this insect over the year. The tent caterpillar nests are getting greater in number each year, but because they are foliage feeders and if sprayed when small after hatching, an effective control can be maintained. DDT is restricted and cannot be used. Methoxychlor was used for the dormant spray for the control of Dutch elm disease. The control was not as good.

We work in cooperation with the Shade Tree Disease Laboratory at the University of Massachusetts in Amherst for the eradication of Dutch elm disease. This year 18 samples were confirmed to have the disease out of 29 samples taken. Six samples were returned as sterile but died back and dried out so rapidly, I had to remove them because they became so hazardous over the streets. We removed 21 other elms not sampled. This was discouraging because the trees were the large old elms 36" to 48" in trunk diameter and 75' to 100' in height in the old section of town. Some had diseases other than Dutch elm disease such as verticillium wilt. We work under laws established by the State Department of Natural Resources. The disease is spread by the European elm bark beetle which burrows into the bark and carries the fungus from an infected tree to another healthy elm causing it to become infected and die also. The department takes cuttings or twig samples to send to the state laboratory to make cultures to have proof of the disease. Then the town begins its eradication program, which consists of cutting the afflicted trees flush to the ground, trucking to the dump and burying completely. The highway trees are often removed below electric wires when weather conditions are favorable, and the heavy trunks are removed during the winter months when the ground is frozen. The stumps are removed 12" or 15" below the grade of the sidewalks or street level with a "stump cutter." This year, as in past years, because some of the trees that were condemned dried out so rapidly, it was dangerous to put men into the tree, but with the cooperation of the Light Department it was possible to use the hydraulic bucket which saved time and money. We rented a large hydraulic bucket that would reach 65' for the removal of dangerous trees unsafe for the men to climb. Sanitation is the trimming of all dead wood in an elm tree keeping the tree healthy and destroying the breeding place of the beetle. This is a great task because of the number of large elms all over town. These are measures which I deem necessary to keep this dreaded disease under restricted and limited control.

This year was the same as last year. I had all of the leaves from the streets trucked by the Highway Department to the Tree Department nursery. When they decay and make leaf mold, we will use it with the loam for tree planting and mix it with the soil in the town nursery where we grow trees and shrubs for our tree planting and landscaping of the town's public buildings and grounds. This year we purchased a large shredder. The leaves decay rapidly when ground up fine and can be used in a short time.

The Tree Department work is difficult because we are working with living trees and shrubs which grow in seasons and the care depends on the elements. Work such as spraying must be completed or squeezed in during the periods of no winds or rains.

Electric Light Department

The wire clearance program was continued as in other years. The Light Department supplied the truck with the bucket lift and the Tree Department sent a man to do the trimming. This crew worked closely between both departments. They trimmed all wires and also street lights. The results were fine; there was less wire trouble or electrical failure caused by trees during the storms and a much better lighting effect on the highways.

Highway Department

We removed the sidewalks that were forced up by the roots, and removed the roots or trimmed and treated them, so that the Highway Department could put the new sidewalk surface back properly. We trimmed shrubbery and brush at bad intersections and along roadsides near curves and at the brow of hills for highway safety. We trimmed shrubbery at Brookhouse Drive and Getchell Green. The department helps in snow removal and sanding of sidewalks and streets after storms.

Sewer Department

We gave clearance of roots and limbs for the contractor for the sewer construction. The limbs were tied back or pulled up higher by ropes to allow for the swinging and lifting of the bucket while doing the trench work. Most of the sewer work this year was done on private roads and private land.

Parks

The trees in all the parks were completely sprayed. Weeping willows at Seaside Park and Reed's Pond receive a special spray for the control of the willow leaf beetle. The brush and shrubbery at the rear of Seaside Park were sprayed. We cleared brush, black cherry and sumac at Joel Reynolds Playground to open up play areas for small children. We planted more white spruce, black, red, white pine, and hemlock at the rear of Seaside Park.

Cemeteries

The mist sprayer now makes it possible to give all the trees in the cemeteries a complete spray program just as the highway trees receive. Other years with the hydraulic sprayer it would leave an unsightly residue.

State Street Wharf

We have planted evergreens and trees in the plot adjacent to the parking lot. This year we planted petunias and the color was outstanding. We weeded, fed and watered these all summer.

Garden Clubs

In cooperation with the Coordinating Council and the Garden Clubs, we planted the traffic islands at Lafayette Street and West Shore Drive, at School Street and Washington Street, at Mugford Street and Elm Street, corner of Maple Street and Lafayette Street, Brown Street and Ballast Lane, and at Harbor Avenue and Ocean Avenue. The Coordinating Council weeded these beds all summer long. The department fertilized and watered all islands.

Abbot Hall Grounds

The Tree Department planted new evergreens, arborvitae, yews, junipers, and azaleas. The lawn was treated for weeds and loamed and seeded, and two beds of red geraniums were planted. We planted red geraniums and white petunias around the Senior Citizens quarters at State Street.

Fire and Police Signal Systems

We trimmed the trees for the fire and police signal systems, and trees that hang low and obstruct the view of the traffic signal lights of which there are many in town.

In closing, I wish to thank the Coordinating Council, garden clubs and all other organizations for their interest and help this year and every year in the past. I wish to thank all town officials, and the town folks for their cooperation. I also wish to thank the men in my department for their support and cooperation.

Respectfully submitted,

Loring E. Clark
Tree Warden

The tree-planting programs described above are not the only successful examples in America. They were chosen because each exemplifies a particularly useful quality that may serve elsewhere. Most state offices of the U.S.D.A. Cooperative Extension Service will provide detailed instructions regarding tree planting and some have prepared extensive bulletins that make careful recommendations with regard to tree selection.

"Jail, Fine, or Plant Trees"

Before looking at other successful tree-planting programs it may be worthwhile to pause briefly on a peculiar arrangement worked out by a town in California.

Judge William J. Wright, of Palmdale, gives offenders who commit minor misdemeanors a choice: pay a fine, go to jail, or plant some trees! Those individuals who breach fish and game laws, vandalize or letter trees in the forest, or are too poor to pay a fine or wish to avoid a jail sentence to circumvent losing status in "security-type positions" and thus their job are allowed to work in the national forest as an alternative.

According to one district forest ranger, the "court crew" works "beautifully." These people are not put on "make-work" details but on specific projects including the planting of trees.

As the choice of working or paying the fine or serving a jail sentence is up to the guilty party there appears to be no dangerous unconstitutional precedent in this unique arrangement.

Plant a Christmas Tree

Each year millions of beautiful young evergreens are slaughtered in the name of a very holy man. To reverse this mob psychology the city of Raleigh, North Carolina, has devised an interesting program.

Individuals are encouraged to purchase living Christmas trees, which are kept alive in a planting box. By watering them during the holiday season, keeping the roots wrapped in burlap, and reducing the time and temperature indoors, the trees will survive in good condition. After New Year's Day, when millions of trees are burned up or thrown into garbage trucks throughout America, the people of Raleigh have the choice of contributing their living trees to the Department of Recreation, which plants them in the eight hundred acres of city parks. As an added incentive the cost of the tree qualifies as a federal income-tax deduction.

Perhaps this small seed of change will reverse the wasteful slaughter of millions upon millions of trees. As Frank Evans, Raleigh Parks Director, stated, "Recycling Christmas trees is a good economy of natural resources and can help a great deal with citywide beautification."

Arbor Day

Preceding "Earth Day" by over 85 years this most ecological celebration was created with the specific goal of regreening one of the plains states:

Resolved, that Wednesday, the 10th day of April, 1872, be, and the same is hereby, especially set apart and concentrated for tree planting in the State of Nebraska, and . . . name it Arbor Day; and to urge upon the people of the State the vital importance of tree planting, hereby offer a special premium of one hundred dollars to the agricultural society of that county in Nebraska which shall . . . plant properly the largest number of trees; and a farm library of twenty-five dollars' worth of books to that person who, on that day, shall plant properly, in Nebraska, the greatest number of trees.

The result of these economic and practical incentives was that over *one million trees* were planted in Nebraska on that first Arbor Day!

The practice of planting trees took such hold of the people that by 1895 the state legislature designated Nebraska the "Tree Planter's State."

In light of the present interest in replanting America, would it be unreasonable for every city to offer appropriate dollar incentives and libraries of plant books to the community that plants the greatest number of trees in their own *or other neighborhoods* on a designated day?

Each state presently has an Arbor Day, the date of which may vary across the nation, however. Earth Day, conceived during a time of great "eco-awareness," is uniformly observed throughout the country. Perhaps local tree-planting contests, based on the original day of tree planting in Nebraska, could be federally supported on future Earth Days?

The price might be costly (if genuine, and not token, dollar and library awards were offered) but the results would be felt through several generations.

Time to Revive the CCC?

There are tens of millions of acres east of the Mississippi River alone in abandoned farms, in cutover land, now growing up in worthless brush. It is clear that economic foresight and immediate employment march hand in

The author's son, Russell Goldencloud, tending his first Christmas tree three years after receiving it. The Norfolk Island Pine thrives on many Pacific islands.

hand in the call for reforestation of these vast areas. In so doing, employment can be given to a million men.

So stated Franklin D. Roosevelt in his acceptance speech before the Democratic National Convention in 1932. Several foresters conceived this movement as a means of relieving unemployment "through the performance of useful public work." The Forest Service furnished shelter while state and county governments provided food and clothing for work in the national forests.

Henry Clepper summarized the work accomplished during the nine years' existence of the Civilian Conservation Corps in a recent issue of *American Forests*:

In general, they worked on fire prevention jobs, such as fire hazard abatement and the construction of firebreaks. They helped put out hundreds of wood fires. They planted millions of trees and provided timber stand improvement on tens of thousands of acres. They built thousands of miles of roads, truck and foot trails, and telephone lines. They developed hundreds of recreational sites and park facilities. They improved extensive areas of grazing lands and wildlife habitat.

Spurred by its example, private and industrial forest owners began similar improvements and practices on their holdings . . . many CCC "graduates" subsequently studied forestry, fisheries management, watershed management, wildlife management, and recreation management. Thus, some of the nation's leaders in resource administration, education, and research got their start as $30 a month enrollees.

Perhaps a revival of the CCC would satisfy both the needs of those wanting time in the forest, and the nation's tree reserves.

"Drive a Datsun . . . Plant a Tree"

One of America's most successful tree-planting programs to date was initiated and financed by a foreign corporation, the Nissan Motor Corporation.

In cooperation with the U.S. Forest Service over 250,000 trees were planted in seven major national forests across the country: Shasta-Trinity, Sequoia, San Juan, Black Hills, Medicine Bow, Nicolet, and Monongahela.

The concept that resulted in this massive planting is simple. The U.S. Forest Service has had an existing program (ongoing) whereby seedlings are planted in selected national forests for a fee of fifteen cents each. Nissan Motors developed an ad campaign whereby they offered to plant a tree in a national forest (by paying the Forest Service) for every Datsun test drive undertaken during the promotion period, July 15 through October 15, 1972.

Thus, this foreign-based corporation has contributed more in direct funds to this nation's forests than any national corporation.* Rather than accept this highly beneficial marriage between industry and environment and backing similar programs themselves, lobbyists for U.S. automobile manufacturers did the very opposite.

Out of blind envy, anti-Datsun trade protectionists objected to U.S. governmental participation in a program designed to help sell Japanese automobiles! Thus, by closing their eyes to the national *benefits* of this brilliant campaign, domestic manufacturers chose instead to block a continuation of the program.

At this time, manufacturers and distributors of domestically produced products who care to show the same respect for the nation as Datsun did, while greatly increasing public awareness of their products, may still participate in the U.S. Forest Service tree-planting program. Donald B. Pritchard, who oversaw this program for Nissan Motors, suggests that interested parties write to Mr. Pat Sheehan at the U.S. Forest Service in Washington, D. C.

The Izaak Walton League of Arlington, Virginia, reports that in a related U.S. Forest Service program individuals may obtain seedlings for use in reforestation through forestry agencies located in the state capitals.

By a cooperative program with the federal government, states operate forest nurseries that grow and sell planting stock at cost to private landowners for forest, watershed, or wind-barrier purposes. In some states, trees and shrubs for wildlife are also available. These trees may not be planted for ornamental or shade purposes, while some states prohibit their use as Christmas trees.

The American Forestry Association recently published an editorial announcing a national tree-planting "effort" entitled "Target: 40 Million Acres of Trees." This figure represents the total number of acres pledged to be planted during the next ten years by forestry

---

* *The Datsun program was preceded by Hunt-Wesson, an American company, which has offered to plant a tree in the national forests for every label of "Big John's Beans" that is mailed in. While this offering has resulted in the planting of many trees, the number is less than those planted as a result of the Datsun program.*

agencies in Georgia, Florida, Louisiana, Alabama, Virginia, Pennsylvania, Missouri, Illinois, and Wyoming, as well as federal agencies and forest industries.

Trees will reportedly also be planted in urban areas in addition to the forests.

With regard to the national forests the prospects are not encouraging. Current Presidential spending restrictions inhibit the expenditure of the 65 million dollars voted by Congress for replanting almost five million acres of logged and burned-over areas on public forest lands.

[The same executive forces also eliminated the Rural Environmental Assistance Program (REAP), which provided cost-sharing assistance for tree planting on private, nonindustrial forests.]

According to Richard Pardo, Programs Director for the American Forestry Association, the greatest hope for retreeing urban, suburban, and rural environments rests with individuals who take it upon *themselves* to plant a tree.

Israel: "Plant a Tree with Your Own Hands"

There have been major reclamation achievements throughout the world. Even Mussolini managed to eliminate thousands of acres of malarial swampland, converting them into productive, arable land.

However, no nation has achieved so much in so short a time as Israel.

The thirty-fifth chapter of Isaiah prophesied, *The desert shall rejoice and blossom as a rose. It shall blossom abundantly, and rejoice even with joy and singing.*

The number of trees planted does not adequately transmit a feeling for the actual work achieved, although 120 *million* trees is an impressive count. As most of us have learned by now, the soil in Israel has not always been a waiting medium of fertile earth.

The Southern Negev Desert regions, for example, were not fertile, even in biblical times. The soil in this region is extremely saline because, for one reason, this low-lying area lacks natural drainage outlets.

To combat this "impossible" problem the JNF (Jewish National Fund—the organizers of agrarian reform in Israel), and the Ministry of Agriculture, successfully applies the "rinsing" method, which consists of flooding the surface of future fields with water. This fresh water quickly percolates into the ground, dissolving the salts and carrying them to depths where they are no longer available to plant roots, thus no longer noxious to crops and sheltering trees.

Think of our Mohave Desert one hundred years from now as a blossoming production center of fruit, flowers, and vegetables. Should this "miracle" come about, necessitated by our burgeoning population, which is forever devouring fertile farmland for homesites, it will be created by techniques pioneered in the sands of Israel.

In the other extreme, Israeli workers have drained marshes and stagnant, saline lakes to create further expanses of arable land. The Hula Valley project, completed in 1957, is the largest of the drainage projects.

This valley is a deep basin hemmed in by high mountains on three sides. The only opening, in the south, was blocked by lava flows of the recent geologic past. Thus, a stagnant lake of Jordan River waters with malarial swamps to the north existed for centuries as one of the most useless regions on earth.

The southern outlet was opened, while three canals were cut through the valley. These canals permit a free flow of water, which eliminates the problem of stagnation, prevents flooding of fields by winter floods, and also lowers a too-high underground water table that ruined many crops.

Today, the Hula Valley, with rich peat soil, has become one of the most productive agricultural regions in Israel. As an added bonus for this horticultural engineering, large quantities of water, which had previously evaporated uselessly from the lake and swamp surface, are now utilized for irrigating other parts of the country.

In addition to the above examples of need, coupled with ambition yielding a proliferation of green plants, including 120 million trees, other "unconquerable" problems have also been solved.

Water has been drained off from oversaturated subsoils; the basalt plateau of the Golan was made fertile by removing the huge boulders and breaking the hard, deep subsoil crust; slopes have been terraced; and villages with vegetable, fruit, and flower gardens built on poor and rocky sites.

In addition to providing timber and its many products, trees are also useful for impeding erosion, for sheltering crops from desert storms, and for actually *creating new* soil.

The roots of trees penetrate into cracks and fissures in the rocks and, as they thicken, widen cracks and open new ones, eventually grinding the stone into gravel and rock meal, a process intensified chemically by secretion of acids from the roots, which are able to melt away hard limestone. To the rock meal, trees add material of their own. All these factors create living soil. Many forests presently exhibit a thick layer of earth where before there were only bare boulders.

Trees growing in the forests of Israel include Jerusalem pine, cypress, eucalyptus, tamarisk, long-leaf acacia, and carob. A fairly inclusive introduction to the growth of these and other forest trees is contained in a booklet available from the Jewish National Fund in Jerusalem.

These great accomplishments bring to mind one question appropriate to the purposes of this book: can the organizational principles employed by the JNF be duplicated, or modified to work for the regreening of America?

Before analyzing this important question it must be borne in mind that the *need* present in Israel is in no way *yet* apparent in America. Further, the *unity* of the Israeli people and their willingness to use their own muscle power (rather than paying some other indifferent souls to perform the task) are no doubt *the* key elements in their tree-planting successes. Further, the Israelis *love* their land, for it is their own if enough historical perspective is applied to the question of time and territoriality.

America never belonged to her present inhabitants (except the native Americans) and she is still mistreated, as are most newly conquered territories. Would a sane man bulldoze a site that contains the graves of his *own* ancestors, or pave over fertile farmlands to create nonproductive (distribution is to be distinguished from production) shopping deserts?

In spite of the apparently soulless relationship between the American soil and her people, as compared with the Israelis' love for their land, no matter how inhospitable it was at first (though the signs of soulless land relationships have recently appeared in their lands too), we must evaluate the methods employed in Israel for raising funds for the planting of trees and attempt to adapt them to our own needs in the urban, suburban, rural, and forest environments in need of repair.

The human desire to leave one's name on earth in association with worthwhile enterprises seems to be the prevailing theme in the JNF financing of agrarian projects. Contributions for tree planting in Israel are used solely for this purpose. Donors around the world receive small plaques, which have their name and the number of trees they have "planted" by proxy. All such gifts are recorded in the Tree Register at the JNF

Head Office in Jerusalem. Contributions may be made for individual trees or for gardens (100 trees), groves (1,000 trees), woods (2,500 trees), and entire forests (10,000 and over).

Forests are marked with permanent individual stone markers at the sites or with a plaque at a Commemorative Center. In addition, the donor receives a handsome certificate for future generations of his family to share.

Some of the forests created with outside financial support include the "Queen Elizabeth Coronation Forest," in Upper Galilee (1956), the "John F. Kennedy Memorial and Peace Forest" (1966), and most recently the "Governor Tom McCall Oregon Friendship Forest," near Nazareth in Galilee (1973). Interestingly, two native American species, ponderosa pine and incense cedar, were flown 15,000 miles from Oregon to Israel to be planted in this newest of memorial forests.

In addition to these memorial trees, funds are raised by more traditional means: by a fee for inscribing on a register the names of children on the occasion of their birth, birthday, recovery from illness, or religious "coming-of-age"; by the sale of stamps that reflect some of the accomplishments of afforestation; by fund raising on special flag and flower days, at dinners, concerts, and theater parties; through bequests, gifts, and insurance policies made payable to a tree-planting foundation, the deposits in which earn interest but whose profits are plowed into the soil; and from special projects established in the name or memory of communities, organizations, or persons in the country and abroad.

Behind all this money and energy there lies a genuine need for new trees as well as a commitment to having them without depending on the government for direct support.

Both elements need to be recognized in America before any nationwide organization can begin to look toward successfully incorporating any of the tree fundraising means outlined above. On local levels this has been done to some extent (as the street tree programs in San Francisco and Boston) however, nowhere has there been a *nationwide* effort to create a nongovernmental organization that truly raises the funds, selects the sites that have priority, and sets about to plant the trees.

Perhaps when the need becomes strong enough (after we suffer the fate of the ancient Chinese?) such an organization will be generated on its own.

·II·
Selecting a Tree

Key Questions Important to the Survival of the Tree

1. Can the tree survive the minimum temperature of your locale for prolonged periods of time?
2. Can the tree tolerate the fumes, dust, smoke, and road salt it may be subject to?
3. Will it be able to thrive in the soil it is planted in?
4. Is the rainfall adequate for optimum growth, or will watering be required?
5. How resistant is the tree to diseases common to the area?

Key Questions Important to the Planter

1. What are you hoping to achieve with this tree? Do you want shade, a buffer from noise and electric lights, a landscape effect, flowers in the spring, brilliant colors in the fall, or what have you?
2. How large do trees of the species you have in mind eventually become? How wide the trunk? How long-lived, in general?
3. What shape will the tree assume? Will it be narrow and conical, fastigate, columnar, broad, oval, globe-shaped, spreading-branched, or vaselike?
4. Does the tree bear fruit that is edible or desirable because it attracts birds, squirrels or other wildlife, or will it create a noxious mess that requires constant cleaning?

Even the least green-thumbed among us knows not to expect a palm to grow in Minnesota or a sugar maple in a canefield, but from among the hundreds of trees that will grow in a specified locale we must bear in mind the above nine questions and make the proper choice.

If all nine questions were to be reduced to just one simple rule regarding success in tree planting it would be that held foremost in the mind of settlers new to any country: plant trees that are found growing *naturally* in the region because they are usually best adapted to the local conditions.

But most of us are not new to this country, nor are conditions of living that simple any more. We inhabit terribly complex worlds that are difficult enough for us to live in, without worrying about the survival of trees, birds, dogs, cats, goldfish, and our common zoo animals. Yet, who among us would argue that human life in isolation from any other life forms is worthwhile, or even emotionally possible, for any great length of time?

Conical tree

Man associates himself with the nonfood-supplying animals for the same reasons that he needs ornamental and shade trees. Both groups serve to remind him of his *place in nature*, to show him his relative size, his place in the sequence of evolution, and to remind him of his hardy nature.

When we feel particularly mortal and frail we might

glance at a passing bird or climbing squirrel and instantaneously, without great conscious effort, realize that they, too, are composed of flesh and blood. Out there in a world of horns, smoke, soot, and other very real dangers, somehow the bird, the squirrel, the mouse, the rat, even the cockroach, has a lesson for us in our frail moments. That of survival. All living things existing on the earth have survived because they contain a marvelous configuration of characteristics inherited from a chain of ancestors. Whoever or whatever put us here meant for us to *live*, and we are all doing so despite the threats of disease, war, accident, or contamination, which are also part of our living world, as they apparently have been for many ages.

So too must the trees we select remind us of the inherent strength of all living beings. Has anyone ever studied the tranquilizing effects of green plants?

Big Trees Versus Small Trees

Trees should, *wherever possible*, be the hardiest, longest-lived species possible in an area if we are to draw our lessons of support from their very spreading roots. Can a tiny, "neat" hybrid teach us anything we want to know about our lives?

A large group among the present generation of commercial tree growers seems intent on rectifying the "mistakes" of the past generations of tree planters. They argue that it is expensive to continually prune the "mammoth forest species," which now dominate some of America's best-treed, most aesthetically pleasant sections. Some of these arbo-businessmen are avid article writers. They suggest the replacement of our pin oaks, London planes, maples, ginkgos, etc., with "low-maintenance" species, which just happen to be available from their own nurseries. We are led to believe that our city-owned nurseries, which may contain excellent stocks of "forest giants," should be plowed under and replanted with small, manageable hybrids, purchased, of course, from those who "contributed so much . . . by developing them."

Not only does this evoke Huxleyan images of a not so "Brave New World," where clones of people as well as trees are bred in controlled environments that are alien to life, but the arbo-business arguments are faulty from an economic point of view as well.

Globe-shaped tree

Fastigate tree

In a recent article, the costs of purchasing, planting, and maintaining modern and traditional trees are compared. We learn, with surprise, that the traditional trees, "the standard tall-growing types," actually cost

Vase-shaped tree

Oval tree

less initially than the modern varieties. We are then bombarded with comparative maintenance costs that show the modern trees requiring less than one-fifth the funds necessary to service the "old standbys." We sadly realize that the cost of the modern varieties over a twenty-year period is fully one-half that of the sad, old giants, which, alas, must be forgotten in our ever-growing new world.

In looking deeper into the picture we realize that the dollar facts may be distorted.

For one, the major cost in the way of maintaining the big trees is for pruning the branches away from overhead utility lines. Further, the cost of removing the giants in the event of disease, old age, or interference

with construction plans or traffic signs is understandably much greater than the price for removing mere sticks in the earth.

Who would believe that overhead utility lines will be with us until the end of time? Does it not make sense to plan on future cities and towns with *all* wiring placed *beneath the ground*? This happens to be the trend already established, and quite usual in the most carefully planned new communities. Then why project maintenance costs for big trees by planning on pruning them over twenty years when, in fact, much of the nation's wiring will be or should be run underground?

By eliminating overhead wires we eliminate *the* main struggle between trees and man's contemporary needs. By placing the wires underground we are once again free to plant a nation of forest giants; big trees that comfort us as we gaze at them, shade us from the summer's heat, filter particles from the air while adding to it cooling moisture; trees that support birds and other animal life, and provide us with a living screen from the mammoth buildings that are here to stay.

A second aspect of the utility line versus big tree controversy that is *always* overlooked is that the truly big trees, with no lower branches, eventually grow *above* these wires. The canopy of a huge monkeypod tree, for example, stands many feet above utility wires after a certain number of years and from that point on requires little maintenance except for removal of dead branches to prevent their falling on pedestrians. In the case of the true "forest-giants," several years of pruning —both in the beginning to eliminate lower branching, and after ten to twelve years of age (American elm) to keep the branches off the wires—are soon rewarded by a great tree that grows up out of the way of all utility lines.

Removal costs for small versus large trees are also inadequately evaluated.

Why assume a dead tree is a useless tree? By planting trees with useful wood (or edible fruits that can be eaten through most of its life cycle), we may look forward to tree "removal" as tree harvest time.

Black cherry trees, for example, are composed of wood highly prized in furniture making. Incense cedar, a native of Oregon and northern California, is made of wood useful in mothproofing and in making chests and cigar boxes. These two examples of trees that may be used to make things with after providing a lifetime of shade are only indicators of the hundreds of trees that provide some useful food or product that may be grown in American soil.

Certainly not every one of them is recommended as a street tree; however, they would do beautifully on lawns, in parks, and wherever else space permits. The point to remember is that trees need not be planted solely for the shade they provide—but for some very useful products as well; products that may be harvested during the life cycle or at the end of the actual living phase.*

Furthermore, how many of us realize that birds eat the fruit of trees and that the growing number of "seedless" tree varieties being planted today may be partially responsible for diminished populations of our bird friends?

Birds are not mere visual and audio ornaments. In the scheme of life most species are actually beneficial to trees because they may eat harmful insects while adding organic matter to the soil with their droppings.

Nevertheless, there are certain advantages to some of the modern trees and these may as well be listed here lest the author be labeled "old-fashioned."

In addition to requiring less pruning (where this is a problem) smaller trees *may* be desirable *if* they possess qualities superior to the forest giants. Ornamental types may be showier, and thus perhaps more interesting, throughout entire seasons. Also, specially created cultivars *may* prove to be better adapted to specialized conditions with regard to soil, moisture, and pollutants. Certain cultivars may prove to be superior to regular seedlings of the many trees listed and illustrated in this book. As one example, there are many

---

* For a list of some of "Man's Useful Plants" see Economic Botany by Albert F. Hill; or Plants for Man by Robert W. Schery.

Spreading branched tree

available *varieties* or cultivars of Norway maple. The interested planter might evaluate the limitations to growth that may be required in his chosen site, or the specialized uses he may demand of his tree (does he want a broad variety for shade, an especially short variety, or a pyramidal-shaped maple?), and select *the* variety that best meets these needs.

As will be obvious by now, the main thrust of this section is toward the careful selection of street and roadside trees.

In addition to being named in the following lists, over 170 trees are treated in an expanded version in Part VI, "Tree Profiles." They are there enumerated alphabetically by common name and many are illustrated with masterful photographs.

Street Trees

The question of selecting street trees has been treated by many. However, one of the clearest writers on the subject is William Solotaroff. In his classic, limited-edition *Shade-Trees in Towns and Cities* (1911) he states:

The tree planter must picture to himself how his work will look a great number of years later . . . the street of mature trees looks quite different from the street of young saplings; yet it is the selection of young trees, their proper setting apart, and their care after planting that make the beautiful street possible.

The Ideal Street

1. One species of tree on the entire street (of course, other streets should contain separate species).
2. The trees are of equal size.

An example in the extreme of "controlled trees." Laurels with contorted stems, Essen, Germany.

3. The distance between each tree is uniform; their mature canopies do not touch.
4. Each tree has an effective, interesting, iron or other guard to protect them from animals, people, and vehicles.
5. All low branches have been pruned to permit a free flow of pedestrians and road traffic.

Particularly Desirable Qualities of Shade Trees

1. The tree must be hardy. In cities it must be able to survive poor soil, little sunlight and water, noxious fumes, dust, soot, road salt, high winds, sleet, snow, and occasional vandalism or other rough treatment.
2. The stem must grow straight while not appearing to have been artificially influenced in its habit of growth.
3. The foliage should be full throughout the summer months to provide the maximum amount of shade, while the leaves should exhibit autumn color changes for interest. Too dense a tree is somewhat undesirable because eliminating all sunlight may

prevent the streets from drying quickly after a summer rain.

4. The branches should have a generally pleasing symmetry to their outline, lending order to the street while being strong enough to support their own weight plus the addition of snow in winter without artificial support such as cables or braces.
5. Fruit and flowers or interesting bark that is easily removed or falls off may be desirable traits for lawn or park trees, but are distinctly troublesome when exhibited on street trees. Littered sidewalks are expensive to keep clean; mushy fruits may emit highly disagreeable odors (the *female* ginkgo, for example, is never planted any more because of this characteristic) while creating dangerous footing for the passerby.
6. The desirable street tree should grow to as great a size as the area will permit, and should be long-lived (see the 800-year-old Oriental arborvitae tree on page 114 as it was photographed in Chung-San Park, in China, by Dr. Tenbroeck). Some planters sacrifice entire streets to an early death by

setting in species such as poplars, which grow remarkably fast initially, but die quickly owing to inherent factors such as soft wood, which is easily broken by wind or the weight of snow.

7. The ideal street tree should be relatively immune from insect or fungal attack.

8. The roots should not heave sidewalks or "strangle" underground wiring and sewer pipes.

Regional Tree Lists

General lists of shade trees for different regions of the United States and Canada follow. Each state is grouped in one of eight "regions," while Canada is treated as Region IX.

The regions are grouped according to the format outlined in the 1949 Yearbook of Agriculture, *Trees*, as follows:

Region I: The Northeast

Connecticut, Delaware, Illinois, Indiana, Iowa, Kentucky, Maine, Maryland, Massachusetts, Michigan, Minnesota, Missouri, New Hampshire, New Jersey, New York, Ohio, Pennsylvania, Rhode Island, Vermont, Virginia, West Virginia, Wisconsin

Region II: The Southeast

Alabama, Arkansas, Florida, Georgia, Louisiana, Mississippi, North Carolina, South Carolina, Tennessee, Texas (Gulf regions)

Region III: The Plains

Colorado (eastern), Kansas, Montana, Nebraska, North Dakota, Oklahoma, South Dakota, Texas (except Gulf regions), Wyoming (eastern)

Region IV: The Rocky Mountains

Arizona, Colorado (western), Idaho, Montana, Nevada, New Mexico, Utah, Wyoming (western)

Region V: California

Region VI: The North Pacific

Oregon, Washington

Region VII: Alaska

Region VIII: Hawaii

Region IX: Canada

British Columbia, Manitoba, Ontario (southern), Quebec, New Brunswick

The number of available species for each state greatly exceeds those enumerated in this section. These lists have been compiled from suggestions made by local municipal arborists or state foresters, those men closest to the environments in which the trees must survive.

In addition to *specific* statewide and local recommendations *general* recommendations for some regions are also included. The International Shade Tree Conference (ISTC) rated trees for each region of the U.S. and Canada according to their relative values (adaptability, degree of required maintenance, longevity, etc.). Preceding each regional tree list are those species rated 100 percent and 80 percent by the ISTC.

Some trees recommended by a local arborist in the following lists may have received a *low* rating by the ISTC. I have chosen to include *all* species recommended to me in my survey of the fifty states and the Canadian provinces without regard to possible objections raised. I do not presume to know more about the needs of a particular town or city than those closest to the soil in so vast a continent.

While a tree such as the hackberry may be considered a nuisance by some individuals, it may be the *only* tree able to withstand the arid plains environment and therefore be highly recommended for cities in this region.

A tree may thrive in one part of a town but not in another, or even grow differently along the same street! Thus, the lists for each state, and for cities within some states, are presented without criticism or evaluation. An individual interested in selecting a tree or trees for a particular site should use the following lists as an initial *guide*. After you discuss the subject with local tree wardens and nurserymen, a final selection should be forthcoming. But please bear in mind that *you* may be the only person arguing for a big tree. The other people may be "sold" on smaller trees and you must then stick to your original choice. If you are told the species you would like is not locally available please consult the handbook *1200 Trees and Shrubs—Where to Buy Them*, available from the Brooklyn Botanic Garden, 1000 Washington Avenue, Brooklyn, New York 11225, for $1.25. This useful guide contains descriptions of most trees listed in this book and the addresses of nurseries that stock them.

Urban dwellers requiring especially tough trees will find notes highlighting desirable species in the Tree Profiles.

To a large extent conifers and colorful flowering trees are excluded from the following lists even where some might grow quite well. The main concern has been to coordinate a series of workable lists of street and shade trees.

Tree Villains. All large trees are not desirable. (Courtesy,
Georgia Power Company)

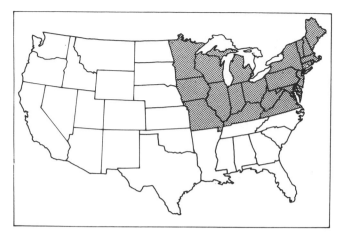

Region I: The Northeast

While states as far central as Minnesota, Iowa, and Missouri, and those southernmost in this group, Kentucky and Virginia, are seldom thought of as "northeastern states," climatic and geographic factors do in fact favor their being grouped together. Since separate tree lists are provided for most states, there is little likelihood that a suggested species for northern Vermont will be confused as suitable for an Appalachian city.

Before enumerating the state lists, the ISTC recommendations for "New England" (Connecticut, Maine, Massachusetts, New Hampshire, Rhode Island, and Vermont) and "Eastern States" (New Jersey, New York, and Pennsylvania) follow.

New England

Class No. 1—100%

BEECH, AMERICAN (*Fagus grandifolia*)
BIRCH, EUROPEAN WHITE (*Betula pendula*)
HEMLOCK, CANADA (*Tsuga canadensis*)
HONEY LOCUST, COMMON (*Gleditsia triacanthos*)
MAPLE, SUGAR (*Acer saccharum*)
OAK, EASTERN RED (*Quercus borealis maxima*)
OAK, PIN (*Quercus palustris*)
OAK, SCARLET (*Quercus coccinea*)
OAK, SWAMP WHITE (*Quercus bicolor*)
OAK, WHITE (*Quercus alba*)
PINE, EASTERN WHITE (*Pinus strobus*)
SERVICEBERRY, SHADBLOW (*Amelanchier canadensis*)
TULIP TREE (*Liriodendron tulipifera*)
TUPELO, BLACK (*Nyssa sylvatica*)

Class No. 2—80%

APPLE, COMMON (*Malus pumila*)
ASH, BLACK (*Fraxinus nigra*)
ASH, EUROPEAN MOUNTAIN (*Sorbus aucuparia*)
ASH, GREEN (*Fraxinus pennsylvania lanceolata*)

ASH, RED (*Fraxinus pennsylvanica*)
ASH, WHITE (*Fraxinus americana*)
BIRCH, RIVER (*Betula nigra*)
BIRCH, SWEET (*Betula lenta*)
HICKORY, BITTERNUT (*Carya cordiformis*)
HICKORY, MOCKERNUT (*Carya tomentosa*)
HICKORY, PIGNUT (*Carya glabra*)
HICKORY, SHAGBARK (*Carya ovata*)
MAPLE, RED (*Acer rubrum*)
OAK, CHESTNUT (*Quercus montana*)
PEAR, COMMON (*Pyrus communis*)
PINE, RED (*Pinus resinosa*)
SASSAFRAS, COMMON (*Sassafras albidum*)
SPRUCE, BLACK (*Picea mariana*)
WALNUT, BLACK (*Juglans nigra*)

Eastern States

Class No. 1—100%

BALDCYPRESS, COMMON (*Taxodium distichum*)
BEECH, AMERICAN (*Fagus grandifolia*)
BEECH, EUROPEAN (*Fagus sylvatica* var.)
CRABAPPLES, FLOWERING (*Malus* sp. and var.)
DOGWOOD, FLOWERING (*Cornus florida*)
ELM, AMERICAN (*Ulmus americana*)
GINKGO (*Ginkgo biloba* var.)
HAWTHORN, PAULS SCARLET (*Crataegus oxyacantha pauli*)
HAWTHORN, WASHINGTON (*Crataegus phaenopyrum*)
HEMLOCK, CANADA (*Tsuga canadensis*)
HOLLY, AMERICAN (*Ilex opaca*)
HONEY LOCUST, MORAINE THORNLESS (*Gleditsia triacanthos moraine*)
HORNBEAM, AMERICAN (*Carpinus Caroliniana*)
KATSURATREE (*Cercidiphyllum japonicum*)
MAGNOLIA, CUCUMBERTREE (*Magnolia acuminata*)
MAPLE, ERECT NORWAY (*Acer platanoides erectum*)
MAPLE, RED (*Acer rubrum*)
MAPLE, SUGAR (*Acer saccharum*)
OAK, EASTERN RED (*Quercus borealis maxima*)
OAK, PIN (*Quercus palustris*)
OAK, SHINGLE (*Quercus imbricaria*)
OAK, SHUMARD (*Quercus shumardi*)
OAK, WHITE (*Quercus alba*)
OAK, WILLOW (*Quercus phellos*)
SOURWOOD (*Oxydendrum arboreum*)

Class No. 2—80%

ASH, GREEN (*Fraxinus pennsylvanica lanceolata*)
ASH, WHITE (*Fraxinus americana*)
CORKTREE, AMUR (*Phellodendron amurense*)
GOLDENRAIN TREE, PANICLED (*Koelreuteria paniculata*)
HAWTHORNS (*Crataegus* sp.)

HICKORY, SHAGBARK (*Carya ovata*)
HORSECHESTNUT, COMMON (*Aesculus hippocastanum*)
HORSECHESTNUT, RED (*Aesculus carnea*)
LINDEN, LITTLELEAF (*Tilia cordata*)
MAPLE, NORWAY (*Acer platanoides*)
MAPLE, SCHWEDLER NORWAY (*Acer platanoides schwedleri*)
OAK, OVERCUP (*Quercus lyrata*)
OAK, SCARLET (*Quercus coccinea*)
OAK, SWAMP CHESTNUT (*Quercus prinus*)
OAK, SWAMP WHITE (*Quercus bicolor*)
PAGODATREE, JAPANESE (*Sophora japonica*)
PINE, EASTERN WHITE (*Pinus strobus*)
PLANETREE, AMERICAN (SYCAMORE) (*Platanus occidentalis*)
PLANETREE, LONDON (*Platanus acerifolia*)
SERVICEBERRY, SHADOW (*Amelanchier canadensis*)
SWEETGUM (*Liquadambar styraciflua*)
TULIP TREE (*Liriodendron tulipifera*)
TUPELO, BLACK (BLACKGUM) (*Nyssa sylvatica*)
WALNUT, BLACK (*Juglans nigra*)
YELLOWWOOD (*Cladrastis lutea*)

Connecticut: (See ISTC tree list, this section. See adjacent states.)

Edwin D. Carpenter of the Connecticut Cooperative Extension Service has prepared a publication entitled *Trees and Shrubs Adaptable to Street, Mall, and Other Public Planting Areas.* Although small trees are favored, this list should be valuable to people in downtown districts who refuse to plant anything except species suitable for planting boxes.

The town of Westport, Connecticut, has a Beautification Committee, which has begun to replant trees along U.S. Route 1. Previously, solid rows of majestic oaks, maples, and elms were destroyed when the road was widened. The Committee hopes to restore the appearance of a "traditional New England community" and has planted the road with honey locust, London plane, Norway maple, red oak, hawthorn, Hopa crabapple, and fastigate ginkgo.

Delaware: (See "New Jersey" tree list, this section.)

Permits to plant trees on public property (streets, roadways, etc.) vary throughout Delaware. An ordinance of the city of Dover, for example, *prohibits* tree planting in these areas by individuals, while the city of Wilmington will issue permits that allow the pavement to be broken for the purpose of tree planting, at the expense of the applicant.

The following list of trees was recommended by the Wilmington Department of Parks and Recreation: ash, ginkgo, linden (littleleaf), locust (shademaster), maple (red), maple (sugar), pagodatree (Japanese), planetree (London), oak (willow), and zelkova.

The Extension Service also recommends the following trees: goldenrain tree, Washington hawthorn, saucer magnolia, and Russian olive.

Illinois:

Trees for Your Community, by Nelson and Porter, Circular 934 of the Cooperative Extension Service, from which the following list of trees is derived, is an excellent booklet for any individual or group interested in developing a tree-planting program in the state of Illinois.

An asterisk indicates trees that are especially hardy in city conditions.

Small Trees: (20–35 feet tall when mature)
DOGWOOD, FLOWERING (*Cornus florida*)
*GOLDENRAIN TREE (*Koelreutaria paniculata*)
*HAWTHORN, WASHINGTON (*Crataeugus phaenopyrum*)
HORNBEAM, AMERICAN (*Carpinus caroliniana*)
MAPLE, AMUR (*Acer ginnala*)
REDBUD (*Cercis canadensis*)
SILVERBELL, CAROLINA (*Halesia carolina*)
Medium Trees: (35–60 feet tall when mature)
*ASH, GREEN (*Fraxinus pennsylvanica lanceolata*)
*CORKTREE, AMUR (*Phellodendron amurense*)
*LINDEN, CRIMEAN (*Tilia euchlora*)
*LINDEN, LITTLELEAF (*Tilia cordata*)
*MAPLE, NORWAY (*Acer platanoides*)
MAPLE, RED (*Acer rubrum*)
*OAK, PIN (*Quercus palustris*)
*PAGODATREE, JAPANESE (*Sophora japonica*)
SWEETGUM (*Liquidambar styraciflua*)
ZELKOVA (*Zelkova serrata*)
Large Trees: (greater than 60 feet tall when mature)
*GINKGO (MAIDENHAIR TREE) (*Ginkgo biloba*)
*HACKBERRY (*Celtis occidentalis*)
*HONEY LOCUST, THORNLESS (*Gleditsia triacanthos inermis*)
MAPLE, SUGAR (*Acer saccharum*)
*OAK, RED (*Quercus borealis maxima*)
*SYCAMORE, AMERICAN (*Platanus occidentalis*)
TULIP TREE (*Liriodendron tulipifera*)

Indiana:

The "Illinois" list generally applies to Indiana as well. However, the following additions may prove useful:

BIRCH, RIVER (*Betula nigra*)
OAK, SWAMP WHITE (*Quercus bicolor*)
PLANETREE, LONDON (*Platanus acerifolia*)
TUPELO (SOURGUM) (*Nyssa sylvatica*)

Iowa:

The "Illinois" list applies to Iowa with the addition of ironwood trees (*Ostrya virginiana*), which are sometimes planted along city streets.

As learned from the Des Moines City Forester, planting restrictions are very relaxed in comparison with other cities of equal size. An individual can usually obtain a permit to plant on a public right-of-way merely by phoning the City Forester and allowing his inspection of the proposed site. Factors considered include species of tree, soil, underground and overhead wiring, and location. However, tree planting in the downtown area is unfortunately discouraged by (among other things) a requirement for an expensive set of plans.

Kentucky: (See "Illinois" list.)

The Louisville Forester will issue permits to allow planting on city streets after considering variables such as: size and shape of tree; soil and space available at the site; location; and the amount of maintenance required after planting.

Breaking the pavement requires a special permit from the City Hall.

Maine:

In Bulletin 22, issued by the Maine Forestry Department, the following trees are recommended for street planting. An asterisk indicates species that are suitable only for parks and suburban streets, owing to the height and spread each achieves at maturity:

ASH, GREEN ("MARSHALL'S SEEDLESS") (60′)
(*Fraxinus pennsylvanica lanceolata*)
*ASH, WHITE (75′) (*Fraxinus americana*)
ELM, AMERICA (90′) (*Ulmus americana*)
ELM, BUISMAN (90′) (*Ulmus carpinifolia*)
*ELM, ENGLISH (90′) (*Ulmus procera*)
GINKGO (MAIDENHAIR TREE) MALE (75′)
(*Ginkgo biloba*)
HONEY LOCUST, THORNLESS (70′) (*Gleditsia triacanthos inermis*)
*LINDEN, AMERICAN (65′) (*Tilia americana*)
LINDEN, EUROPEAN (45′) (*Tilia europaea*)
LINDEN, LITTLELEAF ("GREENSPIRE") (70′)
(*Tilia cordata*)
MAPLE, COLUMNAR NORWAY (50′) (*Acer platanoides* var. *columnare*)

MAPLE, COLUMNAR SUGAR (60′) (*Acer saccharum* var. *monumentale*)
MAPLE, NORWAY (60′) (*Acer platanoides*)
MAPLE, RED (SWAMP) (65′) (*Acer rubrum*)
*MAPLE, SUGAR (ROCK) (75′) (*Acer saccharum*)
*OAK, NORTHERN RED (70′) (*Quercus rubra borealis*)
OAK, PIN (70′) (*Quercus palustris*)
*OAK, WHITE (75′) (*Quercus alba*)

Maryland: (See "New Jersey" list, this section.)

In this state, street tree plantings can only be made with the permission and approval of the county governments. If the community is incorporated, the individual must also seek permission from the beautification committee of the city government.

The city of Baltimore *does* allow individuals to break the pavement and plant a tree at their own expense. However, the Department of Recreation and Parks must be notified; on approving the site and species, the Bureau of Consumer Services will issue the permit.

City of Baltimore Tree List

Acceptable—plant spring only

*Red Maple
Gerling Red Maple
Scanlon Red Maple
Tilford Red Maple
Sargent Cherry
Kwanzan Cherry
Yoshino Cherry
Purpleleaf Flowering Plum
Chanticleer Pear
Callery Pear
Silver Linden
Japanese Zelkova
October Glory Maple
Shirofugen Cherry
Village Green Zelkova
Milky Way Flowering Cherry
Lavalle Hawthorn
Scanlon Cherry
*Northern Red Oak
Washington Hawthorn

Acceptable—plant spring or fall

Cleveland Norway Maple
Summershade Maple
Almira Norway Maple
Olmsted Columnar Norway Maple

---

* *Recommended only for larger grassy areas such as median strips or wide tree lawns.*

Pyramidal Sycamore Maple
Wineleaf Sycamore Maple
Pyramidal European Hornbean
Eley Crabapple
Almey Crabapple
Redbud Crabapple
Hopa Red Flowering Crabapple
Ginkgo—male only
Wilson Columnar Mountain Ash
Chinese Scholartree (Japonica)
Rancho Littleleaf Linden
Crimean Linden
Augustine Ascending Elm
Amur Cork
Greenspire Linden
European Mountain Ash
Pyramidal Oakleaf Mountain Ash
Littleleaf Linden XP110
*Hackberry
Bauman's Horsechestnut
*American Linden
Ruby Red Horsechestnut
*Sugar Maple
*Green Mountain Sugar Maple

Not Acceptable

Pauls Scarlet Hawthorn—does poorly
Christine Buisman Elm—poor form, very susceptible to
   elm leaf beetle
Silver Maple—too large, roots tend to get in sewer lines,
   brittle
Willow—roots get in sewer lines
Tulip Poplar—too large
Ash—is subject to very severe insect attacks (borers)
Black Locust—very brittle, subject to insect attack (borers)
White Oak—too large
American Elm—Dutch elm disease
Sycamore—brittle, too large, fruit nuisance

Massachusetts: (See ISTC tree list. See tree lists for "Illinois," "Maine," "Michigan," and "Minnesota.")

The Extension Service recommends *avoiding* the following species: catalpa, Chinese elm, willow, poplar, silver maple, and horsechestnut. The branches of these trees break easily and their roots often plug drains and envelop pipes.

For a list of "Desirable Shade Trees" for the state, contact the state Extension Service.

Michigan: (See tree list for "Illinois.")

Maples, ashes, ginkgo, honey locust, London plane-

* Recommended only for larger grassy areas such as median strips or wide tree lawns.

tree, sweetgum, sycamore, oaks, and lindens are planted along Detroit streets. The Department of Parks and Recreation will plant on request, charging about "one-half of the average actual cost to the city," or approximately $25, for a tree two inches in diameter, with two replacements guaranteed during the first five years, if necessary.

Unfortunately, permits to plant are denied simply if overhead wiring passes the proposed site!

The following list of shade trees was published jointly by the Michigan Forestry and Park Association and the Michigan State University Forestry Department.

Intended primarily to enable professional horticulturists to assign a dollar value to shade trees, depending on several qualities (character and growth habit, longevity and hardiness, disease immunity, usefulness, and maintenance costs), the list is also useful for selecting appropriate trees for shade. By choosing trees with relatively high "percent values" (60 percent–100 percent) the individual is certain to make a desirable selection.

The classification as set up below for the lower peninsula of Michigan is determined according to the following qualities: character and habit of growth, length of life and durability, immunity from diseases and insects, usefulness, cleanliness, and hardiness:

Species	Percent Value
Abies balsamea: Balsam Fir	80
Abies concolor: White Fir	100
Acer campestre: Hedge Maple	100
Acer ginnala: Amur Maple	80
Acer griseum: Paperback Maple	80
Acer negundo: Box Elder Maple	20
Acer nigrum: Black Maple	100
Acer palmatum: Japanese Maple	80
Acer platanoides: selected varieties	100
Acer platanoides columnare: Columnar Norway Maple	100
Acer pseudoplantanus and varieties: Sycamore Maple	60
Acer rubrum: selected varieties	100
Acer saccharum: Sugar Maple	100
Acer saccharinum and varieties: Silver Maple	40
Acer tataricum: Tatarian Maple	80
Aesculus carnea Brioti: Ruby Red Horsechestnut	80
Aesculus species: Horsechestnut	60
Ailanthus altissima: Tree of Heaven, or Ailanthus	40
Alnus glutinosa: European Alder	60
Amelanchier species: Serviceberry or Shadblow	80
Betula lenta: Sweet Birch	60

Species	Percent Value
Betula lutea: Yellow Birch	60
Betula species and varieties: Birch	80
Carpinus betulus: European Hornbeam	100
Carpinus betulus fastigiata:	
Upright European Hornbeam	100
Carpinus caroliniana: American Hornbeam	100
Carya species: Hickory	60
Castanea mollissima: Chinese Chestnut	80
Catalpa species: Catalpa	40
Celtis species: Hackberry	80
Cercidiphyllum japonicum: Katsura Tree	100
Cercis canadensis: Eastern Redbud	100
Cladrastis lutea: American Yellowwood	100
Cornus alternfolia: Pagoda Dogwood	80
Cornus florida and varieties: Dogwood	100
Crataegus species: Hawthorn	80
Crataegus phaenopyrum and varieties:	
Washington Hawthorn	100
Elaeagnus angustifolia: Russian Olive	60
Fagus species: Beech	100
Fraxinus species: Ash	60
Ginkgo biloba (male): Ginkgo (male tree)	100
Ginkgo biloba (female): Ginkgo (female tree)	40
Gleditsia triacanthos: Honey Locust	60
Gleditsia triacanthos inermis:	
Thornless Honey Locust	60
Gleditsia triacanthos selections:	
Patented Honey Locust	80
Gymnocladus dioicus: Kentucky Coffeetree	80
Juglans species: Walnut	60
Juniperus virginiana: Eastern Red Cedar	60
Koelreuteria paniculata and varieties:	
Goldenrain Tree	80
Larix species: European Larch	80
Liquidambar stryaciflua: American Sweetgum	100
Liriodendron (tulipifera): Tulip Tree	100
Maackia amurensis: Amur Maackia	60
Maclura pomifera: Osage-Orange	40
Magnolia species: Magnolia	80
Malus species: Flowering Crabapple	80
Metasequoia glyptostroboides: Dawn Redwood	80
Morus alba and varieties: White Mulberry	40
Morus rubra: Red Russian Mulberry	20
Nyssa sylvatica: Black Tupelo	100
Ostrya virginiana: American Hop Hornbeam	100
Oxydendrum arboreum: Sourwood	100
Phellodendron species: Corktree	80
Picea species: Spruce	80
Pinus banksiana: Jack Pine	60
Pinus nigra: Austrian Pine	100
Pinus ponderosa: Ponderosa Pine	80
Pinus resinosa: Red Pine	80

Species	Percent Value
Pinus strobus: Eastern White Pine	100
Pinus sylvestris: Scot's (Scotch) Pine	100
Platanus species: Planetree	80
Populus species: Poplars	20
Populus alba and varieties: White Poplars	40
Prunus—ornamental and cultivated forms:	
Flowering Cherry	80
Prunus species (native): Native Cherry	40
Pseudotsuga menziesii: Douglas Fir	100
Pyrus species: cultivated forms of Pear	80
Quercus species: Oak	100
Robina species: Locust	20
Salix species: Willow	40
Sassafras albidum: Sassafras	100
Sophora japonica: Japanese Pagodatree	80
Sorbus species: Mountain Ash	80
Syringa amurensis japonica:	
Japanese Tree Lilac	80
Taxodium distichum: Common Baldcypress	80
Thuja species: Cedar	80
Tilia species: Lindens	80
Tilia americana: Basswood	60
Tsuga canadensis: Canadian Hemlock	100
Ulmus americana and varieties: American Elm	
and selections	60
Ulmus carpinifolia Christine Buisman:	
Christine Buisman Elm	80
Ulmus fulva: Slippery Elm	20
Ulmus parvifolia: Littleleaf (Chinese) Elm	80
Ulmus pumila: Siberian Elm	20
Ulmus species: all other Elms	60
Zelkova serrata: Japanese Zelkova	60

Minnesota:

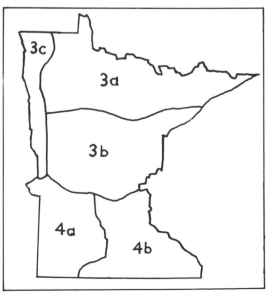

STATE OF MINNESOTA
RECOMMENDED STREET TREES

(From *Horticultural Fact Sheet 22* by M. C. Eisel and L. C. Snyder)

Tree	Height	Spread	Growth rate	4b	4a	3c	3b	3a
Norway Maple (*Acer platanoides*)	M	W	M	*				
Cleveland Norway Maple (*Acer platanoides* 'Cleveland')	M	I	M	*	T			
Emerald Queen Norway Maple (*Acer platanoides* 'Emerald Queen')	M	W	M	*				
Schwedler Norway Maple (*Acer platanoides* 'Schwedleri')	M	W	M	*				
Summer Shade Norway Maple (*Acer platanoides* 'Summer Shade')	M	W	M	*				
Red Maple (*Acer rubrum*)	M	W	M	*			*	*
Sugar Maple (*Acer saccharum*)	L	W	S-M	*	*			T
Ohio Buckeye (*Aesculus glabra*)	M	W	S-M	*	*	T		
Hackberry (*Celtis occidentalis*)	L	W	M	*	*		*	
Russian Olive (*Elaeagnus angustifolia*)	S-M	M	M			T		
White Ash (*Fraxinus americana*)	L	M	M-F	*	*		T	
Autumn Purple White Ash (*Fraxinus americana* 'Autumn Purple')	L	M	M-F	*	*		T	
Green Ash (*Fraxinus pennsylvanica*)	L	W	F	*	*	*	*	*
Marshall Seedless Green Ash (*Fraxinus pennsylvanica* 'Marshall Seedless')	L	W	F	*	*	*	*	*
Summit Green Ash (*Fraxinus pennsylvanica* 'Summit')	L	W	F	*	*	*	*	*
Blue Ash (*Fraxinus quadrangulata*)	M	W	S	T	T			
Ginkgo (*Ginkgo biloba*)	M	W	S	*	T			
Imperial Honey Locust (*Gleditsia triacanthos* 'Imperial')	L	W	F	*	T			
Skyline (*Gleditsia triacanthos* 'Skyline')	L	W	F	*	T			
Kentucky Coffeetree (*Gymnocladus dioicus*)	M-L	W	S	*	*			
Flame Flowering Crabapple (*Malus* 'Flame')	S	I	M	*	*	*		
Radiant Flowering Crabapple (*Malus* 'Radiant')	S	I	M	*	*	*		
Vanguard Flowering Crabapple (*Malus* 'Vanguard')	S	N	M	*	*	*		
Ironwood (*Ostrya virginiana*)	M	I	M	*	*		*	*
Amur Corktree (*Phellodendron amurense*)	M	W	M	*				
Swamp White Oak (*Quercus bicolor*)	L	W	S-M	*	*	T		
Pin Oak (*Quercus palustris*)	M	I	M	*	T			
Sovereign Pin Oak (*Quercus palustris* 'Sovereign')	M	I	M	*	T			
Showy Mountain (*Sorbus decora*)	S	I	M				*	*
Japanese Tree Lilac (*Syringa amurensis japonica*)	S	W	S	*	*	*		
American Linden (*Tilia americana*)	L	W	M	*	*		*	*
Littleleaf Linden (*Tilia cordata*)	M	W	S	*	*	T		
Greenspire Linden (*Tilia cordata* 'Greenspire')	M	I	S	*	*	T		
Redmond Linden (*Tilia* x *euchlora* 'Redmond')	L	I	S	*	T	T		

Height	Spread	Growth rate	Planting Zones
S = small (25 ft. and smaller)	N = narrow (15 ft. and less)	F = fast	* = recommended
M = medium (25-50 ft.)	I = intermediate (15-25 ft.)	M = medium	T = trial planting (protected sites)
L = large (50 ft. and over)	W = wide (25 ft. and wider)	S = slow	

Missouri: (See "Illinois" list.)

The Division of Forestry of the city of St. Louis will plant the following species for a minimal fee:
ASH, GREEN
ASH, 'MARSHALL SEEDLESS'
LINDEN, AMERICAN
LINDEN, EUROPEAN
MAPLE, 'EMERALD QUEEN'
MAPLE, NORWAY
MAPLE, RED
OAK, PIN
PEAR, BRADFORD'S CALLERY (*Pyrus calleryana*)
PLUM, 'PURPLE LEAF' (*Prunus blireiana* and others)
REDBUD (*Cercis* spp.)

New Hampshire: (See ISTC tree list, this section. See "Maine" and "Illinois" tree lists.)

Permission to break the pavement for tree planting must be obtained from the City Manager, the City Council, or the Public Works Department. In most towns the Highway Department will assist in planting.

Several towns have Conservation Commissions, which organize public support for tree-planting programs.

New Jersey:

Trees for New Jersey Streets, a publication of the New Jersey Federation of Shade Tree Commissions (Rutgers College of Agriculture, New Brunswick) is one of the best booklets of its kind and should be obtained by *any* group interested in selecting, planting and maintaining street trees.

The Federation was among the first groups to recognize the shortcomings of tree planting in America when they wrote:

City planners of the post-World War I era decreed that all projections (trees, poles, permanent awnings) along the streets of the business sections were passé, a nuisance and unsightly. The nudity of these streamlined avenues has become drab and monotonous. Trees are being welcomed back into the picture either as surfaced container installations or planted.

The Federation recommends the following trees as "preferred selections":
Tall: attain height of more than 40 feet

GINKGO
HACKBERRY
HONEY LOCUST, THORNLESS 'SHADEMASTER'
HONEY LOCUST, THORNLESS 'SKYLINE'

LINDEN, SILVER
MAPLE, RED
MAPLE, 'WALTER'S COLUMNAR'
MAPLE, 'OCTOBER GLORY'
MAPLE, SUGAR
MAPLE, SUGAR, 'TEMPLE UPRIGHT'
MAPLE, SUGAR, 'GREEN MOUNTAIN'
MAPLE, NORWAY
MAPLE, NORWAY, 'SUMMERSHADE'
MAPLE, NORWAY, 'CLEVELAND'
OAK, RED
OAK, SCARLET
REGENT SCHOLAR TREE and CHINESE SCHOLAR TREE (*Sophora japonica*)
SWEETGUM

Medium-Sized Trees: 30 to 40 feet at maturity

ASH, MODESTO (*Fraxinus velutina* var. *glabra*)
CHERRY, 'RANCHO' COLUMNAR (*Prunus sargentii* 'Rancho')
CRABAPPLE, SIBERIAN (*Malus baccata*)
LINDEN, EUROPEAN, 'LITTLELEAF'
LINDEN, 'GREENSPIRE'
MOUNTAIN ASH, KOREAN (*Sorbus alnifolia*)
PEAR, BRADFORD'S CALLERY
MAPLE, NORWAY, 'MOUNT HOPE'
MAPLE, UPRIGHT SYCAMORE
MAPLE, SCANLON RED
YELLOWWOOD (*Cladastris lutea*)

Small Trees: less than 30 feet tall at maturity

ASH, FLOWERING
CHERRY, KWANZAN (*Prunus serrulata* 'Kwanzan')
DOGWOOD, FLOWERING
DOGWOOD, PINK FLOWERING
HAWTHORN, LAVALLE
HORNBEAM, EUROPEAN (*Carpinus betulus*)
HORNBEAM, UPRIGHT EUROPEAN
MAGNOLIA, KOBUS (*Magnolia kobus* var. *borealis*)
MAPLE, HEDGE
MAPLE, GLOBE NORWAY
WASHINGTON THORN (*Crataegus phaenopyrum*)

Permits for planting on a New Jersey right-of-way would usually be obtained from the County or Municipal Shade Tree Commission. Even a property owner is "urged . . . to wait" on planting a tree until county funds are available. This ruling, no doubt, discourages much incentive for replanting New Jersey streets.

New York: (See "New Jersey" and "Illinois" lists.)

The city of Buffalo uses species common to other states in their street tree-replanting program. In addition, the following varieties are also being experimented with:

HORSECHESTNUT, RUBY RED (*Aesculus carnea briotti*)
HORSECHESTNUT, BAUMAN (*Aesculus hippocastaneum baumani*)
LINDEN, 'GLEN LAVEN'
MAPLE, 'BOWHALL'
MAPLE, 'ARMSTRONG'
MAPLE, 'DRUMMONDS'
MAPLE, 'AMUR'
MAPLE, 'OLMSTEAD' NORWAY
MAPLE, 'PRINCETON' RED
MAPLE, 'CRIMSON' KING
MAACKIA (*Maackia amurense*)

Permission to plant a tree on a public street is granted by the Parks Commission on recommendation by the City Forester.

Permission to break pavement must be obtained from the Department of Public Works.

The city of New York lists the following species as "highly recommended":
ASH, 'MARSHALL'S SEEDLESS'
CALLERY PEAR
CHERRY, KWANZAN
DAWN REDWOOD (*Metasequoia glyptostroboides*)
ELM, BUISMAN
GINKGO
HONEY LOCUST
LONDON PLANETREE
LINDEN, SILVER
OAK, RED
OAK, WILLOW
REGENT SOPHORA (Pagodatree, Scholartree, etc.)
ZELKOVA 'VILLAGE GREEN'

The New York City Department of Parks encourages neighborhood tree planting and distributes an excellent diagram that describes how a sidewalk should be cut and the proper methods for planting trees.

Ohio: (See "Illinois" and "New Jersey" tree lists.)

As a result of the devastating loss of over 25,000 American elms, over a period of years, the city of Toledo now utilizes many more varieties of species than any other city.

Rather than enumerate all the horticultural varieties of maple, honey locust, and linden that are being tried along Ohio streets, a few species of shade trees not yet listed for any state in the Northeast region but that are planted in Toledo follow:
ASH, FLAME (*Fraxinus oxycarpa*)
ASH, GOLDEN DESERT (*Fraxinus oxycarpa aureafolia*)
GOLDENCHAIN TREE (*Laburnum vosii*)

In Toledo, individuals who wish to do so are encouraged to conduct sidewalk tree plantings. The Division of Forestry will pay two-thirds of the cost of planting and then assume all maintenance and replacement costs. An encouraging program, indeed.

Funds for tree planting are derived from all property owners who are required to pay an assessment of five cents per front foot. *All* of this money is used solely for the purpose of retreeing the city.

Pennsylvania: (See ISTC tree list, this section. See "Illinois," "New Jersey," and "Michigan" lists.)

Since varying climatic conditions exist in different regions of this and other states, advice about the adaptability of any species to a particular area should be sought from the Extension Service before trees are finally selected.

The city of Williamsport, one of the smaller cities in the state, has a progressive tree-planting program in which individuals are encouraged to plant between sidewalks and curbs. Applications for permits must be made through the Bureau of Recreation and Parks, and must be approved by the City Forester or Superintendent of Parks.

Rhode Island: (See ISTC tree list, this section. See "Illinois," "Michigan," "New Jersey," and "Maine" lists.)

In addition to species included in the above lists, Rhode Island streets sometimes include the following:
CAROLINA SILVERBELL (30 ft.) (*Halesia carolina*)
GREAT SILVERBELL (60 ft.) (*Halesia monticola*)

The city of Providence has been planting hawthorns, plums, cherries, maples, crabapples, locusts, lindens, and other standard urban selections on its sidewalks for the past ten years.

Individuals wishing to plant a tree (at their own expense) must obtain a permit from the Forestry Department.

Vermont: (See ISTC tree list, this section. See "Maine," "New Jersey," "Michigan," and "Illinois" tree lists.)

Not all species in the above lists will grow throughout Vermont, because of the extremes in temperature, especially in northern areas. Nevertheless, the following trees will grow even where the temperatures sometimes fall as low as −35° F.: Amur maple, American hornbeam, pagoda dogwood, Russian olive, flowering crab, Norway maple, Marshall's seedless ash, Amur corktree, and littleleaf linden.

Further, the Agency of Environmental Conservation in Montpelier recommends that the following trees *not* be planted along *roadsides*, for the following reasons:

ASH, MOUNTAIN—insect problems
BIRCHES—severe insect problems
BOX ELDER—weak wood
ELMS—insect and disease
HAWTHORN—disease
LOCUST, BLACK—insect problems
MAPLE, RED—salt sensitive
MAPLE, SILVER—weak wood
MAPLE, SUGAR—salt sensitive
POPLARS—weak wood
WILLOWS—weak wood

The Bennington Chamber of Commerce recently organized a program that resulted in the planting of 100 trees in the main section of town.

Working with funds from the local garden club as well as individual donations the sidewalks were cut, new soil added, and a layer of sand, topped off with bricks imbedded at the sidewalk level. In a manner similar to the successful reforestation program practice in Israel (discussed in Section 1) stainless-steel plaques bearing the name of donors or deceased individuals were placed next to the trees.

Some potential for vandalism was eliminated by utilizing the labor of male students of a local school.

Virginia: (See tree lists for "West Virginia" and other adjacent states of the northeast region.)

James T. Oates, City Arborist for Richmond and past President of the International Shade Tree Conference, suggests that "trees that are planted in various cities are . . . almost without exception, trees that landscape people use which are easiest to transplant and fastest in growth. Cities end up with a hodgepodge of the wrong trees in the wrong place."

This tends to be confirmed. As one example, the city of Newport News reports that several hundred sycamores (*Platanus orientalis*) that were planted during the early 1920s have had to be removed in recent years, owing to unspecified problems.

The same city reports that of a total population of 18,000 street trees, it was found that the American linden (*Tilia americana*) has best withstood city conditions. In the past ten years over two-thousand crape myrtles (*Lagerstroemia indica*) have been planted be-

cause of their attractive bright pink flowers. Although these trees exhibit some of the desirable traits listed at the beginning of this chapter (the roots do not buckle sidewalks, the branches do not interfere with utility lines), they are very small trees (about twenty feet tall at maturity) and fail to evoke the grandeur of Old Virginia.

The city of Richmond lists the following trees as acceptable for planting on city streets:
Male Ginkgo
Winged Elm
Augustine Elm (ascending)
Red Maple
Norway Maple (pyramidal and small globe)
Pin Oak
Linden
Ash

Smaller shade trees (some of which are not yet available in any quantity) acceptable and to be used when they are available are:
Small conventional Maples, Redbud, Hornbeam, Beech,
  Crape Myrtle (tree form), Sourwood
Hop Hornbeam
Koelreuteria Paniculata
Hawthorn
Thornless Honey Locust (podless)
Amur Privet
Dogwood (tree form)
Flowering Crab

Trees disapproved for planting on city streets are:
Female Ginkgo
Silver Maple
Fruit trees, including Wild Cherry, Mulberry
Sweetgum
Chinaberry
Ailanthus
Cottonwood
Black Locust
Elm (large varieties), Chinese and Siberian

West Virginia:

Clifford W. Collier, the State Extension Specialist for Landscape Architecture, recommends the following trees to fit the "tree zones" illustrated in the following diagram:

Zone 1 (Small Trees)
FLOWERING CRABAPPLES
GLOBE NORWAY MAPLE
WASHINGTON HAWTHORN
KOREAN MOUNTAIN ASH
UPRIGHT EUROPEAN HORNBEAM

JAPANESE FLOWERING CHERRY
LAVALLE HAWTHORN
HEDGE MAPLE
FLOWERING GLOBE LOCUST *(Robinia hispida* x *macrophylla)*

Zone 2 (Medium-Sized Trees)

LITTLELEAF LINDEN
COLUMNAR RED MAPLE
BRADFORD'S CALLERY PEAR
GINKGO
RUBY RED HORSECHESTNUT
SORREL TREE
SCANLON RED MAPLE
SAWTOOTH OAK
YELLOWWOOD
KATSURA TREE
EUROPEAN WHITE BIRCH

Zone 3 (Large Trees)

RED MAPLE
NORWAY MAPLE
PIN OAK
TEXAS RED OAK *(Quercus shumardi)*

SWEET GUM
THORNLESS HONEY LOCUST
AMERICAN LINDEN
ZELKOVA

Unfortunately, citizens of this state are discouraged from planting along a public right-of-way. Since "the sidewalks belong to the city," individual tree-planting efforts on these areas are forbidden.

Wisconsin: (See "Illinois," "Michigan," and other tree lists for this region.)

The Extension Service of this northern state, in Circular #129, recommends the larger trees because of their durability in the cold. Thus, recommended trees for Wisconsin city and village streets include the Buisman elm, sycamores, ginkgos (these three species are adapted only to southern and eastern Wisconsin), as well as most maples, lindens, oaks, honey locusts, ash, hawthorn, serviceberry, Baumann horsechestnut, ironwood, and Amur corktree.

Trees to be avoided, and reasons, include:

Black Locust—subject to borers

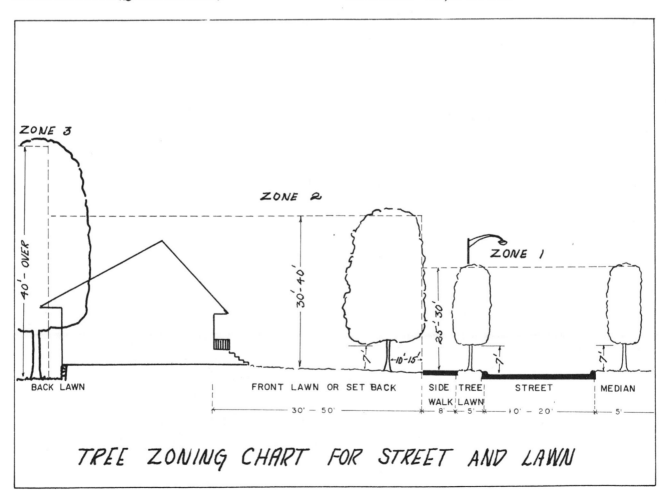

TREE ZONING CHART FOR STREET AND LAWN

Box Elder—weak wooded, female trees attract the box elder bug

Catalpa—litter of flowers, fruits, and leaves

Elms—subject to Dutch elm disease

Poplar—roots block sewers, weak wooded, litter of fruits

Silver Maple—weak wooded, buttress roots heave pavements

Willows—roots block sewers, weak wooded, litter of twigs

Nut-bearing trees—litter of nuts

Region II: Southeast

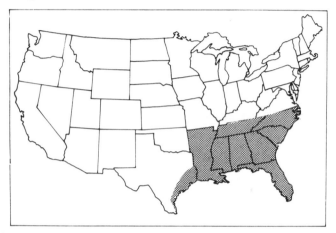

Before enumerating the recommended street trees for each state in this regional grouping it may prove valuable to list those species given a "100 percent" rating for the southern states by the International Shade Tree Conference (ISTC):*

BEECH, AMERICAN
BEECH, EUROPEAN
DOGWOOD, FLOWERING
GINKGO
HOLLY, AMERICAN *(Ilex opaca)*
HONEY LOCUST, 'MORAINE' THORNLESS
MAGNOLIA, SOUTHERN *(Magnolia grandiflora)*
MAPLE, RED
OAKS (WHITE, SCARLET, SHINGLE, LAUREL, OVERCUP, BUR, WILLOW, SHUMARD, LIVE)
PINE, LOBLOLLY *(Pinus taeda)*
PINE, LONGLEAF *(Pinus palustris)*

The same committee rated the following species at the "80 percent" value:

BALDCYPRESS, COMMON *(Taxodium distichum)*
ELMS (AMERICAN, CEDAR, ROCK, WINGED)
GOLDENRAIN TREE
HEMLOCK, CANADA

---

* Latin names are provided for those species not yet so identified.

HEMLOCK, CAROLINA
HONEY LOCUST, THORNLESS
MAPLE, FLORIDA
MAPLE, SUGAR
OAK, SWAMP CHESTNUT *(Quercus prinus)*
PECAN *(Carya illinoensis)*
PINE, EASTERN WHITE
SWEETGUM
TULIP TREE
TUPELO, BLACK
WALNUT, BLACK *(Juglans nigra)*

The recommendations of individual states in this region follow.

Alabama: (See ISTC tree list, as well as "Georgia" and "Florida.")

Arkansas: (See other southern regional tree lists.)

The City Forester for Little Rock suggests such trees as ash, arborvitae, elm, cedar (red), dogwood, hickory, magnolia, maple, mimosa, oak (red and white), pine, redbud, sycamore, and willow.

Florida:

This state offers nearly limitless possibilities for the tree planter.

Of the three distinct zones of growth that cross the state, the southernmost portion will allow any number of excellent subtropical shade trees their place in the sun. (See "Hawaii" tree list for additional selections.)

The Florida Cooperative Extension Service lists the following species as "the most popular trees and palms for street and roadside plantings":

The following trees were rated "first order" if they appeared on lists of "the 10 best" prepared by 75–100 percent of leading Florida plantsmen; "second order" if they were on 50–75 percent of the lists; and "third order" if they appeared on less than 50 percent of the lists. Although the lists were for "ornamental plants," only trees appropriate for streets and roadsides are listed below:

Statewide Trees

First Order
MAPLE, RED
OAK, LIVE
SABAL PALMETTO

Second Order
BOTTLEBRUSH *(Callistemon* spp.)
DATE PALM, CANARY ISLAND
HOLLY, AMERICAN
LOQUAT *(Eriobotrya japonica)*

	Height in Feet	Section of Florida to Which Adapted:		
		North and West	Central	South
AFRICAN TULIP TREE	60			x
BENJAMIN FIG (WEEPING LAUREL)	50			x
CABBAGE PALM	90	x	x	x
CAJEPUT TREE	80		x	x
CANARY ISLAND DATE PALM	60	x	x	x
COCONUT PALM	100			x
FLOWERING DOGWOOD	35	x	x	
LAUREL OAK	100	x	x	x
LIVE OAK	60	x	x	x
MAHOGANY	75			x
QUEEN PALM	40		x	x
RED MAPLE	80	x	x	x
ROYAL PALM	60			x
SOUTHERN MAGNOLIA	100	x	x	

OAK, LAUREL
QUEEN PALM (*Arecastrum romanzoffianum*)
YAUPON (*Ilex vomitoria* and var.)
YEW, JAPANESE

Third Order

BRAZILIAN BUTIA PALM (*Butia capitata*)
JERUSALEM THORN (*Parkinsonia aculeata*)
WASHINGTON PALM (*Washingtonia robusta*)
WATER OAK (*Quercus nigra*)

The city of Gainesville has a municipal requirement that "a minimum of 10 percent of the total developed area of any parcel of property . . . be devoted to landscape development."

Further, this progressive code of legislation, rare in America, where developers usually plant nothing or a token shrub on multimillion-dollar sites, provides a schedule for computing how much a particular species of tree contributes to fulfilling the landscape area requirements.

Thus, trees such as live oak and slash pine count for 200 square feet of a developed landscape (at maturity), while loquat, cherry laurel, Chinese evergreen elm, Jerusalem thorn, Japanese myrtle, and ligustrum are credited with a contribution of 100 square feet.

Trees that are *preserved* (instead of being destroyed to facilitate construction) also receive credit against the landscape-area requirements, according to a fixed schedule. This provision encourages thoughts about the economic advantages of tree preservation among devel-

opers who need only file a request to destroy such trees in other cities.

Georgia:

The Atlanta City Arborist has approved the following trees for the streets of Atlanta:
CRABAPPLE, FLOWERING
CHERRY LAUREL (*Prunus caroliniana*)
CRAPE MYRTLE
DOGWOOD
GINKGO
HAWTHORN, WASHINGTON
HOLLY, AMERICAN
HONEY LOCUST, THORNLESS
LINDEN, LITTLELEAF
MAPLES, FLORIDA, NORWAY, RED, SUGAR
OAKS, WATER, PIN, WILLOW
REDBUD
SOURWOOD
SWEETGUM
SYCAMORE
ZELKOVA

Permits are *not* required to break sidewalks for tree planting; however, approval must be granted by the Arborist and the Public Works Department.

The city of Savannah Park and Tree Commission will plant a tree for individuals who establish a proper bed on city property. Arrangements for opening the pavement for this purpose must be obtained through the traffic engineering department.

Louisiana:

The city of New Orleans is peculiar in that extremes in weather, ranging from subfreezing temperatures (as low as 12° F. for a 72-hour period in 1962), to hot, subtropical temperatures limit rather severely the choice of trees that can be expected to survive.

Lawrence M. Kuhn, of the New Orleans Parkway and Park Commission, recommends that "hardy native and escaped exotics" be used because they generally survive with a minimum of care.

Trees recommended by this Commission include the following:

Large Trees

BALDCYPRESS
ELM, AMERICAN AND CHINESE
HACKBERRY
MAGNOLIA
OAK, LIVE AND SHUMARD
PALM, CANARY DATE *(Phoenix canariensis)*
PALM, WASHINGTON
PECAN *(Carya illinoensis* var. 'Elliott' and 'Candy')
REDWOOD, DAWN
SWEETGUM
SYCAMORE

Medium-Sized Trees

BIRCH, RIVER
CEDAR, RED
CHINESE TALLOW *(Sapium sebiferum)*
ELM, WINGED
GOLDENRAIN
GINKGO
MAPLE, RED
PALM, COCOS *(Butea capitata)*
PALM, WINDMILL *(Trachycarpus fortunei)*
PARASOL TREE, CHINESE *(Firmiana simplex)*
PINE, SPRUCE
TREE OF HEAVEN *(Ailanthus aetissima)*

Small Trees

CRAPE MYRTLE
HOLLY, AMERICAN
HORNBEAM, AMERICAN
LAUREL, CHERRY
MAGNOLIA, SWEET BAY

The city of Baton Rouge has abundant rainfall and nearly consistent humidity, factors that make life uncomfortable for most humans, but that are ideal for growing plants, even under urban conditions.

Using many of the same species as listed for New Orleans boulevards, the Baton Rouge (City Parish) Beautification Commission has begun to replant many streets, particularly in the long-neglected Riverside area. Streets have been completely rebuilt and are now lined with trees.

Individuals may plant on public streets, but the species should be consistent with the "Master Planting Plan" of this city; maintenance must be continued by the individual or group undertaking such planting.

Mississippi: (See ISTC tree list this section; also "Georgia.")

The Cooperative Extension Service includes the following "street trees" in their general list of "Landscaping Plant Materials" by Wallace C. Gordon:

Large Trees (above 40 feet)

BALDCYPRESS
CEDAR, EASTERN RED
ELM, WINGED
HACKBERRY, SUGAR
HONEY LOCUST, 'MORAINE'
MAGNOLIA, SOUTHERN
MAPLE, RED
MAPLE, SILVER
MAPLE, SUGAR
OAK, LIVE
OAK, WATER
OAK, WILLOW
PECAN
PINE, SLASH
PINE, YELLOW
PINE, LOBLOLLY
PLANETREE
TULIP TREE

Small Trees (15–40 feet)

CRAB, JAPANESE FLOWERING *(Malus floribunda)*
DOGWOOD, FLOWERING
GOLDENRAIN TREE
REDBUD, EASTERN

North Carolina: (See ISTC tree list. See other states in this region.)

South Carolina: (See ISTC tree list; also "Georgia.")

The Cooperative Extension Service at Clemson University does not have a standard list of recommended trees that will apply to all regions of the state.

Trees are recommended on an individual basis, decisions being based on population density, industrial needs, amount and proximity of traffic, geographical location, and horticultural demands of the site.

Where general recommendations *are* made the following trees are often recommended:

ASH, GREEN
CRAPE MYRTLE
DOGWOOD, FLOWERING
ELM, WINGED
GOLDENRAIN TREE
MAGNOLIA, SOUTHERN
MAPLE, RED
MAPLE, NORWAY
OAK, WILLOW
PEAR, BRADFORD'S CALLERY
SYCAMORE

Tennessee: (See ISTC tree list; also other states in this region.)

The Tennessee Department of Conservation recommends the following trees for urban planting:

ASH
DOGWOOD
MAPLE, RED AND SUGAR
REDBUD
SWEETGUM
SYCAMORE
TULIP TREE
WILLOW OAK

Knoxville commonly plants:

MAPLE, SILVER
MAPLE, SUGAR
OAK, PIN
PINE, WHITE

The Cooperative Extension Service issues a list of "Trees for the Landscape" but prefers not to make a standard list that would be applicable for all regions of the state.

Individuals are apparently free to plant trees anywhere in the state, as restrictive or protective ordinances are apparently not enforced to any degree. However, before the expense of breaking the pavement is undertaken it might be wise (and legal) to contact the Street Department.

Texas (coastal plain along the Gulf of Mexico): (See ISTC tree list; list of trees for southern Florida and Hawaii. For trees suitable for other regions of Texas see "Plains States.")

Soil and climatic conditions vary widely in Texas, from the grassland plains in the North, to semiarid and arid regions in the West, to subtropical in the South.

According to the Cooperative Extension Service the following trees are desirable for the coastal plain, which experiences short winters, moderate summer

temperatures with an annual rainfall of about thirty to forty inches, and has a generally high water table:

BALDCYPRESS
ELM, AMERICAN
GINKGO
HACKBERRY, SUGAR
HOLLY, AMERICAN
MAGNOLIA, SOUTHERN
MAPLE, RED
OAK, LAUREL
OAK, LIVE
OAK, SOUTHERN RED
OAK, WILLOW
PALM, CANARY DATE
PALM, CHINESE FAN
PALM, SABAL PALMETTO
PALM, WASHINGTON
PECAN
PINE, LONGLEAF
PLANETREE, AMERICAN
PLANETREE, LONDON

The city of Corpus Christi Parks Department reports that there are no restrictions on the trees that may be used and the following are most frequently planted:

ASH, RIO GRANDE *(Fraxinus texensis)*
CHINESE TALLOW
OAK, LIVE
PALMS (above listed plus the DATE PALM)

To obtain permission to break concrete for the purpose of planting street trees a permit must be obtained from the Building Section of the Department of Engineering Services of the city.

Region III: The Plains

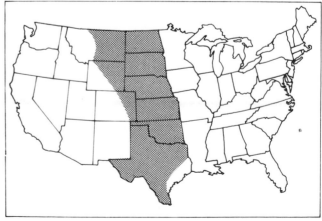

The International Shade Tree Conference rates the following trees as "100 percent" on their value scale for this region of the country. (The region termed

"Midwestern" by the ISTC encompasses most of the states grouped here in the "Plains" category.)

BEECH, AMERICAN
HONEY LOCUST, 'MORAINE'
HOPHORNBEAM, AMERICAN
MAPLE, NORWAY
MAPLE, RED
MAPLE, SUGAR
OAK, BUR
OAK, EASTERN RED
OAK, PIN
OAK, WHITE

These species are rated 80 percent:

ASH, GREEN
ASH, WHITE
GINKGO
HACKBERRY, COMMON
HICKORY, SHAGBARK
HONEYLOCUST, THORNLESS
LINDEN, LITTLELEAF
WALNUT, BLACK

A separate list "For Dry Plains Areas" (3,500 to 5,000 feet) is also provided in the ISTC ratings, as follows:

Large Trees

Class No. 1—100%
ELM, SIBERIAN (*Ulmus pumila*)
HACKBERRY, COMMON
HONEY LOCUST, COMMON
POPLAR, PLAINS (*Populus sargenti*)

Class No. 2—80%
ASH, GREEN
ELM, AMERICAN
MAPLE, SILVER

Small Trees

Class No. 1—100%
RUSSIAN OLIVE (*Eleagnus augustifolia*)

Class No. 2—80%
RUSSIAN MULBERRY (*Morus alba tatarica*)

Colorado (eastern): (See ISTC tree list.)

The city of Denver has very specific ordinances regarding the planting, care, removal, and selection of trees. The following species may be planted on public street right-of-ways upon receipt of an approved permit from the office of the City Forester under the Manager of Parks and Recreation:

Medium Trees (40 feet tall at maturity)

ASH, GREEN

BUCKEYE, YELLOW (*Aesculus octandra*)
CATALPA, WESTERN (*Catalpa speciosa*)
HACKBERRY, COMMON
HONEY LOCUST, THORNLESS
KENTUCKY COFFEETREE
LINDEN, AMERICAN
LINDEN, EUROPEAN
MAPLE, NORWAY
OAK, BUR
OAK, ENGLISH
OAK, RED

Smaller Trees

ASH, EUROPEAN (*Sorbus aucuparia*)
BUCKEYE, OHIO
CATALPA, CHINESE
CRABAPPLES, FLOWERING
HAWTHORN, DOWNY
HAWTHORN, WASHINGTON
LINDEN, LITTLELEAF

Kansas: (See ISTC tree list and "Colorado," this section.)

The Extension Service issues a booklet, *What Shall I Plant?* In it are listed shrubs, trees, and vines that do well in various regions of Kansas. However, a separate listing of trees for streets or for shade has not yet been prepared.

The Topeka City Forestry Department issues permits that enable individuals to plant trees on public streets, providing the species is adaptable to the site and the tree will not interfere with utility lines, traffic signs, etc.

Montana: (See ISTC tree list and "Colorado," this section.)

The Cooperative Extension Service issues a beautifully produced bulletin (#323), *Trees and Shrubs for Montana*. This booklet is written to make the *identification* of foliage an easy assignment.

A separate report lists "Street Trees Adapted to Montana Conditions," as follows:

ASHES
BOX ELDER
CATALPA
CRABAPPLES
ELM, AMERICAN
ELM, CHINESE
FIR, CONCOLOR
HACKBERRY
HAWTHORNS
HONEY LOCUST

HORSECHESTNUTS
LOCUST, BLACK
LINDENS
MAPLE, NORWAY
MAPLE, SYCAMORE
POPLAR, LOMBARDY
POPLAR, SILVER
RUSSIAN OLIVE
SPRUCE, COLORADO

Since regional recommendations within the state are not made for the above "street trees" it is difficult to evaluate these species in relation to the ISTC lists, which cover several regions of Montana.

Ordinances regarding trees are not strict in Montana. Consequently many older trees are being indiscriminantly cut back (and exposed to disease), especially in Billings. Typical of many cities in America Billings is "undertreed," especially in suburban tracts developed in the past twenty years and the downtown areas. Those sections of the city that were heavily planted with trees twenty-five to fifty years ago are still among the most attractive (and expensive) of all local residential districts.

Nebraska: (See ISTC tree list, this section. See other states, this section.)

Of the trees recommended as good "yard trees" by the State Extension Service the following species should do well (with attention) as shade trees for Nebraska's towns and cities:

ASH, GREEN, 'MARSHALL'S SEEDLESS'
GINKGO (central and eastern Nebraska)
HACKBERRY
HAWTHORN
HONEY LOCUST
KENTUCKY COFFEETREE
LINDEN, LITTLELEAF
MAPLE, NORWAY (eastern Nebraska)
MAPLE, SUGAR (eastern Nebraska)
OAK, BUR
OAK, PIN (eastern Nebraska)
OAK, RED (eastern Nebraska)

North Dakota: (See ISTC tree list, this section; also adjacent states, this section.)

For mountainous regions of North Dakota see separate listing, "The Rocky Mountains."

The Cooperative Extension Service at Fargo recommends the following species. Forester Robert H. Heintz states, "We are limited to the species that will grow and survive on the northern prairie":

ASH, GREEN
BASSWOOD (AMERICAN LINDEN)
BOX ELDER
COTTONWOOD
ELM, AMERICAN
HACKBERRY
MAPLE, SILVER (southeastern North Dakota)

Forester Heintz reports that "street tree planting in North Dakota's cities and towns has been left to the individual homeowner. Very few of our cities have an ordinance covering shade tree species. However they all agree that shrubs, conifers, and the small trees such as the various flowering crabs and chokecherry are *not* to be planted on that area between the city sidewalk and the curb."

Oklahoma: (See ISTC tree list, this section.)

Paul J. Mitchell of the Oklahoma State University Extension Service has published suggested lists of tree species for different regions of Oklahoma as follows (only deciduous shade trees are listed here):

Northeastern Region

ASH, GREEN, 'MARSHALL'S SEEDLESS'
ASH, WHITE, 'ROSEHILL'
GINKGO
GOLDENRAIN TREE
HACKBERRY, WESTERN
KENTUCKY COFFEETREE—MALE
OAK, SHUMMARD
OAK, WATER
OAK, WILLOW
PAGODATREE
PEAR, 'BRADFORD' CALLERY
PISTACHIO
REDBUD, EASTERN

Eastern Region

Medium Shade Trees (40 to 50 feet)
BALDCYPRESS
DAWN REDWOOD
GINKGO
HACKBERRY, WESTERN
MAPLE, SILVER
MAPLE, SUGAR
MULBERRY, FRUITLESS
OAK, LIVE
OAK, WATER
OAK, WHITE
OAK, SHUMMARD
SWEETGUM (CULTIVARS)
SYCAMORE
TULIP TREE

Northwestern Region

ASH, GREEN, 'MARSHALL'S SEEDLESS'
CRABAPPLE, 'SPRING SNOW'
*GINKGO, 'AUTUMN GOLD'
GOLDENRAIN TREE
HACKBERRY, WESTERN
HONEY LOCUST
KENTUCKY COFFEETREE—MALE
MULBERRY, FRUITLESS
*OAK, SAWTOOTH
*OAK, WATER
*OAK, WILLOW
PAGODATREE
PEAR, 'BRADFORD' CALLERY
PISTACHIO, CHINESE
*REDBUD, EASTERN
*SOAPBERRY (*Sapindus drummondi*)

Western Region

Medium Trees (40 to 50 feet)

ASH, GREEN
COTTONWOOD, MALE
ELM, LACEBARK
HACKBERRY, WESTERN
HONEY LOCUST
KENTUCKY COFFEETREE
MAPLE, SILVER
MULBERRY, FRUITLESS
OAK, BLACKJACK
OAK, BUR
OAK, SHUMMARD
POPLAR, WHITE—MALE
POPLAR, BOLLEANA
SYCAMORE

Small Trees (20 to 30 feet)

GOLDENRAIN TREE
JUJUBE
MULBERRY, FRUITLESS WEEPING
PAGODATREE
PEAR, BRADFORD ORNAMENTAL
PISTACHE, CHINESE
PLUM, PURPLE LEAF
REDBUD, EASTERN ('ALBA,' 'FOREST PANSY')
RUSSIAN OLIVE
SOAPBERRY

Central Region

Medium Trees (40 to 50 feet)
ASH, GREEN
BALDCYPRESS

---

*Doubtful in Panhandle.

DAWN REDWOOD
ELM, LACEBARK
GINKGO, 'AUTUMN GOLD' OR A MALE
HACKBERRY, WESTERN
MAPLE, SILVER
MAPLE, SUGAR ('CADDO')
MULBERRY, FRUITLESS
OAK, BUR
OAK, LIVE
OAK, SHUMARD
OAK, WATER
SYCAMORE

Individuals who wish to break the pavement of a sidewalk or other public right-of-way must first contact the City Engineering Department and then the Parks Department. Unfortunately, most municipalities in Oklahoma do not plant trees in public right-of-ways.

The city of Tulsa has prepared the best "Tree Planting Guide" of any American city. In addition to planting and maintenance instructions, there is information on tree selection and 39 illustrated species recommended for Tulsa streets.

If Tulsa has been able to raise the funds necessary for this superior tree-planting program there is no reason why *every* other city in America should not be able to learn how the program was organized, financed and produced.

South Dakota: (See ISTC tree list, this section. For mountainous regions of South Dakota see separate listing "The Rock Mountains.")

The Cooperative Extension Service at Brookings has available a very complete booklet, *Deciduous Trees for South Dakota Landscapes* (Bulletin #578). Over 44 species are treated, including "descriptive features" (landscape uses, disease and insect susceptibility, water and soil requirements, hardiness, etc.), height and spread, and zone of growth in South Dakota. Since this tree list is not limited to species suitable for street or shade purposes, but also for shelter purposes, park plantings, lawns, etc., the interested tree planter would do well to read through the entire publication.

Street tree planting in the state is rare at this time. Although cities will sometimes replace dead trees, this is usually left to the property owner.

For example, the city of Pierre does have a brief ordinance regarding street trees, but recommended or prohibited species are not enumerated, nor is there a permit system.

Bruce Webster, Pierre Community Forester, states

that the four most common trees in most South Dakota cities are green ash, box elder, and American and Siberian elm.

Texas (North, East, Central and Western): (See ISTC tree list, this section.)

The Extension Service at College Station publishes *Selected Lists of Trees for Regions of Texas* as follows (only deciduous trees are included here):

East Texas ("most of the cotton country")

ASH, WHITE
ELM, AMERICAN
ELM, WINGED
GINKGO
MAPLE, RED
OAK, BUR
OAK, LAUREL
OAK, OVERCUP
OAK, SOUTHERN
OAK, WILLOW
PECAN
PLANETREE, AMERICAN
SWEETGUM
TULIP TREE
TUPELO

Central Texas ("subhumid . . . with black and chocolate colored soils")

ASH, GREEN—south only
CHINQUAPIN *(Quercus muhlenbergi)*
ELM, CEDAR
ELM, CHINESE
FLAME BOTTLETREE *(Brachychiton acerifolium)*
GOLDENRAIN TREE
HACKBERRY, SUGAR
OAK, BUR
OAK, POST
OAK, SOUTHERN RED
OAK, SHUMARD
OAK, WILLOW
PECAN
PLANETREE, AMERICAN
PLANETREE, LONDON

North (Texas plains)

"Satisfactory . . . for all parts" [of this region]:
ASH, GREEN
ELM, CHINESE
HACKBERRY
LOCUST, BLACK

"Likely to succeed over most of region":
ASH, RED

PLANETREE, AMERICAN
POPLAR, SILVER

"Less desirable trees that may be useful under especially difficult conditions in this region":
BOX ELDER
OSAGE ORANGE
RUSSIAN MULBERRY
RUSSIAN OLIVE

Western Texas ("arid plateau conditions")

"Most promising":
ASH, GREEN
HACKBERRY
LOCUST, BLACK
LOCUST, HONEY
POPLAR, EASTERN
WALNUT, NOTHA
WILLOW, DESERT

"Less desirable but satisfactory":
BOX ELDER
CHINABERRY

Texas cities differ in their regulations regarding the planting of street trees.

For example, Dallas encourages planting on *private* property but allows planting on public streets after the "appropriate department" is notified. There are no formal tree-planting permits.

Wyoming (eastern): (See ISTC tree list, this section.)

For recommendations in mountainous regions of the state see Wyoming under "The Rocky Mountains."

Region IV: The Rocky Mountains

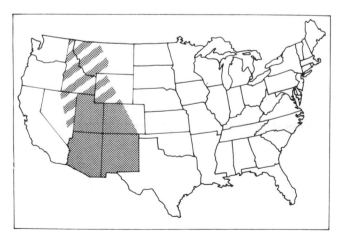

The International Shade Tree Conference (ISTC) rates "Rocky Mountain Shade Trees for Irrigated Areas 4,000 to 6,000 Feet" as follows. (Only "Large

Trees" in the 100 percent and 80 percent categories are included; trees rated 60 percent and lower and "Small Trees" are omitted.)

Class No. 1—100%

BUCKEYE, YELLOW
ELM, AMERICAN
HACKBERRY, COMMON
HONEY LOCUST, THORNLESS
HORSECHESTNUT, COMMON
KENTUCKY COFFEETREE
LINDEN, AMERICAN
LINDEN, EUROPEAN
MAPLE, SILVER
OAK, BUR

Class No. 2—80%

ASH, GREEN
BIRCH, GRAY (Betula populifolia)
BIRCH, CUTLEAF EUROPEAN (Betula pendula gracilis)
BIRCH, EUROPEAN WHITE (Betula pendula)
CATALPA, NORTHERN
ELM, ENGLISH
MAPLE, CUTLEAF SILVER
MAPLE, NORWAY
MAPLE, SCHWEDLER NORWAY
MAPLE, SUGAR
OAK, EASTERN BLACK
OAK, ENGLISH
OAK, PIN
OAK, SOUTHERN RED
OHIO BUCKEYE
WALNUT, EASTERN BLACK

A second list is recommended by the ISTC "For High Altitudes Mountain Areas, 6,000 to 9,000 feet." . . . "In many very high towns, the native evergreens are the only street trees possible."

Class No. 1—100%

POPLAR, LANCELEAF (Populus acuminate)
POPLAR, NARROWLEAF (Populus angustifolia)

Class No. 2—80%

FIR, ALPINE (Abies lasiocarpa)
PINE, BRISTLECONE (Pinus aristata)
PINE, LIMBER (Pinus flexilis)
PINE, LODGEPOLE (Pinus contorta latifolia)
POPLAR, CAROLINA (Populus canadensis eugenei)
POPLAR, SOUTHERN (Populus deltoides missouriensis)
SPRUCE, COLORADO (Picea pungens)
SPRUCE, ENGELMANN (Picea engelmanni)
WILLOW, SHARPLEAF (Salix acutifolia)
WILLOW, YELLOWSTEM (Salix alba vitellina)

Arizona:

The University of Arizona Cooperative Extension Service recommends shade trees in two categories; for northern and for southern regions of the state:

Northern Arizona

ASH, ARIZONA
ASH, GREEN (MAPLE)
COTTONWOOD, GREAT PLAINS
COTTONWOOD, NARROW-LEAVED
ELM, AMERICAN
ELM, CHINESE
LOCUST, BLACK
LOCUST, MORAINE
LOCUST, THORNLESS HONEY
MAPLE, RED (SCHWEDLER)
MAPLE, SILVER
MAPLE, SUGAR
MULBERRY, KINGAN FRUITLESS
OLIVE, RUSSIAN
PLANETREE, EUROPEAN
POPLAR, BOLLEANA
POPLAR, CAROLINA
POPLAR, LOMBARDY
WILLOW, WEEPING

Southern Arizona

ASH, ARIZONA
ASH, MODESTO
COTTONWOOD
ELM, CHINESE
HACKBERRY
LOCUST, BLACK
LOCUST, THORNLESS HONEY
MESQUITE
MULBERRY, KINGAN FRUITLESS
OLIVE, RUSSIAN
PECAN
PISTACHIO, CHINESE
POPLAR, BOLLEANA
POPLAR, CAROLINA
PLANETREE, LONDON
TREE OF HEAVEN (Ailanthus)
WILLOW, DESERT
WILLOW, WEEPING GOLDEN
WILLOW, WEEPING GREEN

Colorado Rockies: (See ISTC tree list, this section.)

Idaho:

"The City of Trees," also known as Boise City, has a very specific approved tree list. Fortunately, most streets in the city have wide-enough nonpaved strips of soil that allow for street tree planting. Individuals *may* break the pavement and plant a tree on paved streets if they have permission of the City-County Road District and a permit from the City Forester.

Montana, Mountains: (See ISTC tree list, this section.)

Nevada, Mountains: (See ISTC tree list, this section.)

New Mexico: (For mountainous regions see ISTC tree list, this section.)

Circular 447 of the Cooperative Extension Service of New Mexico State University, *Ornamental Trees for New Mexico*, lists both deciduous and evergreen trees for home landscaping. New Mexico laws do not restrict any type of tree that may be planted on streets, with the exception of height limitations on trees placed beneath power lines.

Permission to break sidewalks "is not easily" secured.

Interested planters would best obtain a copy of the circular listed above before selecting species for the wide geographic extremes in the state.

Utah: (For mountainous regions see ISTC tree list, this section.)

Salt Lake City recommends the following shade trees for streets:

ASH, WHITE
ASH, EUROPEAN (MALE)
CRAB, FLOWERING
ELM, AUGUSTINE ASCENDING
GOLDENRAIN TREE
HORSECHESTNUT (hybrid only)
KENTUCKY COFFEETREE (male)
LINDEN, LITTLELEAF
MAPLE, NORWAY
MAPLE, SYCAMORE
OAK, BUR
PAGODATREE
PLUM, PURPLE FLOWERING,
 'THUNDERCLOUD'

Permits to plant and/or to break existing pavement must be obtained from the Shade Tree Department.

Carl M. Johnson, Extension Forester at Logan, reports the following trees are commonly planted in Utah:

Gymnosperms
CEDAR, EASTERN RED
CEDAR, NORTHERN WHITE
*FIR, DOUGLAS ROCKY MOUNTAIN
*JUNIPER, ROCKY MOUNTAIN
PINE, AUSTRIAN
PINE, MUGO
*PINE, PONDEROSA
PINE, SCOTCH
*SPRUCE, BLUE
SPRUCE, NORWAY

Angiosperms
ASH, GREEN
ASH, MOUNTAIN (EUROPEAN)
ASH, WHITE
*ASPEN, QUAKING
BASSWOOD, AMERICAN
BASSWOOD, EUROPEAN
BIRCH, PAPER
*BIRCH, WATER
BIRCH, WEEPING
*BOX ELDER
CATALPA, NORTHERN
*CHOKECHERRY
COTTONWOOD, EASTERN
*CRAB, FLOWERING
*DOGWOOD, RED-OSIER (shrub)
*HACKBERRY
*HAWTHORN, ENGLISH
*HAWTHORN, NATIVE
HAZEL
HORSECHESTNUT
KENTUCKY COFFEETREE
LOCUST, BLACK
LOCUST, HONEY
*MAPLE, BIGTOOTH
MAPLE, NORWAY
MAPLE, RED
MAPLE, SILVER
MAPLE, SYCAMORE
MULBERRY, RED
MULBERRY, WHITE
OAK, BUR
*OAK, GAMBEL
OAK, NORTHERN RED
OAK, WHITE
OLIVE, RUSSIAN
*PLUM
POPLAR, WHITE
*SUMAC
SYCAMORE, AMERICAN
TAMARISK (shrub in area)
WALNUT, BLACK
WILLOW, WEEPING

* *Native to Utah.*

Wyoming: (For mountainous regions see ISTC tree list, this section.)

E. Blair Adams, Extension Forester at Laramie, reports: "an individual who wants to break the pavement and plant a tree, this is no problem here since we have few situations where this would be necessary. . . . We are still working on individual awareness of tree values and urging additional tree plantings *anywhere, anytime,* and by anyone. We do, however, caution in the use of varieties which can grow in each area."

In the following tree list, each species is keyed by altitude as follows:

A. Areas below 5,000 feet.
B. Areas between 5,000 feet and 6,500 feet.
C. Areas over 6,500 feet.

CONIFEROUS TREES

Altitude	Name	Height	Space	Exposure
ABC	Rocky Mountain Juniper *Juniperus scopulorem*	6–20'	8'	sun
ABC	Scopulorem Junipers—Medora, Moffet, Welch, Pathfinder, Cologreen, Platinum, Grey Gleem, et al. *Juniperus scopulorem* varieties	6–10'	5–6'	sun
ABC	Utah Juniper *Juniperus utahensis*	6–10'	6'	sun
A	Eastern Red Cedar *Juniperus virginiana*	20–30'	8'	sun, part shade
AB	Red Cedar varieties—Canaerti, Burki, Hills Dundee, Cupressifolia, et al. *Juniperus virginiana* varieties	6–10'	5–6'	sun, part shade
C	Concolor Fir (White Fir) *Abies concolor*	50'	20'	sun, part shade
C	Subalpine Fir *Abies lasiocarpa*	50'	20'	sun, part shade
C	Douglas Fir *Pseudotsuga menziesii*	50'	20'	sun
AB	Austrian Pine *Pinus nigra*	50'	20'	sun
BC	Limber Pine (Western White Pine) *Pinus flexilis*	30'	15'	sun
BC	Lodgepole Pine *Pinus contorta*	40'	10'	sun, shade
AB	Scotch Pine *Pinus sylvestris*	50'	20'	sun, part shade
ABC	Ponderosa Pine (Bull Pine) *Pinus ponderosa*	50'	20'	sun, part shade
ABC	Blue Spruce (Colorado Spruce) *Picea pungens*	50'	20'	sun, part shade
AB	Black Hills Spruce *Picea glauca densata*	40'	15'	sun, part shade
BC	Engelman Spruce *Picea engelmannii*	50'	20'	sun, shade
ABC	American Larch *Larix decidua*	50'	25'	sun, part shade

DECIDUOUS TREES

Altitude	Name	Height	Space	Exposure
ABC	Ash (Green Ash)	40–50'	40'	sun, part shade

Altitude	Name	Height	Space	Exposure
BC	Alder (Thinleaf Alder)	10–20'	10'	part shade, shade
	Alnus tenuifolia			
ABC	Birch (European White and Cutleaf Weeping)	30–40'	30'	part shade
	Betula pendula and *Betula laciniata pendula*			
BC	Birch (Water Birch or Mountain Birch)	15–25'	15'	sun, shade
	Betula occidentalis			
AB	Black Locust	30–40'	20'	sun
ABC	Box Elder	40–50'	20'	sun, part shade
ABC	Buckeye (Ohio Buckeye)	15–20'	15'	part shade, shade
ABC	Buckthorn	10–20'	10'	sun, shade
	Rhamnus cathartica			
ABC	Chokecherry	15–20'		sun, part shade
	Prunus virginiana melanocarpa			
ABC	Cottonless Cottonwood	50–60'	50'	sun
BC	Lanceleaf Cottonwood	40–50'	40'	sun
BC	Narrowleaf Cottonwood	50–60'	50'	sun
AB	Plains Cottonwood	50–60'	50'	sun
ABC	Crabapple (Flowering Crabs) varieties Hopa, Dolga	15–20'	15'	sun
AB	Elm (American Elm)	40–50'	40'	sun
ABC	Elm, Siberian (Chinese Elm)	40–50'	40'	sun
A	Goldenrain Tree	25–30'	25'	sun, part shade
ABC	Hackberry	30–35'	30'	sun
ABC	Hawthorn	10–20'	10'	sun, part shade
AB	Honey Locust (numerous thornless seedless varieties)	35–40'	40'	sun
AB	Horsechestnut	40–50'	40'	sun
BC	Larch (Western Larch)	40–50'	30'	sun, part shade
AB	Linden (Basswood)	40–50'	30'	sun
	Maples:			
AB	Amur Maple	15–20'	15'	sun
BC	Mountain Maple	10–15'	10'	part shade, shade
AB	Silver Maple (Soft Maple)	40–50'	50'	sun
ABC	Mountain Ash (European Mt. Ash)	25–30'	20'	sun, part shade
AB	New Mexico Locust	15–20'	10'	sun, part shade
	Oaks:			
AB?	Bur Oak	40–60'	30'	sun
BC	Bambel Oak (Scrub Oak)	15–25'	20'	sun
ABC	Plum (Purpleleaf Plum)	10–15'	10'	sun
	Poplars:			
BC	Balsam Poplar	50–80'	50'	sun
	Populus balsamifera			
ABC	Bolleana Poplar	40–50'	10'	sun
	Populus alba pyramidalis			
AB	Carolina Poplar	40–50'	40'	sun
	Populus canadensis			
ABC	White Poplar (Silver Poplar)	35–40'	40'	sun
	Populus alba			
A	Lombardy Poplar	40–50'	6–10'	sun
	Populus nigra italica			

BC	Quaking Aspen *Populus tremuloides*	30–50'	6–20'	sun, part shade
ABC	Russian Olive	25–40'	5–20'	sun
ABC	Staghorn Sumac *Rhus typhina*	15–20'	10'	sun, shade
AB	Walnut (Black Walnut) *Juglans nigra*	40–50'	30'	sun
	Willows:			
AB	Golden Willow *Salix vitella aurea*	40–50'	40'	sun
ABC	Laurel Willow *Salix pentandra*	30–40'	40'	sun
ABC	Peachleaf Willow *Salix amygdaloides*	25–30'	25'	sun, part shade
A?	Weeping Willow *Salix babylonica*	40–50'	50'	sun

Region V: California

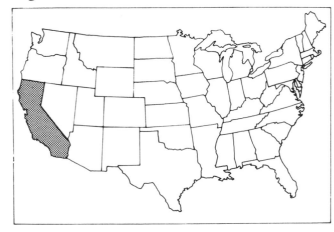

First, the ISTC tree lists for those species rated "100 percent" and "80 percent":

Northern California—Coastal Regions

Class No. 1—100%

BEECH, PURPLE
GINKGO
HAWTHORN, ENGLISH
HAWTHORN, LAVALLE
HAWTHORN, WASHINGTON
HORNBEAM, AMERICAN
HORSECHESTNUT, RED
INCENSE CEDAR, CALIFORNIA
LINDEN, LITTLELEAF
LYONTREE, FERNLEAF
MAGNOLIA, SOUTHERN
OAK, HOLLY
OAK, PIN
PLUM, BLIREIANA
SWEETGUM, AMERICAN
TULIP TREE
YEW, IRISH ENGLISH

Class No. 2—80%

ASH, VELVET
BIRCH, EUROPEAN WHITE
CAJEPUT TREE
CAROB
CEDAR, ATLAS
CEDAR, DEODAR
DATE, CANARY
ELM, CHINESE
EUCALYPTUS, SCARLET
GOLDENRAIN TREE, PANICLED
HOLLY, ENGLISH
MADRON, STRAWBERRY
MAPLE, RED
PINE, CANARY
PINE, ITALIAN STONE
PLANETREE, LONDON
PLUM, PURPLELEAF MYROBALAN
PRIVET, GLOSSY
REDWOOD
SEQUOIA, GIANT
TEATREE, VICTORIA

Northern California—Inland Regions

APRICOT, JAPANESE
ASH, VELVET
CAMPHOR TREE
CHERRY, CATALINA
CHERRY, HIGAN
CHERRY, ORIENTAL
CHERRY, YOSHINO

CRABAPPLES, FLOWERING
ELM, CHINESE
ELM, ENGLISH
ELM, SIBERIAN
ELM, SMOOTHLEAF
EUCALYPTUS, MOITCH
EUCALYPTUS, PINK MULGA IRONBARK
EUCALYPTUS, RIBBON
GOLDENRAIN TREE, PANICLED
JERUSALEM THORN
LABURNUM, WATER
LOCUST, DECAISNE BLACK
MULBERRY, WHITE (FRUITLESS)
OAK, BUR
OAK, CALIFORNIA WHITE
OAK, ENGLISH
PEACH, FLOWERING
PERSIMMON, KAKI
PINE, CANARY
PINE, COULTER
PLUM, FLOWERING
SWEETGUM, AMERICAN
TANOAK
WALNUT, PERSIAN
WILLOW, BABYLON
WILLOW, YELLOWSTEM WEEPING
ZELKOVA, JAPANESE

Northern California—Inland Section

Class No. 1—100%
ALBIZIA, SILKTREE
CAROB
CEDAR, BLUE ATLAS
CHERRY, HOLLYLEAF
CRAPE MYRTLE, COMMON
EUCALYPTUS, PINK MULGA IRONBARK
GINKGO
HACKBERRY, CHINESE
HACKBERRY, EUROPEAN
HAWTHORN, PAUL'S SCARLET
HAWTHORN, WASHINGTON
HONEY LOCUST, THORNLESS
LAUREL, GRECIAN
LOQUAT
MAGNOLIA, SOUTHERN
MAYTEN, CHILE
OAK, CALIFORNIA LIVE
OAK, CANYON LIVE
OAK, EUROPEAN TURKEY
OAK, HOLLY
OAK, INTERIOR LIVE
OAK, SHUMARD
OLIVE, COMMON
PAGODATREE, JAPANESE

PECAN
PINE, ALLEPO
PINE, ITALIAN STONE
PISTACHE, CHINESE
PITTOSPORUM, WILLY
PODOCARPUS, YEW
PRIVET, GLOSSY
REDBUD, EASTERN
TULIP TREE

Class No. 2—80%
BIRCH, EUROPEAN WHITE
HORSECHESTNUT, RED
MAPLE, TRIDENT

Southern California Shade Trees

Class No. 1—100%
ASH, SHAMEL
CAROB
CEDAR, DEODAR
MAGNOLIA, SOUTHERN
OAK, HOLLY
ORANGEBERRY, PITTOSPORUM
SWEETGUM, AMERICAN
WASHINGTON PALM, MEXICAN
YEW, PODOCARPUS

Class No. 2—80%
ASH, VELVET
CAMPHOR TREE
CRAPE MYRTLE, COMMON
DATE, CANARY
DIAMONDLEAF, PITTOSPORUM
ELM, CHINESE
EUCALYPTUS, PINK MULGA IRONBACK
GINKGO
PEPPERTREE, BRAZIL
PRIVET, JAPANESE

Of the hundreds of possibilities, the city of San Francisco lists the following deciduous trees as "suitable for street tree planting" in that city (based on the local climate, the fact that each is relatively free of insects or disease, their roots are not "voracious or gross feeders," and they do not create major litter problems). An excellent list of evergreens suitable for San Francisco streets is also contained in the booklet *Trees Make Good Neighbors,* available from the San Francisco Department of Public Works:

ASH, EVERGREEN (*Fraxinus uhdei*)
CHERRY TREES
CRABAPPLE SPECIES
GINKGO
HORSECHESTNUT, RED
PLANETREE, LONDON

PLUMS
SWEETGUM
TULIP TREE

The city of Eureka, Parks and Recreation Department, does allow individuals to plant street trees, after checks have been made for sewage, gas lines, electric lines and other underground utilities. The following street trees are currently recommended by this city:

ACACIA, LONGLEAF
CHILE MAYTEN TREE (Maytenus boaria)
OLIVE
PEAR (P. kawakami)
PHOTINIA (P. frazerii)
PITTOSPORUM (P. tenuifolium & P. crassifolium)
PRIVET (GLOSSY AND JAPANESE)
SWEET BAY

The Los Angeles County Department of Parks and Recreation provides a relatively large list of trees suitable for streets and roadsides. Their publication lists not only recommended species, but evaluation ratings, tree type, characteristics, adaptability, useful life-expectancy, and possible problems. Unfortunately, the list was prepared through the courtesy of a local electric company and subsequently truly large trees (sixty feet and over at maturity) are few in number.

The list is available from the above department located at 155 West Washington Boulevard, Los Angeles, 90015.

Region VI: North Pacific

The ISTC shade tree lists for Oregon and Washington represent those species best adapted for *all* regions of these states. In general, the giants are omitted, and those such as Oregon white oak, northern red oak, pin oak, maple, Atlas cedar, Deodar cedar, black walnut, American sweetgum, and tulip trees should be considered where adequate space is available.

Class No. 1—100%
MAPLE, MONTPELIER (Acer monspessulanum)
MAPLE, SCHWEDLED NORWAY
PLANETREE, CALIFORNIA (SYCAMORE)
TULIP TREE

Class No. 2—80%
BIRCH, CUTLEAVED EUROPEAN
CEDAR, BLUE ATLAS
CHERRY, ORIENTAL
CHESTNUT, JAPANESE
CYPRESS, HINOKI (Chamaecyparis obtusa)
HAWTHORN, WASHINGTON
HORNBEAM, AMERICAN
HORSECHESTNUT, RED
INCENSE CEDAR, CALIFORNIA
    (Libocedrus ducurrens)
LABURNUM, SCOTCH (Laburnum alpinum)
MAGNOLIA
MAPLE, HEDGE
MAPLE, JAPANESE
MAPLE, NORWAY
MAPLE, PLANETREE
MAPLE, RED
OAK, ENGLISH
PLANETREE, LONDON
PLUM, BLIREIANA
PLUM, PURPLELEAF MYROBALN
    (Prunus cerasifera pissardi)
SPRUCE, BLUE COLORADO (Picea pungens glauca)
SWEETGUM

Oregon: (See ISTC tree list, this section.)

The city of Portland, Bureau of Parks, issues tree-planting permits free of charge. After site inspection one of the following species (or others, suggested by the planter) are usually suggested.

Street Trees Suggested for Extra-Wide Planting Spaces
BEACH, COPPER (Fagus sylvatica atropunica)
BEACH, EUROPEAN (Fagus sylvatica)
BIRCH, PAPER
HORNBEAM, EUROPEAN
LINDEN, MONGOLIAN (Tilia mongolica)
MAPLE, OREGON (Acer macrophyllum)
PLANETREE, LONDON
SYCAMORE, ORIENTAL
TULIP TREE

Suggested Varieties of Street Trees for Lawn Spaces of Six- to Eight-Foot Widths
ASH, AMERICAN WHITE
ASH, ROSE HILL
BIRCH VARIETIES (exclude the Paper Birch)

ELM, AMERICAN
GINKGO
HACKBERRY, COMMON
HORSECHESTNUT, PINK
HORSECHESTNUT, RUBY RED
LINDEN, CRIMEAN
LINDEN, GREENSPIRE
LINDEN, LITTLELEAF
MAPLE, NORWAY ('GREENLACE,' 'CLEVELAND,'
    'IRISH,' 'ROYAL CRIMSON')
MAPLE, SYCAMORE
OAK, ENGLISH
OAK, RED
OAK, SCARLET
OAK, SHUMARD
OAK, WILLOW
SWEETGUM TREE
TUPELO
ZELKOVA, JAPANESE

**Suggested Varieties of Street Trees for
Tree Lawn Widths of Three to Four Feet**
ASH, GLOBE EUROPEAN
ASH, GOLDEN DESERT
ASH, MODESTO
ASH, ROUND HEAD
BOX ELDER
DOGWOOD, NATIVE
EVODIA, KOREAN (Evodia hupehensis)
GINKGO
GOLDENRAIN TREE
HAWTHORN, CARRIER'S
HAWTHORN, CHINESE BIGLEAF
HAWTHORN, DOUBLE WHITE ENGLISH
HAWTHORN, GRIGNONENSIS
HAWTHORN, LAVELLE
HORNBEAM, OAKLEAF EUROPEAN
HORNBEAM, PYRAMIDAL EUROPEAN
MAPLE, ARMSTRONG'S COLUMNAR
MAPLE, SCANLON
MAPLE, SENECA SUGAR
MAPLE, TILFORD'S RED
RED BUD
WASHINGTON THORN

The city of Medford, Oregon, has an active tree-planting program and now requires that one tree be planted per lot in all new subdivisions.

Individuals may apply for a *free* permit to plant by contacting the City Planning Department. A Master Street Tree Plan has recently been devised which designates specific species for every street in the city.

Washington: (See ISTC tree list, this section.)

Plant Materials for Landscaping (Extension Bulletin 592) is available from the College of Agriculture of Washington State University at Pullman. One of the most useful booklets for the property owner interested in replanting, it contains recommendations for Washington, Oregon, and Idaho.

The Board of Public Works of the City of Seattle recommends the following street trees:

Street Trees for Business District
BIRCH, EUROPEAN WHITE
ELM, AMERICAN ASCENDING
ELM, BUISMAN
GINKGO
HONEY LOCUST, THORNLESS
HOPHORNBEAM, AMERICAN
HORNBEAM, UPRIGHT EUROPEAN
LINDEN, LITTLELEAF EUROPEAN
MAPLE, PLANETREE
MAPLE, PYRAMIDAL NORWAY
MAPLE, SCHWEDLERI
OAK, NORTHERN RED
SWEETGUM, AMERICAN
TULIP TREE

Street Trees for Residential District
CHERRY, FLOWERING
CHERRY, KWANZAN FLOWERING
CRABAPPLE, RIVER'S
HAWTHORN, PAUL'S SCARLET
HORNBEAM, AMERICAN
HORSECHESTNUT, RED
KATSURA TREE
MAGNOLIA, KOBUS
MAPLE, DAVID'S
MAPLE, HEDGE
OAK, PIN
OAK, SCARLET
PLUM, PURPLELEAF
WASHINGTON THORN

The city of Spokane will issue permits allowing the planting of street trees, but only after liability insurance has been purchased by the planter!

The Spokane regulations are so unique in America (and in general, discourage private groups from re-greening the city) that a brief extract of these regulations is included:

_____

Before such permit shall issue, the person proposing to make such installation as aforesaid, shall furnish proof of liability insurance coverage covering such sidewalk and the proposed installation. Whereby in such insurance coverage the City of Spokane is co-insured for *liability limits of not less than $100,000 for any one personal injury, $300,000 for all personal claims in any one accident and $25,000 for property damage. The limit herein prescribed may be increased from time to time by the Corporation Counsel of the City of Spokane by filing with City Clerk an order increasing the insurance limits required. Any person aggrieved by such order may appeal the same to the City Manager whose decision will be final.*

Region VII: Alaska

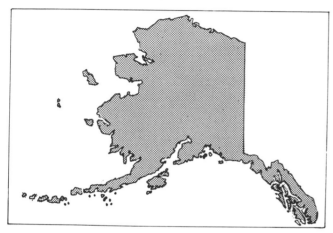

At the present time most Alaskan towns and cities have not truly considered the value of street trees. Many villages, such as Fort Yukon, are without sidewalks and trees are not planted in the gravel streets, even where many native varieties such as white birch, poplar, and many coniferous species would grow.

The city of Anchorage recommends the planting of birch (native) and mountain ash in established planting strips only. Permits to plant are required, even for these few patches of earth, and may be obtained from the Department of Public Works.

In no case are the following species, which may damage the pavement, to be planted: cottonwood, lombardy poplar, and maples.

Region VIII: Hawaii

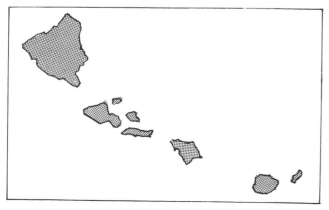

Hawaii is unique in that of the *thousands* of trees that *could* be grown in shade and street plantings scarcely one dozen species are utilized in any numbers. The ever-popular coconut palm is cheapest and finds its way onto most every new construction site, almost as an afterthought.

The defoliation of Miami Beach's "trademark"— the coconut palm—by "lethal yellowing" disease is somewhat akin to the widespread loss of American elms to Dutch elm disease. In both cases, where large areas have been planted in only *one* species, these same large areas now exhibit treeless streets. One species planting may be cheap in the short run, but expensive when viewed backward over the years. For this and other reasons, the Hawaiian tree planter must take advantage of his blessed environment and plant many, many species on the streets and yards of his state.

Must every relationship with trees be calculated by using the denominator "cleanliness with low initial cost and low maintenance"? This effectively diminishes the numerator "beauty" to a negligible position. The beauty of many trees cannot be compromised.

Ironwood trees, which suggest a sweeping seascape, are considered unworthy street trees by some owing to their tiny seed containers, which can be annoying when stepped on barefooted. Should the beauty of these trees be lost simply because of the inconvenience of one part of their anatomical structure? If we are to incorporate some of the *wildness* of nature in our daily life we must be willing to accept some of her tough edges.

Similarly, mango trees which bear so much delicious fruit (the large bearers were planted thirty or so years ago) are seldom planted on newly developed properties, for they are considered "dirty trees." If people want the delicious fruit they will have to learn to clean up much unwanted fruit as well. Must every "civilian" tree bear nothing but shade?

Keawe is often the only tree that can survive on windy hillsides. Yet they are not being planted because they drop a "messy fruit" (which was once the basis of a honey industry, is a nutritious cattle feed, and attracts birds) and sometimes sharp thorns. A thornless Keawe of intricate structure may be just the tree to wake up state streets of regular, vertical species of much less interest.

While the hotel industry is often criticized by environmental groups for detracting from the inherent beauty of the islands it should be noted that some new hotels far outshine the University of Hawaii in terms of sidewalk and interior courtyard tree plantings.

Sadly enough, the newest suburban tracts often remain unplanted for years—even though the city of Honolulu will plant trees for homeowners on request. Few new homeowners associate trees with a "good or exclusive" neighborhood. They prefer instead stunted, tidy trees, or carefully controlled "bonzai" gardens. Yet, the most expensive older homes in the city are all surrounded by *big* trees.

While the following tree list is a good guide for new plantings and several of the species might be tried in each neighborhood, a walk through Foster Botanic Garden will suggest at least a dozen other species that would add beauty to any setting.

Official Street Tree List

ALIBANGBANG (BUTTERFLY) (*Bauhinia binata*)
ALLSPICE (*Pimenta officinalis*)
BOTTLEBRUSH, DROOPING (*Callistemon viminalis*)
BOTTLEBRUSH, UPRIGHT (*Callistemon lanceolatus*)
BUTTONWOOD, SILVER (*Conocarpus erectus* var. *argenteus*)
CABBAGE TREE (*Andira inermis*)
CAMPHOR TREE (*Cinnamomum camphora*)
CAROB TREE (*Ceratonia siliqua*)
CASSIA BARK TREE (*Cinnamomum cassia*)
CINNAMON TREE (*Cinnamomum zeylanica*)
CRAPE MYRTLE (*Lagerstroemia indica*)
CRAPE MYRTLE, GIANT (*Lagerstroemia speciosa*)
DEGAME TREE (*Calycophullum candidissimum*)
FALSE OLIVE (*Elaeodendron orientale*)
FERN TREE (*Filicium decipiens*)
FIDDLEWOOD TREE (*Citharexylum spinosum*)
GOLDENRAIN TREE (*Koelreuteria formosa*)
GOLDEN SHOWER TREE (*Cassia fistula*)
GOLDEN SHOWER TREE (*Cassia javanica*)
HAOLE KOU (*Cordia sebestena*)
JACARANDA (*Jacaranda acutifolia*)
JASMINE TREE (*Ervatamia orientalis*)
LIGNUM VITAE (*Guiacum officinale*)
MAGNOLIA, SOUTHERN (*Magnolia grandiflora*)
MOCK, ORANGE (*Murraya exotica*)
MONKEY POD (*Samanea saman*)
ORCHID TREE, HONG KONG (*Bauhinia blakeana*)
ORCHID TREE, RED (*Bauhinia purpurea*)
ORCHID TREE, WHITE (*Bauhinia variegata* var. *candida*)
PALM, COCONUT (*Cocos nucifera*)
PALM, QUEEN (*Arecastrum romanzoffianum*)
PALM, ROYAL (*Roystonea regia*)
PAPER BARK (*Melaleuca leucadendron*)
PARAGUAY TEA TREE (*Ilex paraguayensis*)

PITTOSPORUM "ALII SHORES" (*Pittosporum* sp. Alii Shores)
PODOCARP, CYPRESS (*Podocarpus cupressina*)
PODOCARP, OLEANDER (*Podocarpus neriifolius*)
POLYALTHIA (*Polyalthia longifolia*)
RAINBOW SHOWER TREE (*Cassia hybrida*)
ROYAL POINCIANA (*Delonix regia*)
SATIN LEAF (*Chrysophyllum oliviforme*)
TACOMA, MOIR'S PINK (*Tabebuia pallida* var. *Moir*)
TACOMA, PALMER'S (*Tabebuia palmeri*)
TAHITIAN GARDENIA (*Gardenia taitensis*)
TIPU (*Tipuana tipu*)
TRUMPET TREE, GOLDEN (*Tabebuia chrysotricha*)
TRUMPET TREE, SILVER (*Tabebuia argentea*)
TRUMPET TREE, YELLOW (*Tabebuia chrysea*)
WISTERIA, THODESIAN (*Bolusanthus speciosus*)

Region IX: Canada

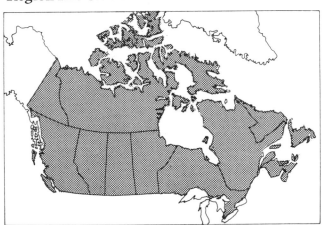

The recommendations of the ISTC for regions of Canada fortunately contain some large trees, as follows:

British Columbia

Class No. 1—100%

BEECH, EUROPEAN
DOGWOOD, PACIFIC
ELM, AMERICAN
HAWTHORN, ENGLISH
MAPLE, HEDGE
MAPLE, RED
MAPLE, VINE
OAK, NORTHERN RED
OAK, PIN
OAK, SCARLET
SWEETGUM
TULIP TREE

Class No. 2—80%

ASH, FLOWERING
DOUGLAS FIR, COMMON (*Pseudotsuga taxifolia*)
HOLLY, ENGLISH (*Ilex aquifolium*)

HORSECHESTNUT, RED
LOCUST, BLACK
MAPLE, NORWAY
MAPLE, SILVER
MAPLE, SUGAR
PLANETREE, LONDON
PLUM, BLIREIANA
PLUM, PURPLELEAF MYROBALAN (*Prunus cerasifera pissardi*)
RED CEDAR, EASTERN

→ Ontario, South of Ottawa

Class No. 1—100%

BEECH, PURPLE EUROPEAN (*Fagus sylvatica atropunicea*)
LINDEN, LITTLELEAF
MAPLE, NORWAY
MAPLE, SCHWEDLER NORWAY
MAPLE, SUGAR
OAK, EASTERN RED (*Quercus borealis maxima*)

Class No. 2—80%

ASH, WHITE
BEECH, EUROPEAN
ELM, AMERICAN
HICKORY, BITTERNUT (*Carya cordiformis*)
HONEY LOCUST, THORNLESS
HORNBEAM, AMERICAN
MOUNTAIN ASH, EUROPEAN
OAK, PIN
PLANETREE, AMERICAN (SYCAMORE)
WALNUT, BLACK

Montreal and Vicinity

Class No. 1—100%

ELM, AMERICAN
LINDEN, CRIMEAN
LINDEN, LITTLELEAF
MAPLE, NORWAY
MAPLE, SCHWEDLER NORWAY
MAPLE, SUGAR
OAK, EASTERN RED

Class No. 2—80%

ASH, WHITE
GINKGO (MALE)
HACKBERRY, COMMON
HAWTHORN, WASHINGTON
HICKORY, BITTERNUT (*Carya cordiformis*)
HONEY LOCUST, THORNLESS
HOPHORNBEAM, AMERICAN
LILAC, JAPANESE TREE (*Syringa amurensis japonica*)
PEAR, CALLERY
PINE, SCOTCH (*Pinus sylvestris*)
SPRUCE, BLUE COLORADO (*Picea pungens glauca*)

British Columbia: (See ISTC tree list, this section.)

Unfortunately for the people of Vancouver the Board of Parks is replacing "the huge old elms, London planes, maples, horsechestnuts, etc., with the smaller trees." The little, "untrees" have been declared more suitable for urban needs (even though the grand, old specimens are hardy and do so much more in the way of cleaning the air, shielding ugly urban views, muffling sounds, etc.).

The city of Vancouver seems to have lost its role as Canada's frontier, both treewise and with regard to individualism. "Individuals are *not allowed* to plant trees on city streets, even at their own expense."

If some of the magnificence of old Vancouver is to be retained and incorporated into the city of new buildings which is continually under construction then the *big trees* must once again be planted! Maples, oaks, elms, planetrees, tulip trees, sweetgums, and some large conifers are definitely in order. Only the citizens of Vancouver can prevent a major error in tree selection that will, if continued, create a pitiful sight for the next fifty years.

Manitoba:

The city of Winnipeg Parks and Recreation Department has planted annually, for the years 1970–72, between 1,300 to 1,800 trees. The planting of boulevard trees by individuals is *not* encouraged.

Of the species enumerated below the Japanese tree lilac and littleleaf linden would be used more widely by the Parks Department if they were available in larger planting size:

BOULEVARD TREE PLANTINGS ON WINNIPEG'S MAJOR STREET SYSTEM

Species	Percentage of Total Trees Planted in 1972
ASH, GREEN	24%
BASSWOOD	18
BIRCH, PAPER	1
CHOKECHERRY, SHUBERT	8
CRABAPPLE, ROSYBLOOM	.5
ELM, AMERICAN	3
ELM, SIBERIAN	25
JAPANESE TREE LILAC (*Syringa amurensis japonica*)	3
LINDEN, LITTLELEAF (Hardy strain)	.1
MAPLE, SILVER	5
POPLAR, BERLIN	.1
POPLAR, NORTHWEST (*Populus deltoides* x *P. balsamifera*)	.1
RUSSIAN OLIVE	.2
WILLOW, LAUREL	7

The Inner City of Winnipeg is administered by a separate government. The Parks and Recreation Department for these sections of the city has planted 80 percent ash and 20 percent elm on newly treed streets. As elms die off they are replaced with elms while ash trees are replaced with ash.

Planting by individuals is discouraged.

Ontario: (For list of trees for Southern Ontario see ISTC recommendations, this section.)

The northern city of Thunder Bay has a relatively active tree-planting program and looks forward to becoming known as the "City of Trees" by the year 2000.

The following was taken from a recent policy statement by the Parks and Recreation Department:

The departmental philosophy of tree planting might best be summed up in two cliches: "Planting trees is for tomorrow" and "Rome was not built in a day." For many years prior to 1963 no attempt was made to introduce trees on boulevards and properties by civic bodies resulting in some areas virtually void of any substantial tree growth. This decade undoubtedly will establish the value of past years' endeavours and substantiate the true worth of trees in urban areas. Two to three thousand specimens planted annually certainly is meager in relation to the size of the present City; however, over the long range programme instituted by the department by the year 2000 we may be considered the "City of Trees."

Desirable trees such as red maple, arborvitae, elder, gray birch, paper birch, red oak, linden, and green ash are among those planted by this conscientious department.

Toronto parks' people report that, based on a ten-year trial of a limited number of species, the following are the most successful species for the city:
ASH, 'MARSHALL'S SEEDLESS'
HONEY LOCUST, THORNLESS, 'SHADEMASTER'
JAPANESE LILAC
LINDEN, 'GREENSPIRE' AND 'GLENLEVEN'
   ("Where salt is no problem")
MAPLE, NORWAY
MAPLE, SUGAR ("In residential areas where sufficient
   protected turf is available")

Quebec: (For Montreal and vicinity see ISTC tree list, this section.)

New Brunswick:
   Mr. C. C. Smith, chairman of the Frederickton, N. B. Tree Commission, reports that the following

species are most commonly planted along the streets of that city:
ASH, AMERICAN
HONEY LOCUST, THORNLESS
LINDEN, LITTLELEAF
MAPLES (NORWAY, RED, SUGAR, etc.)
OAK, RED

Individuals who wish to plant trees on city property must obtain permission from the City Engineer's Office or the Parks Superintendent.

PART

·III·
How to Plant a Tree

When you bait your hook with your heart the fish always bite ... when you plant a tree with love it always lives; you do it with such care and thoroughness.
                                                            John Burroughs

Sites

All tree species are planted in about the same way. Soil and site requirements vary widely, but the actual planting of a tree, whether it be in a forest, or along a city street requires the same approach. Instead of repeating similar planting instructions for each situation (forest, rural woodlot, shelterbelt, suburban, and urban) a general guide to planting all types of trees is provided. Preceding the generalized planting instructions are some useful concepts to consider about the various sites.

Forests and Rural Woodlots

Trees planted to establish or reestablish a dense woodlot in a rural setting, or for reforestation, are planted in the range of 400 to 1,200 per acre. They may be planted 6 feet apart, on all sides, creating "plots" of 6 feet by 6 feet if they are comparatively narrow in form; while larger species usually require at least 10-foot-by-10-foot plots.

Woodlots and forestland may be planted with young *seedlings* or by *direct seeding*.

Seedlings may be obtained from most agricultural extension service offices, free of charge, or for cost. These seedlings are grown in nurseries, or "tree farms" for differing lengths of time depending on the species and the locale in which they are grown.

Red spruce seedlings, the common spruce of the northeast, usually need three to four years in the ground before they are large enough for transplanting (6 to 12 inches high); while slash pine seedlings, a southern species, require only eight or nine months to reach a height of 10 to 18 inches, at which time they are ready for transplanting.

Direct seeding is less costly and produces trees more quickly than does the seedling method. Instead of having to plant seeds in a nursery and later transplant the seedlings, seeds are sown directly into the soil of the area needing a retreeing.

Seeds are sown by two methods: broadcast and partial seeding.

Broadcast seeding is usually accomplished by dropping huge numbers of seeds from an airplane or helicopter. This method is, of course, easier. However, very few seeds "take" in relation to the great number that are dropped.

Partial seeding of a woodlot has several advantages. Less seed is used, the seeds are better protected because they are each covered with soil, selected sites within a locale may be chosen, or avoided, on passing, and the number of seeds that actually grow into trees is relatively higher.

Windbreaks

Rows of trees are often needed to shelter buildings, roads, or railroads from dust storms, snow drifts or plain high-wind conditions. In these situations such rows are usually known as *shelterbelts.*

Rows of trees that are planted to provide shade for cattle while protecting crops and topsoil by reducing the velocity of high winds are known as *windbreaks.* Windbreaks may be effectively created with a single row of trees, though high wind conditions generally require several rows. Multiple-row windbreaks are often planted as follows: a row of conifers to deflect the wind upward, a row of deciduous or broad-leafed trees to trap whatever wind breaks through the conifers, and a third row of conifers to carry upward any remnants of a powerful blow that manages to break through.

While each windbreak environment favors the growth of different species, spacing is generally consistent in all locales. Conifers need 8 to 12 feet between themselves, while broad-leafed trees must be between 8 to 18 feet apart. The space *between* each row of trees, in a multiple-row windbreak, should range from 10 to 20 feet wide. This allows farm machinery to pass between the rows of trees to suppress weeds and grass from growing until the tree canopies are large enough to block the sunlight and inhibit competitive plants in a natural way.

In Nevada growing conditions are so difficult that windbreak seedlings need to be watered once or twice each week for the first few years of growth. The Nevada State Tree Nursery now offers only Russian olive and golden willow trees as well as a few evergreens such as ponderosa, Jeffrey and Scotch pine, Engelmann spruce, and Sierra redwood sequoia, for the trying desert environment.

In California, the eucalyptus is widely used for windbreaks because of its dense, tough foliage.

Windbreaks in Florida can be created with the following trees that are recommended by the state extension service (N = for northern regions of the state; C = central regions; S = southern regions). Arizona cypress (N), Australian pine (C-S), cajeput (C-S), eucalyptus (C-S), pongam (S), southern red cedar (N-C), and cypress pine (N-C-S).

In the East, evergreens such as arborvitae, balsam, cedar, and spruce adapt themselves well to the role of wind-deflectors.

The northern Great Plains is a very trying environment for any tree. Very cold winters and very dry summers require trees with a special hardiness and adaptability. The U.S.D.A., in a long term study, reports that box elder, green ash, and the silver buffaloberry (a shrub) were best adapted for their role as farm windbreaks.

Shade Trees

The expense of "air-conditioning" a house can be drastically reduced, if not eliminated entirely, by placing at least one huge shade tree on the property. Several smaller trees along the edge of a property line can reduce the velocity of cold winds during the winter months, thereby reducing the fuel bill.

Alfred W. Boicourt and Tom S. Hamilton, Jr., of the University of Massachusetts, recommend the following procedure for determining the all important location of a large shade tree:

Because of the customary high temperature, mid-summer is an excellent time to see where you need trees. Measure off 40–50 feet diagonally from the southeast corner of your house. By holding one arm straight above your head, see if your shadow points toward the house at about 11 A.M. If not, change your location. A tree placed diagonally off the corner usually does not interfere with the view outside. However, there may be other factors which may alter the placement of the tree such as poor drainage, gravelly or dry soil or nearness to sidewalk, driveway, pipelines, overhead wires or other trees. Repeat your shadow testing in early and late afternoon . . .

Shade trees should be spaced with enough distance between them and buildings, wires or other trees to allow their mature limb spread to develop without crowding.

Approximate distances between a few sample trees are:

Live Oaks	80 to 100 feet apart
American Elms	60 feet apart

Oaks (Black, Red, Scarlet, Water, White, Willow)	60 feet apart
Oriental Planes, Maples (Red, Sugar)	50 feet apart
Norway Maples, Littleleaf Lindens, Pin Oaks, Southern Magnolias	40 feet apart
Ginkgos, Flowering Dogwoods, Catalpas	30 feet apart

Street Trees

Lists of recommended species for most states are included in another section. Here we must evaluate the amount of area available and the type of street on which the selected tree will be expected to grow.

Many mistakes have been made in the planting of American streets that would now be traumatic to rectify. Some avenues lack the definitive beauty individual trees are capable of projecting because the trees were planted too close together.

One classic example of tree crowding is Commonwealth Avenue, in Boston. As Solotaroff wrote in 1911:

The planting-space on this prominent thoroughfare is one hundred feet wide, and the plans provided for the planting of four rows of American elms, the trees in the rows to stand opposite each other. In 1880, Professor Charles Sprague Sargent and Frederick Law Olmsted proposed the removal of the four rows of trees . . . and the planting in their place of two rows of trees . . . In 1880 and 1881 . . . the planting of four rows of trees was continued in this avenue up to Massachusetts Avenue. The Park Commissioners of Boston are now confronted with the problem of thinning out the trees.

The same basic questions remain that were raised with regard to city street tree planting over sixty years ago.

Where should the trees be planted? How far apart? Should they be opposite each other on the two sides of a street or be placed alternate to one another? How should corners be treated? How many rows should be set?

Although few cities now plan a strip of soil between sidewalk and curb, many older streets (which may need replanting) often do have this valuable soil which "adds materially to the beauty of the street, serves to help protect pedestrians from the dust and mud of street traffic, and affords the necessary area for trees and their root development." (Solotaroff)

This area has traditionally been the preferred location for street trees. With the demands of wider streets, over the years America has lost so many grand old trees in these planting strips that it seems almost dangerous to plant there once again. Yet, where there is no alternative site (except a barren street) these "parking strips" must be utilized. Where space is available, as in suburban communities, people are encouraged to plant trees on their front lawns, instead of between the sidewalk and curb. However, when left to the individual homeowner a hodgepodge of trees usually results, with an irregular, uncoordinated effect. Besides, trees planted in the lawn area leave a hot, unshaded roadway in summer and an uninteresting effect in any season.

Since lawn areas do not exist in cities, this alternative site and its problems are not a factor.

Narrow streets usually require the *alternate* placement of trees. This pattern allows the mature trees full canopy development.

Broad streets permit full crown development at maturity and therefore *opposite* planting is possible.

Of course, opposite planting can also be achieved on narrow streets with trees of columnar or fastigate shape, but since broad-spreading trees are generally more beautiful, in their wide, arching way, the narrow trees are less preferred.

With both planting patterns, alternate and opposite, uniform spacing is highly desirable. While we may look to the trees themselves for their individual beauty, entire streets somehow transmit a greater sense of orderliness when trees are evenly spaced. Obstacles such as fire hydrants, street lamps, telephone poles, water, and gas and electric connections must be considered before staking out a street with distances distributed as uniformly as possible.

The starkness of so many business districts has for so long overwhelmed people that ugliness and "downtown" have practically become synonymous.

To remedy this word-thought association many chambers of commerce have attempted to beautify the streets by organizing tree-planting programs. In some cases, where trees have actually been set directly into cuts in the concrete and been allowed to spread their roots directly in the subsoil (often gravel), true beautification is in progress. Often, however, to eliminate the expense of breaking pavement, or to avoid conflict with underground utilities, "trees" have been planted in concrete or wooden tubs set on the sidewalk. Although the *initial* cost of such installations is less than breaking up the sidewalk and planting directly in the ground, over the years maintenance and tree-replacement costs greatly exceed the traditional soil planting.

The tree in this illustration has its roots in a concrete vault below the sidewalk. This permits use of larger trees than would be possible with use of above-the-ground tubs. Also notice the well-designed light standard and trash receptacle. (Courtesy, University of Illinois, Cooperative Extension Service)

Aesthetically, tub plantings are generally unpleasant. The plants that grow in these limited environments cannot be considered trees in the truest sense of the word because their growth is so restricted that often shrublike effects are created. Another negative factor for tub planters is the disconcerting fact that people use them as ashtrays and trash baskets. Whether this behavior may be considered one method by which the average passerby comments on his opinion of such installations is difficult to state with authority.

Of course, it might be pointed out that tub planters are better than nothing at all, which is certainly true.

However, an alternative installation permits the use of larger trees than are possible with tub planters and should *always* be considered where underground planting is not at all possible.

The *underground vault* system permits the root system of small trees to develop to the point where the tree looks somewhat like a tree and generates some of the natural benefits of life.

While vault planters are convenient where difficult underground situations exist, direct soil planting, after breaking the pavement, is the preferred street-planting method. This allows for larger trees that live for longer periods of time at lower maintenance costs.

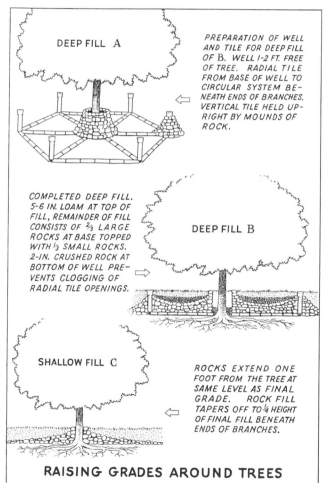

DEEP FILL A

PREPARATION OF WELL AND TILE FOR DEEP FILL OF B. WELL 1-2 FT. FREE OF TREE. RADIAL TILE FROM BASE OF WELL TO CIRCULAR SYSTEM BENEATH ENDS OF BRANCHES. VERTICAL TILE HELD UPRIGHT BY MOUNDS OF ROCK.

COMPLETED DEEP FILL. 5-6 IN. LOAM AT TOP OF FILL, REMAINDER OF FILL CONSISTS OF ⅔ LARGE ROCKS AT BASE TOPPED WITH ⅓ SMALL ROCKS. 2-IN. CRUSHED ROCK AT BOTTOM OF WELL PREVENTS CLOGGING OF RADIAL TILE OPENINGS.

DEEP FILL B

SHALLOW FILL C

ROCKS EXTEND ONE FOOT FROM THE TREE AT SAME LEVEL AS FINAL GRADE. ROCK FILL TAPERS OFF TO ¼ HEIGHT OF FINAL FILL BENEATH ENDS OF BRANCHES.

RAISING GRADES AROUND TREES

(Courtesy, Maine Forestry Department)

Concrete cutters can be rented in most urban areas. The planting hole should be at least 3 feet by 3 feet and 3 feet deep.

Soil Compaction and Grade Alteration Around Trees

Few people consider the fact that the small rootlets of a tree absorb not only water but also *air*. Compacting the soil beneath the trunk causes an increased density of soil, which results in inadequate soil aeration. Eventually, compaction may suffocate the roots entirely and kill the tree. At the very least, soil compaction encourages rootlets to grow near the surface, which increases the risk of root drying while diminishing the strength of the soil anchor that is created by a deep root system.

The same effects result when asphalt or concrete is poured to join the tree trunk at its base. A three- to four-foot soil or gravel "foundation" or a set of open grates is necessary to permit entry of air, water, and fertilizer.

Heavy construction equipment often compacts the soil around construction sites or causes injury by tearing bark or roots. Another common problem often seen around construction areas is the mounding of soil or excavated material at the base of existing trees. Frequently, though these trees were meant to be "saved," they often weaken or die before the building or roadwork is completed, as a result of carelessness.

Construction sometimes demands that the soil level of an existing site be altered. While methods exist that will permit existing trees to survive, such changes are expensive and will often only be undertaken where the tree is of good size and in good health. The opposite diagram outlines methods for "raising grades around trees."

Lowering the level of soil around trees will expose the tiny rootlets and encourage them to dry out. Where the soil must be lowered, a retaining wall built around the root system will protect the roots and keep the soil from washing away.

Buying a Tree

Before investigating soil preparation, staking, and gratings it may be wise to pause and think about the trees themselves. While types of trees to be considered are enumerated in a state by state list, the actual purchase of the tree itself must be carefully considered.

What kind of tree to select and how to tell if a young seedling is healthy are two important questions.

In selecting a shade tree, Solotaroff writes, a compact root system is more important than a spreading top, while both characteristics are desirable. Many roots yield quick growth while an abundant system of branches with a skimpy bunch of roots usually yields poor growth, if any.

Trees that are tall-growing are the author's personal choice *wherever* the tree will truly be able to "sprout its wings" and grow into an inspiring specimen. Trees native to an area are often the hardiest for local soil and moisture conditions. Where this rule does not hold (owing to raging tree diseases, radically altered environment, etc.) select those species that already thrive in the neighborhood.

To see what does well, walk around the streets or visit the city arboretum. Stop and gaze at those trees that command your attention. Is it their great size you like? Well, remember you may have to wait many years before your little seedling grows to that size (a worthwhile wait). Are you attracted by the scent, the sheen of the leaves, the flowers, the interesting bark, or the song of the birds on the branches? Only *you*

Buying a Tree.

can decide what your specific preferences consist of.

Once you have decided you like a certain tree you will have to learn its name, if you hope to order it from a nursery.

While trees in botanical parks are often labeled, a neighbor's bell may have to be rung to inquire after the tree's name. Since your neighbor may not know any more about the tree than you, you might ask permission to snip off the tip of a branch. Be sure to get a few flowers and fruits (if any). Most local university biology departments have a botanist who can tell you the name of your tree.

If the tree is commonly available at a nearby nursery, you will have the great joy of choosing the tree yourself. If the species is only available from a mail-order nursery (see Brooklyn Botanic Garden handbook *1200 Trees and Shrubs—Where to Buy Them*), you will have to take your chances on receiving healthy individuals.

At the nursery, you should examine the tree carefully before buying it. Buds should be filled with optimism and be green inside. By piercing the bark with your thumbnail you should see healthy green tissue. Avoid trees with shriveled bark on trunk, branches, or twigs. Likewise, abrasions or inconsistent coloring on the bark indicates injury that may be difficult for the tree to repair while it is recovering from the shock of transplanting. Twig ends should be springy, not brittle. Bareroot trees must have a few main roots that are covered with a tangle of tiny fibrous threads. These tiny rootlets actually do the work of absorbing water from the soil and are most important. If the tree is "balled and burlapped" insist on inspecting the root system at the nursery. Too often it is at the most inopportune moment of just setting the tree into soil that the planter discovers (upon removing the burlap and spreading out the root system) a broken main root or two.

Many people attempt to grow trees that they themselves dig up in the woods. While this may work in a rural or suburban lawn situation, these trees are generally poor risks for the city.

Under natural conditions of growth, as occurs with a wild tree that takes up life on its own from a fallen seed, a large *tap root* appears. It is extremely difficult to transplant trees with large tap roots with any success. In nursery-grown stock both the tap root and the lateral roots are cut back through one or two growing seasons to encourage a compact root system that increases the chances for successful transplanting.

It is best to buy well-adapted, well-established trees from a local reputable nursery, or where a particular tree is unavailable locally, from a reputable mail-order grower.

Preparing the Soil
Urban Sites

While rural sites often need little soil modification, city and town soils have frequently been so neglected and maltreated that total replacement is almost always required for success in tree-growing.

By looking backward in time I have found that conditions of growth faced in Manhattan (one of the toughest of urban locales?) in 1916 were similar to those we face today. Perhaps urban planters might benefit from this "ancient" wisdom, practical at a time when commercial fertilizers were not yet a way of life and when horses teeth, not automobile fenders and pedestrian vandalism, were the major threat of physical injury.

According to the planner of "A Street Tree System for New York City, 1916," the problems of urban soils were five in number. By substituting the name of any large American city or town for "Manhattan" a set of viable guidelines appears for securing correct urban soil conditions in any city:

———————

(1) **A sufficient amount of good soil.**

In some cities no consideration has to be given to this matter as the existing soil is satisfactory both as regards quality and amount. In Manhattan this is practically never the case, and generally speaking we must figure on providing at least two cubic yards of first-class loam or topsoil and this even when there is a subsoil of some value. When, as in the case of the restricted tree pit, we must provide the entire soil supply of the roots the minimum requirement should be three cubic yards, while five would be better. In Paris three cubic yards of good soil is the standard requirement in planting new trees.

(2) **Sufficient moisture.**

In the writer's opinion this is the most important element in successful tree growth. In the case of trees planted in very restricted areas this can only be supplied by artificial means. Even where a good subsoil exists, it is doubtful if the tree can secure, unaided, sufficient moisture for its needs even after being established. The reason for this is that the continuous pavement of the ground surface prevents the ground water from being replenished from natural sources. To secure successful street trees in Manhattan, continuous irrigation is advised in practically all cases. There are various ways of provid-

Guarding and Staking (From Solotaroff)

Guards and Grills (From Solotaroff)

ing this, such as by tile and dry wells, or by some form of underground pipes as in the so-called "automatic" lawn sprinkling systems in use in the arid regions of the southwest.

A method of irrigation advocated by some authorities is to pierce the gutter curb opposite the tree and secure in this way the water from street flushing and storms. Before the advent of the automobile and the use of oil as a dust layer or in road construction this method was of value, but today the injury from the oil and grease which would be thus washed into the soil around the tree roots would more than offset the value of the water received. This has been found to be the case by German tree experts who formerly made use of this practice.

Where a grating is used over the surface of the tree pit some water is secured from the rains by way of the sidewalk and the rest can be provided by weekly or fortnightly flooding with a hydrant hose or sprinkling wagon.

Where bricks laid in sand are used instead of a tree grating as a traffic surface for the tree pit, a tile or dry well system or the underground pipe system of irrigation will be needed. These methods are also suitable for trees in unfenced gravel parkings or continuous strips paved with bricks laid in sand. In the case of trees grown in grass parkings or gravel areas protected from traffic by fences, an occasional heavy surface watering will usually be sufficient if the grading is such that a good supply is held in a depression around the tree trunk.

The amount of water needed by any tree or street of trees will depend upon the species of tree, the physical characteristics of the soil, the drainage below ground, the rainfall, the season of the year, etc., and can only be determined by experience.

(3) Proper drainage.

The securing of proper drainage follows, of course, as a corollary of the above, and if the subsoil does not provide for it adequately, underdrainage in some form must be provided artificially. A layer of loose stones and a tile to the nearest low-lying sewer will provide such drainage in the simplest and most effective way. Sometimes dynamiting the subsoil will provide adequate drainage if the substrata are suitable.

(4) Proper aeration of the soil.

Next to a supply of water, a well aerated soil is the most necessary condition for successful tree growth. Probably more street trees in Manhattan die because of a deficiency in respect to air and water than from any other cause.

Where a tree is not planted in turf, the only way to insure a proper aeration of the soil is by frequent cultivation of the ground surface above the roots. All street trees planted in gravel parkings or in tree pits with or without gratings should receive such treatment at least

every three or four weeks during the growing season. In the case of gravel surfaced tree pits which are protected by a fence from traffic or in the case of tree pits surfaced with brick laid upon a good cushion of loose sand it is probably only necessary to cultivate two or three times a season.

Where gratings are used they should be of a design which permits of easy removal for frequent cultivation. The chief value of the grating lies in its improvement of aeration conditions by protecting the ground surface from becoming compacted by traffic. Hence an immovable grating which prevents frequent cultivation destroys its main reason for existence. There are a number of gratings in Manhattan which are thus largely worthless. The soil beneath a grating, because of the nearly continuous shade, will soon grow sour and prevent proper aeration if not cultivated.

(5) A supply of plant food.

Sufficient food for a successful street tree will be largely secured from good soil, and sufficient air and water without fertilization, but where the soil supply is unusually limited an annual application of fertilizer is advisable. Bone meal, lime, well rotted manure, and various chemical fertilizers rich in phosphates and nitrates may all be used with success. When gratings are used oats or clover may be planted in early summer and dug under when four or five inches high, or dead leaves may be piled under the gratings in the fall and covered with a light dressing of well rotted manure and the whole spaded under the following spring. In the use of fertilizer in growing street trees conditions and experience must guide our practice.

Suburban Sites

In early life, before leaves are spread before the sun to manufacture an independent food supply via photosynthetic pathways, trees derive much of their sustenance directly from the soil. Thus, initial success in growing trees is almost totally dependent on the nature and preparation of the soil. While the soil along city streets or beneath the pavement should always be removed and fresh soil put back, the suburban site needs less preparation.

In sandy or well-drained ground spade the soil to a depth of two or more feet. In heavy clay soil the hole must not be dug too deep because it forms a reservoir of water that will often drown and kill the tree. A general rule is to dig a hole about twelve inches wider than the spread of bare roots or earth ball and at least six inches deeper than the earth ball and three feet deep for bare root trees. The roots of balled and burlapped stock must be freed and spread to their natural growing position. Be sure the hole has straight sides and a flat bottom.

After digging the hole, and before planting the tree, fill it to the required height with loose, rich soil. If the subsoil has poor drainage, dig about one foot deeper and fill this area with crushed stone or gravel. Another method is to dig two or three vertical drainage holes at the bottom of the pit and fill them with coarse gravel.

Some planters recommend the replacement of a loam soil with a mixture of one-quarter peat moss and three-quarters topsoil; others consider a light sandy loam ideal for trees. These opinions depend upon the species being planted. Check with your local extension service or nursery people for their advice *before* digging.

Although some trees (such as the ailanthus) may grow in *any* soil including clay or shale, most experts recommend the replacement of such soil. A dense clay soil is not permeable to air and water (remember, oxygen must penetrate the soil, too) and becomes extremely hard and cracks when it dries.

Remember, even the best soil must be spaded to a fine consistency. Breaking up clumps of soil allows the free entrance of water and plant food after it has been spaded back around the roots of the newly planted tree.

Good topsoil can be purchased at any nursery, but equally fertile soil can be dug up from an abandoned pasture or other land that has once been cultivated. While fertilizers will be discussed later, it is important to note that the addition of inorganic fertilizers, manure, or even compost to replacement soil may injure or kill the tree. These additives can yield a toxic effect if they come into direct contact with roots. Just as an overabundance of certain vitamins ("A," for example) can be harmful to infants, too much of a "good thing" such as organic fertilizers will damage a newly planted tree. Good garden topsoil mixed with peat humus is a good medium for most trees.

For street trees, the New Jersey Federation of Tree Commissions recommends the following soil modification at the time of planting:

Veteran tree arborists have, through years of trial and error, established fertilizer application procedures, one of these being the thorough mixing of one pound of rock phosphate and two pounds of dolomitic ground limestone with the soil in the bottom of the hole. The addition, *by thorough mixing, of one pound of steamed bonemeal to the soil for backfill is also suggested. Fundamentally, clay (heavy) soils should be conditioned with coarse sand and a minimum of humic material. Generous additions of humic materials to such soils, particularly if poorly drained, will add to the sogginess during wet periods. Sandy soils should be conditioned with a loamy soil plus generous (up to 10 percent) humic materials which will improve the water holding properties.*

Rural Sites

Where entire belts of trees are to be grown, or woodlots created—as in abandoned pastures—the ground should be plowed and prepared as for a garden crop. It is best to plow clay soils the fall preceding planting to allow the ground to settle over winter. If subsoiling of such ground is essential it should also precede planting by at least one season. Just before seedlings are planted the ground should be firmed up with a roller. If the planting is to be done in rows, the ground should be marked off lengthwise and crosswise and the trees placed where the lines intersect.

In dry regions furrows should be dug and the seedlings planted in them, so that a maximum amount of rainwater will drain to the trees.

In wet regions it may be necessary, depending upon the species being planted, to plant trees on a raised mound of earth to keep the soil dry enough for them to do well.

When to Plant

The best success in tree planting results if deciduous trees are set as early in the spring season as possible, usually as soon as the ground ceases freezing, or "opens up." Evergreens may be planted later in spring; some even wait until new growth appears.

During the summer—the period of greatest growth —the roots are continuously required to supply the top of the tree with nutriment. If an attempt is made to transplant at this time the leaves dry out, often resulting in fatal injury. During the dormant period, from late autumn to early spring, the tree is in a subdued state of activity and least shocked by transplanting.

Fall planting does not yield as much success as spring does. If the winter that follows is severe the tree may be uprooted or overturned by the motions of a frozen and later thawed earth mass. Secondly, in fall planting, new roots seldom develop before the ground freezes. All the while, moisture continues to

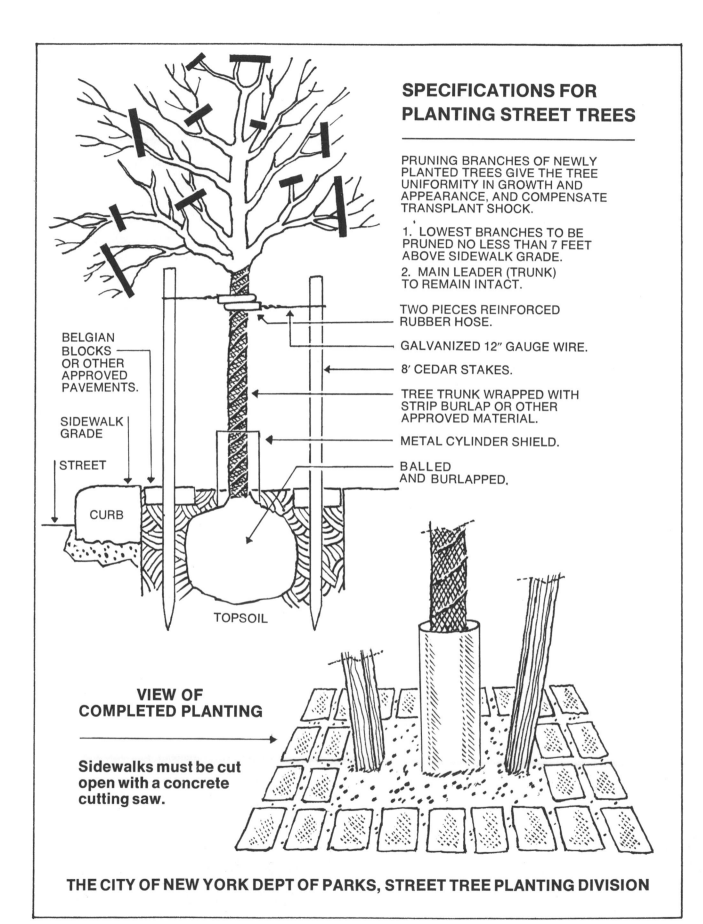

SPECIFICATIONS FOR PLANTING STREET TREES

PRUNING BRANCHES OF NEWLY PLANTED TREES GIVE THE TREE UNIFORMITY IN GROWTH AND APPEARANCE, AND COMPENSATE TRANSPLANT SHOCK.

1. LOWEST BRANCHES TO BE PRUNED NO LESS THAN 7 FEET ABOVE SIDEWALK GRADE.

2. MAIN LEADER (TRUNK) TO REMAIN INTACT.

TWO PIECES REINFORCED RUBBER HOSE.

GALVANIZED 12" GAUGE WIRE.

8' CEDAR STAKES.

TREE TRUNK WRAPPED WITH STRIP BURLAP OR OTHER APPROVED MATERIAL.

METAL CYLINDER SHIELD.

BALLED AND BURLAPPED.

BELGIAN BLOCKS OR OTHER APPROVED PAVEMENTS.

SIDEWALK GRADE

STREET

CURB

TOPSOIL

VIEW OF COMPLETED PLANTING

Sidewalks must be cut open with a concrete cutting saw.

THE CITY OF NEW YORK DEPT OF PARKS, STREET TREE PLANTING DIVISION

evaporate from the trunk and branches, while the roots also suffer.

Of course, the "best" time for planting may vary according to the region.

The New Orleans Parkway Commission, for example, makes the following recommendations:

If the tree is balled or burlapped, planting should be done during the cold months (November 15–March 15). Well rooted trees grown in containers may be planted throughout the year, although the cooler months are preferred for better success. Palms should only be planted from late spring (April) to late summer (the end of August).

In the Yearbook of Agriculture for 1949, *Trees*, it is stated that in Florida and the interior and southern regions of California evergreens are successfully transplanted whenever "abundant" soil moisture is available. In these areas deciduous trees should be planted when they are at their most dormant.

An early farming bulletin (1901) offers the following advice:

If possible, planting should be done on a cool, cloudy day. Unless the day is very moist, the trees should be carried to the planting site in a barrel half filled with water, or a thin mixture of earth and water, and lifted out only as they are wanted. Even a minute's exposure to dry air will injure the delicate roots—the feeders of the tree.

Planting

Before bringing the tree to the site try to complete all digging and soil preparation. This planning reduces the time the tree will be out of the ground. While most people obtain their trees from nurseries, some may want to dig wild trees. The following methods are advised by the Maine Forestry Department.

Obtaining Wild Trees

If wilding trees are to be used, they should be dug in open rather than in wooded areas, and where soil is rich and deep rather than on shallow or poor sites. Trees growing from sprouts or in clumps should not be used. In digging wilding trees, it is important to save as much of the fibrous root system as possible. A tree not over 10–12 feet in height is a good size to plant.

Larger trees are successfully transplanted but this requires experienced help, special methods, and heavy equipment. Small trees (up to 6–8 feet tall, 1½-inch basal diameter) can be dug at once but larger trees (10–12 feet, 2-inch basal diameter and up) respond best if root-pruned a year before transplanting. This involves cutting through the soil around the tree just inside the final digging perimeter. Cut about six inches away from the tree for each inch in diameter of the trunk. The remaining roots will grow a more compact fibrous root system before digging time the following spring. For even larger trees (over 3-inch basal diameter) cut partially around the tree one year with the remainder being done the second year, moving the tree the third year. Evergreens are dug the same as hardwoods with a soil ball but need not necessarily be root-pruned prior to digging. When moving trees with a soil ball, work burlap under and up around the ball, tying the burlap at the top of the ball to hold the soil in place.

Hardwoods may also be dug with the roots bare. In such case dig around the tree as above to cut the roots. Then use a spading fork to loosen the soil gradually away from the roots, working in toward the tree. For moving trees with bare roots put peat moss and burlap around the root area. Whichever way trees are moved the roots should be kept moist until ready for planting.

Pruning at Time of Planting

Hardwood (deciduous) trees should be top-pruned before planting . . . to offset the root loss which results from digging trees. Nursery trees root-pruned prior to digging will necessitate less pruning than will wilding trees dug immediately prior to planting. Pruning should be distributed over the tree instead of removing the ends of all limbs or removing all of the branches on the lower half or third of the tree. Remove all interfering limbs, and space limb crotches so that ample space is provided for diameter growth of each remaining limb. All cuts should be flush to a parent limb to promote rapid healing of pruning wounds. Never cut back the leader unless all but one of the laterals in the top whorl are also removed. Otherwise an undesirable forked tree will result.

Evergreens are not pruned except in case of severe root loss in which case some of the past year's lateral growth should be removed. Do not prune off entire limbs on evergreens or the desirable natural form of the tree will be destroyed.

When pruning the end from a branch, the cut should be made immediately above a bud or twig and slanted down away from the remaining bud or twig. Pruning should be done with a clean, sharp instrument—knife, pruner, or hand-saw. Axes and hatchets should not be used.

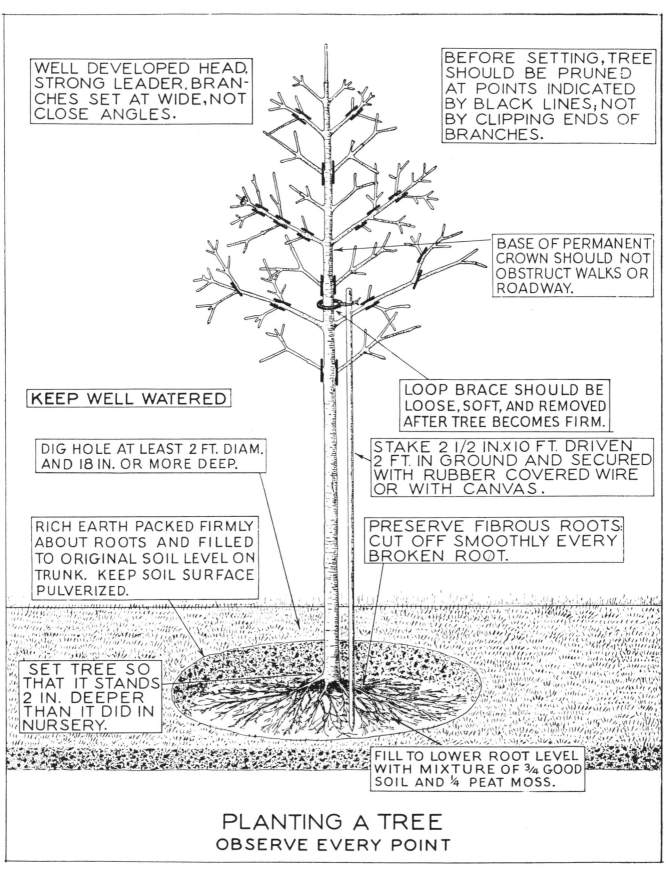

WELL DEVELOPED HEAD, STRONG LEADER, BRANCHES SET AT WIDE, NOT CLOSE ANGLES.

BEFORE SETTING, TREE SHOULD BE PRUNED AT POINTS INDICATED BY BLACK LINES; NOT BY CLIPPING ENDS OF BRANCHES.

BASE OF PERMANENT CROWN SHOULD NOT OBSTRUCT WALKS OR ROADWAY.

KEEP WELL WATERED

LOOP BRACE SHOULD BE LOOSE, SOFT, AND REMOVED AFTER TREE BECOMES FIRM.

DIG HOLE AT LEAST 2 FT. DIAM. AND 18 IN. OR MORE DEEP.

STAKE 2 1/2 IN. X 10 FT. DRIVEN 2 FT. IN GROUND AND SECURED WITH RUBBER COVERED WIRE OR WITH CANVAS.

RICH EARTH PACKED FIRMLY ABOUT ROOTS AND FILLED TO ORIGINAL SOIL LEVEL ON TRUNK. KEEP SOIL SURFACE PULVERIZED.

PRESERVE FIBROUS ROOTS: CUT OFF SMOOTHLY EVERY BROKEN ROOT.

SET TREE SO THAT IT STANDS 2 IN. DEEPER THAN IT DID IN NURSERY.

FILL TO LOWER ROOT LEVEL WITH MIXTURE OF ¾ GOOD SOIL AND ¼ PEAT MOSS.

PLANTING A TREE
OBSERVE EVERY POINT

(Courtesy, Maine Forestry Department)

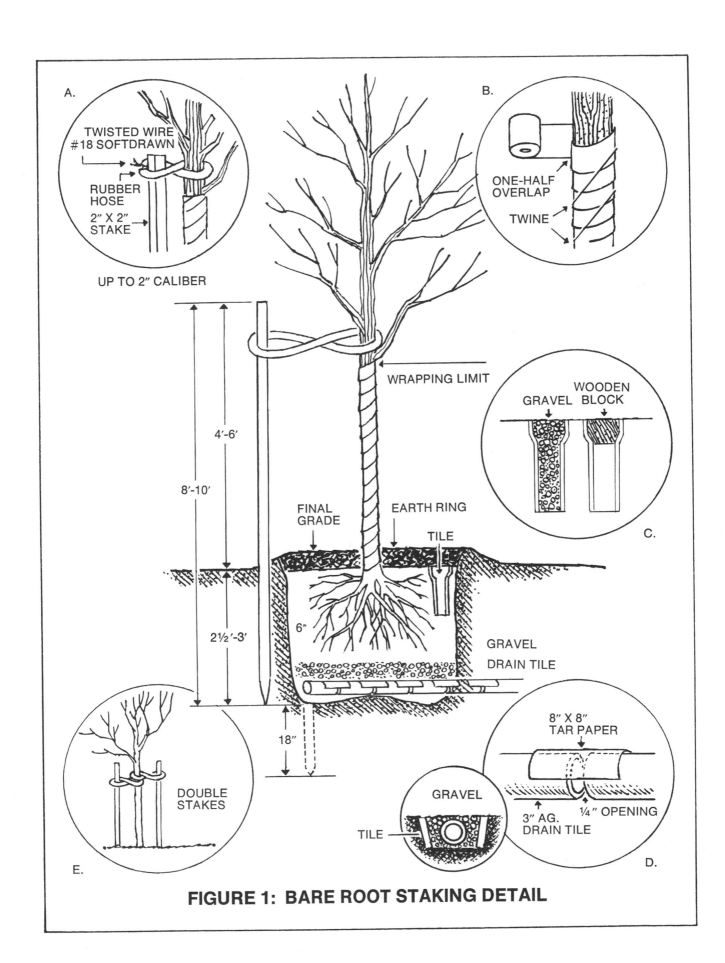

A.
TWISTED WIRE
#18 SOFTDRAWN
RUBBER
HOSE
2" X 2"
STAKE
UP TO 2" CALIBER

B.
ONE-HALF
OVERLAP
TWINE

WRAPPING LIMIT

WOODEN
GRAVEL BLOCK

C.

4'-6'
8'-10'

FINAL
GRADE
EARTH RING
TILE

2½'-3'
6"

GRAVEL
DRAIN TILE

18"

DOUBLE
STAKES

E.

GRAVEL
TILE

8" X 8"
TAR PAPER
¼" OPENING
3" AG.
DRAIN TILE

D.

FIGURE 1: BARE ROOT STAKING DETAIL

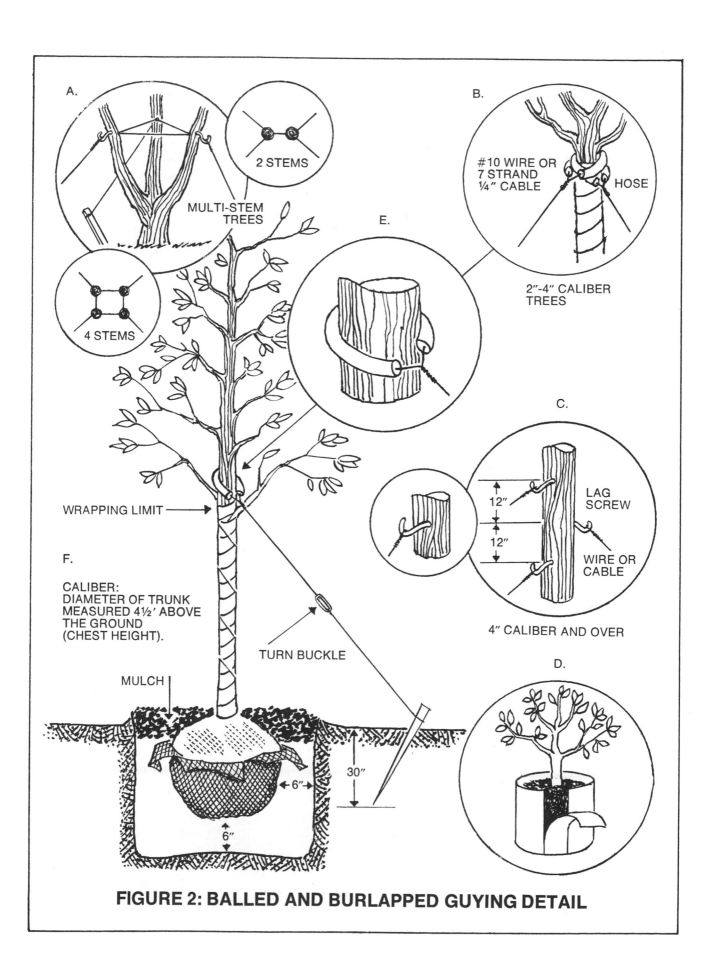

FIGURE 2: BALLED AND BURLAPPED GUYING DETAIL

Planting Bare-Rooted Trees

Spade some of the prepared soil into the pit bottom making certain a slight soil mound is formed in the center. Tamp this backfill with your foot, being careful not to overcompact the soil with too much pressure. The center mound will prevent formation of air pockets by keeping the tree from sinking or shifting.

Just before placing the tree in its new home inspect the roots and prune off all shriveled ends. Check to be sure the hole is large enough to accept the root system without cramping.

Place the tree gently on the center mound and spread the roots out in the directions they most naturally belong, making certain not to twist or crowd them. Align the trunk to a vertical position and begin to spade fine soil around the roots. (This may be the best time to embed supports into the soil. While types of supports are described in greater detail later in this section this is the correct moment to have your supports ready.) To eliminate air spaces, which may kill adjoining roots, soil must be carefully worked around each root. A pointed stick may be a valuable tool for pushing soil firmly beneath and around the roots. It may be necessary to use your hands to place the soil in spaces where the stick or spade cannot enter. Also, the fingers in feeling the soil will seek out any lumps and pulverize them into fine grains.

After successive layers of soil have been added and tamped firm to within three or four inches of the level where the tree stood in the nursery, the hole is heavily watered and the tree gently raised and lowered to allow the soil to fill any remaining air pockets.

While rural planting generally requires no watering during planting, suburban and urban planters generally soak the soil until it is the consistency of a thick mud. Some add water as soon as the roots are covered, while others begin the soaking operation when the hole is two-thirds filled. Older books recommend no watering during planting, but each layer of soil must be tamped and packed firmly to eliminate air pockets. With this method the hole is thoroughly watered *after* planting.

In contemporary planting, after watering and lifting the tree up and down the final three or four inches are filled with a loose layer of soil that permits free aeration of the roots. Soil must *not* be mounded up at the base of the tree. This will smother the roots, causing injury or death.

When finished the tree should stand at the same soil level as originally grown and at the level of the surrounding surface. While some planters set the tree two inches below its former earth level, this may result in root smothering.

After the tree has been planted a rim of earth should be spaded around the hole to act as a basin that catches and retains water.

Planting Balled and Burlapped Trees

This type of prepared tree must be planted so that it finally rests one to two inches *above* soil level. This will allow the tree to settle to the proper depth after planting.

Making certain the planting pit is at least twelve inches wider and six inches deeper than the diameter of the earth ball, a low center earth mound is created to prevent premature settling.

Sufficient soil is spaded in the bottom of the hole (at least four inches of soil is required with an average seven- or eight-foot tree) and the tree is set in and additional soil added to stabilize the ball. Again, stakes should be added at this stage.

Burlap need *not* be pulled out from beneath the roots (this step may even cause some root damage), as it decays after a short while in the ground. It *must* be *loosened* from around the trunk and layed out or cut off with a scissors or sharp blade. Any ropes or attached wire that may restrict growth must also be removed.

While not a requirement, it may be beneficial, at this stage, to spread the roots out to their natural positions, all the while adding prepared soil and tamping it firmly about.

After the hole is one-half to two-thirds full the soil is tamped down firmly and water added. When this has soaked away, additional soil is added and water is again allowed to slowly fill the pit. This process is repeated until the soil level is stabilized at the original base of the trunk.

Making certain the tree now sits *above* soil level, an earth ring is built up around the edge of the ball, or a small circular depression created to retain all available water.

Container-Grown Trees

Trees grown in cans are planted in the same way as balled and burlapped stock. Since the cans must be cut away from the root system, *with the least disturbance,* it is often best to ask the nurseryman to cut the cans using special snippers. The trees can still be transported in their containers, as long as the cans are tied.

At the planting site always cut the can *away* from the roots and earth ball. A tree must *never* be pulled from the container.

After Planting

Mulching

Both bare-rooted and balled stock must be *mulched.* One to two inches of dead leaves, hay, shredded corn stalks, sawdust, or "bagasse" laid over the planting hole after planting will reduce evaporation (of soil moisture), which prevents drying of the soil in summer. Mulching also inhibits the growth of weeds or grass.

This must not be overdone. A large mass of decaying matter may be more harmful than beneficial. Enough mulch to shade the soil is sufficient. Deciduous trees generally require mulching for the first two years, while evergreens do well with a continuous mulch layer.

Wrapping

Trees less than three inches in diameter should be wrapped just after planting to prevent sun scald and to lessen evaporation. Larger trees are generally bark-toughened and need not be wrapped.

To prevent injury special paper or six-inch strips of burlap are twined around the trunk and lower limbs. Begin *below* grade and continue upward in a clockwise direction, overlapping each turn by one-half of the next spiral. The wrapping is best secured with twine, beginning at the lower limbs and spiraling down around the trunk in a counterclockwise direction.

The wrapping should be kept in place for at least one and possibly two years, depending on the tree's growth rate. Fast-growing species need protection for a shorter period of time.

In rural areas, a sleeve of fine mesh wire can also be placed around the trunk to protect the bark from gnawing animals.

City streets harbor other dangerous animals, and to keep them from injuring trees, iron or wooden guards afford excellent protection.

Watering When Planting

While initial watering, during planting, requires a completely saturated soil, waterlogging should be avoided as a general practice.

Heavy watering, once a week, is better than daily sprinkling. Light, daily watering encourages the roots to grow upwards toward the surface to obtain moisture and this encourages a shallow root system that is less stable than deep roots and more susceptible to drought.

Watering must be maintained for at least one but preferably for two to three years after planting.

It is advisable to remove earth rings or fill depressions during winter to prevent water from collecting and freezing and thereby causing trunk damage.

While the above recommendations are advisable for urban and suburban sites an early source recommends that in rural areas *no* watering be practiced:

Trees should be planted neither in very wet nor in very dry soil. If the soil is wet, it is better to wait until it is drier. On the other hand, if good cultivation has been maintained the year previous to planting the soil is not likely to be so dry that trees will not start. Besides insuring a supply of moisture, such cultivation puts the ground in good physical condition for planting.

With this treatment watering will scarcely ever be necessary. If it is, the holes may be dug a few days beforehand and filled with water. They should be refilled as the water soaks away until the soil is fully moistened. A thorough irrigation, when that is possible, is still better. As soon as the soil becomes somewhat dry the trees should be planted. While it is a common custom to water at the time of planting, those who do no watering are usually the most successful. Even in the semiarid regions some successful growers apply no water, but keep up an excellent system of cultivation, thereby retaining the soil moisture. *

Staking

Small trees, with a trunk diameter up to two inches and a height greater than seven feet, generally need only one stake. Trees that are between two to four inches in diameter generally require two or three stakes, while heavy wind conditions may require four stakes.

If a single stake is used it should be placed on the windward side.

Stakes made of metal or wooden supports treated with wood preservatives may be used. An overall stake height of eight to ten feet may be required, depending on the height of the newly planted tree. It should reach up to the base of the crown and be driven into *hard soil* (allow about three feet for the soil side) at least 18 inches from the trunk. *Install the stakes with extreme care, making certain the tender tree roots are not injured.*

---

* *"Planting on Rural School Grounds,"* USDA Farmer's Bulletin #134 (1901).

While it is advisable to drive the stakes three feet into the ground *outside* of the planting pit for maximum stability, if they must be driven within the planting hole they must be one to two feet longer and driven hard into the bottom soil.

The tree is secured to the stake with tough wire that is insulated within old garden hose to prevent bark injury. The hose is usually figure-eighted around the tree and supported with uninsulated wire ends fastened to the stake.

After one growing season check the wire tension and loosen the bind as the tree grows. Tautness is required but the plant must not be inhibited by any pressure if it is to attain a full height and natural shape at maturity.

Guy Wires

Trees larger than four inches in diameter (smaller where additional support is needed) should be secured with three or four guys.

Cables or wire inside garden hose is wrapped around limbs and secured to two-inch by four-inch by four-foot stakes run diagonally into the ground. The stakes should be placed outside the planting pit for maximum support.

Turnbuckles are sometimes used in the center of the guy wires to maintain a tautness but allowing for growth and natural movement by being loosened as required.

Why Trees Sometimes Die After Planting

While the best stock is sometimes selected and all the planting rules followed to a letter, trees sometimes die after being transplanted.

Death is a frightening reality for most humans and is sometimes not understood in relation to the plant world.

While it is true that some trees die "for no reason" it is a general fact that all sane living organisms move toward survival, even under the most impossible conditions. A living organism may not thrive in an environment but yet may "hang on" driven by a universal code of life.

However, young trees sometimes die, and it is often not without good reason. When one begins to wither something is wrong, and the careful planter will watch as a loving parent over the needs of his child.

In some cases a maltreated tree begins to exhibit signs of decay or injury a few days after planting; in other cases the signs are not noticeable for a few weeks.

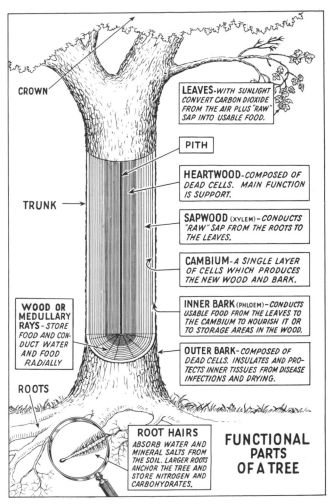

(Courtesy, Maine Forestry Department)

Trees that have been maltreated before planting or improperly set cannot be helped. The only assistance possible is to make the surroundings of the tree as favorable for growth as possible. Only the tree itself can overcome the initial obstacles and "grow" through them.

Some of the causes of death among newly transplanted trees follow:

1. Loss of roots:

a. Have the roots been pruned back too severely?

b. Has the top been pruned back sufficiently to compensate for root loss? Are the leaves evaporating more moisture than the roots can provide?

2. Exposure before planting:

a. Have the roots been exposed to sunlight and winds in handling and allowed to wither and dry out? (This exposure may occur at any point between the time of removal from the ground and subsequent planting; in digging, packing, shipping, unpacking or planting.)

3. *Failure to plant well:*

a. Has the soil been packed about the roots tightly enough to eliminate air pockets and provide stability? The tiny rootlets must be in contact with fine soil to absorb nutriments. Anything that prevents the soil particles from coming into close contact with the roots may be injurious (stones, hard clumps, or manure mixed with the soil may prevent firm packing).

b. Have you planted too shallow, thereby allowing water and wind to lay bare the roots?

c. Have the roots been crowded into too small a pit?

4. *Wet soil:*

a. Is the soil oversoaked, either because the locale is naturally wet or because of excessive watering during planting? Too much water prevents the air from reaching the roots.

5. *Dry soil:*

a. Has the tree not been watered deeply once a week? Dried soil lumps together and causes fissures that admit currents of air that dry the roots. (Roots need a soil *permeable* to air not open crevices.)

b. Have weeds and grass been allowed to grow up in the tree well and draw off the moisture needed by the young tree?

6. *Inappropriate soil reaction:*

Soils range from very strongly acid (pH 3.5) to strongly alkaline (pH 10.0). While a pH value of 5.5 to 7.0 is favorable for most trees, some species prefer acid soils, while others insist upon being placed in an alkaline environment.

Soil-testing kits are available at many garden suppliers, while agricultural chemical corporations often have field agents who will evaluate the soil pH free of charge. Most cooperative extension services also offer this service.

·IV·
Main-
taining
Trees

However rewarding the act of tree planting may be, watching a young tree slowly die can be spiritually defeating. While rural conditions generally require little support from man, trees planted in the suburbs and cities always require outside support if they are to survive.

Trees, especially when they are young, but also in old age, will survive only if maintenance is continued, either by the individuals who plant them or by city tree crews. Since most cities prohibit tree planting without prior approval the time *before* planting is best for deciding *who* will be responsible for maintenance.

The world is in constant struggle. Trees too must "struggle" for survival, especially in strange environments. Insects, blows, vandalism, soot, alkaline soil, insufficient natural water, road salts, obnoxious gases, and the soluble salts of canine rain must be countered.

New buildings are seldom planned without calculating and budgeting adequate funds for maintenance through many years. The same approach must be applied to tree planting. *No trees should be planted without budgeting the time and/or the funds for maintaining them through several years of growth.* Since this may discourage tree planting the wise planter will select relatively low-maintenance species or clones of disease-resistant trees for his site, provided they are of good form and attain a healthy size. Before a final selection is made consult the "tree profiles" in this book, other publications, local agricultural experiment stations, arboretums, city-forestry or parks-department personnel, and nurserymen.

Assuming that a hardy tree is planted and does well the best advice to follow is "leave it alone"! If problems develop, such as wilting, pale green leaves (where this is abnormal), dead twig tips, absence of new foliage, loose bark and slow or zero growth, consult the chart "Diagnosis of Principal Causes of Injury to Trees," which is presented at the end of this section.

While common maintenance procedures that are normally encountered in growing trees are treated here, more detailed discussions are available in other publications. One of the most inclusive books is P. P. Pirone's *Tree Maintenance.*

Dr. Pirone issues the following information form to individuals who submit diseased plant material to him for diagnosis. The questions themselves may be useful guidelines for the maintenance of trees:

———

A. General Questions

1. Kind, age and size of tree.

2. Where is the tree situated—along street, on lawn, in a park? Near body of water, salt or fresh? On level ground or on a slope?

3. How long has the tree exhibited the trouble? If the trouble appeared suddenly, describe the weather conditions occurring just previously. Describe any other unusual conditions.

4. Is the trouble visible all over the tree, on only one side, in the lower or upper branches?

5. Do any other trees of the same species in the near vicinity show the same injury? Do other species show it?

6. How much annual growth have the twigs made during the past 3 years?

7. Has the grade around the tree been raised or lowered during the past 7 years? If so, explain amount of change and describe the procedure and type of fill used.

8. Has any construction work been done nearby within the past 3 years—house, road, driveway, curbstone, garage or ditches for laying water or sewer pipes?

9. What work has been done on this tree recently? Has it been pruned within the past 2 years? If so, how much? Fertilizer treatments—when, what and how much?

10. If a young tree, how long since it was planted in present location? How deeply was it planted? (Use a spade to determine depth of roots.) What treatments were given during the first year after transplanting?

B. Questions About the Soil—*These are extremely helpful, particularly if the tree has been dying back slowly over a period of years.*

1. What kind of soil surrounds the tree? Sandy, loamy, or clayey? What soil cover—asphalt, cement, crushed rock, cinders, sand, grass, mulch, weeds or no cover? How much open area is there?

2. What is the depth to subsoil, to rock or shale, to hardpan?

3. What is the pH reaction of the soil?

4. Does water stand on the soil after a heavy rain?

C. Questions About the Roots—*These are the most difficult to answer, since considerable digging may be required. They are most important, however, especially when a general disorder is involved.*

1. Is a girdling root present? Sometimes such roots are well-below-ground and you may have to dig a foot or so before you can be sure.

2. Are the larger roots normal in color? Do they have rotted bark or discolored wood? If so, submit specimens.

3. What is the appearance of the finer roots? Are root hairs abundant and white? (Dig down a foot or so beneath the outer spread of the branches.)

D. Questions About the Trunk

1. Are there any long, narrow open cracks present? If so, in which direction do they face?

2. Are cavities present? If so, describe size of opening, condition of interior if unfilled. If filled, give details.

3. Is there any bark bleeding? If so, how extensive? (Submit specimens including bark and sapwood.)

4. Are there any swollen areas? Describe.

5. Is there a swollen area completely around the trunk? If so, cut into the swelling with a chisel to determine the presence of some foreign object such as a wire.

6. Are there any fungi (mushrooms or bracket-type) growing out of the bark? (If so, include a few specimens.)

7. Are there cankers (dead sunken areas in the bark)? (Submit specimens.)

8. Are there any borer holes or other evidences of insect work?

9. Is the bark at or just below the soil line healthy? (Use your chisel to determine this.)

10. If wood beneath this bark is discolored, describe color, and extent. Submit several pieces of bark and wood.

E. Questions About Branches

1. Is the bark cracked for some distances? On what side of the branches?

2. Are there any cankers in the branch?

3. Is there any discoloration in the branches or twigs which have wilted leaves, which are leafless?

F. Specific Possibilities

1. Did the trouble appear
   a. immediately after a thunderstorm?
   b. after chemicals were injected into the trunk?
   c. after sprays were applied? (Name the ingredients used and when applied.)
   d. after weed killers were applied in the vicinity?
   e. after treating a nearby cellar for termite control?
   f. after any other chemical treatment?

Watering

Water is one of the primary agents in the nutrition and life activities of a tree. With a decrease in the supply of water growth decreases and leaves are shed in an attempt to survive. If the supply continues to decrease the tree finally withers and dies.

In their demands for water trees differ widely. Some thrive only with their roots in constantly saturated soil —as, for example, the tamarack of the northern and the baldcypress of the southern states. Every degree of variation exists between trees of this "water-loving" nature and those of the desert, where a scant few inches of rain falls each year.

The amount of water required will be determined by appraising the tree's size, existing soil conditions, and the average amount of rainfall.

It is therefore impossible to make generalizations about the water requirements of "trees." In attempting to come up with a formula the planter must first analyze the nature of the tree and the site. Hopefully, advance planning will have coordinated a tree "that does best in moist soil" to a wet soil, and a "tree that prefers dry soil" to dry soil. Those trees that "grow in a wide range of soils" usually do just that and are best left alone, except for a weekly watering, unless signs of disease or injury become apparent.

Overwatering the soil of a newly planted tree is a common mistake. Like a newly acquired puppy that is made to feel at home by being overfed, only to end up with a digestive problem, the newly set tree is often nearly drowned by its new "master." Excessive soil moisture favors the growth of fungi that rots roots because too much water fills up air spaces and drives out oxygen.

Thus, small trees should be watered infrequently in early spring until new leaves appear, when the once-weekly schedule begins. The soil around large, newly planted trees must be kept moist at all times, as they dry out rather quickly.

Rural Plantings

While much artificial watering is not recommended in replanted woodlots or shelterbelts (providing trees well adapted to local conditions have been selected), it is a good idea to keep the soil moderately moist. Without resorting to the garden hose or sprinkler, moisture can be added to the soil by conducting water that drains from adjacent slopes. A small trench made to correspond with the contour lines of a hill or slope will often gather almost all the surface-drainage water.

One of the simplest and most effective ways of retaining moisture, in a limited planting, is by frequently spading the soil to a depth of two or three inches within a circle of a few feet around the trunks. This will keep grass and weeds from draining away water and retarding the tree's growth. The longer this form of cultivation is practiced the better it is for the trees. It should be maintained at least until they are well rooted and able to thrive without any assistance.

Town and City Trees

"When you receive your trees would you be kind enough to water these newly planted trees with a pail full of water about every other day during the dry summer months. We would greatly appreciate it and, without any doubt, would guarantee the life of the trees."

This advice is warmly mailed in a personally signed letter by Loring E. Clark, tree warden of Marblehead, Massachusetts. The property owner who requests tree plantings is expected to contribute some energy (and water) to their survival.

The following note is attached to the tree warden's letter and contains general advice regarding proper watering:

PLEASE...
WATER DEEPLY!

PROPER WATERING: —

ONCE or TWICE a week for 1 to 2 hours water as diagram shows, allowing hose to fill saucer around the plant SOAKING the ground deeply. This keeps the roots down.

Sprinkling 10-15 min. every day does more harm than good as it brings the roots closer to surface of ground.

Where atmospheric soot and dust is a problem it is also a good idea to rinse the leaves once in a while to eliminate particles that block the tiny stomata and inhibit transpiration.

William Solotaroff, a grandfather of American urban tree planting, has very specific advice about the need for and amount of water required by city street trees:

In cities the water from rainfall runs off quickly, and very little finds its way into the soil and subsoil . . . Young trees need more frequent watering than older ones. Trees that have surface roots need more watering than deeply rooted ones; also rapidly growing trees more so than those of slow growth. . . . How much water to give trees, and at what intervals, depend upon the extent of soil occupied by the roots and the nature of the soil and subsoil. Young trees, two or three years after planting, of which the roots occupy a volume of about a cubic yard, require from 20 to 25 gallons at every watering. Older trees require more water. . . . While on the one hand there must be enough watering to maintain a uniform degree of moisture in the soil, on the other hand care

must be taken not to allow too much moisture around the roots. . . . Watering of trees should be avoided during the hottest part of the day. It is best to do it in the early morning and late in the afternoon or evening.

Fertilizing

Of all aspects of tree maintenance the question of fertilization is least clear in the minds of experts and laymen alike. Some recommend using fertilizers both _during_ and _after_ planting, on a regular schedule; others definitely _avoid_ using any fertilizers until after the young tree has grown for one to two years, while a third group condemns the entire question as one promoted by those in the agri-chemical industry.

No doubt, the last group—the cynics—are thinking of forest trees when they say, "Nobody fertilizes the forests yet look how well trees grow there!"

Taking the last point first it is interesting to note that Dr. Dan Neeley, Illinois natural history pathologist, believes that fertilizing may indeed have drawbacks. "You will have to mow your lawn more often. . . . You may need to prune more frequently and you may actually decrease the amount of flowering or fall color. Some plants may develop a weepy appearance."[*]

Few argue with Dr. Neeley's statement that the _correct_ amount of fertilizer (in contrast with too much fertilizer) spurs rapid growth, safeguards against disease, and aids in the reestablishment of a tree after it has been damaged by mechanical means or been attacked by insects or suffered through a drought.

In a forest a tree grows by itself.

Fallen leaves form a useful mulch and later decompose along with twigs, branches, and dead animal matter that covers the forest floor. These fallen elements return mineral nutrients and nitrogen to the soil thus rendering the "ashes to ashes" theme into a physical reality. In this cycle of growth followed by decay the fertility of forest soil is naturally maintained.

While this natural cycle may provide fertilization in a retreed woodlot, shade trees are often denied the benefits of a healthy accumulation of fallen leaves, twigs, and fruit. In the "civilized" areas nature's cycle is interrupted by fierce neatness experts armed with rake and matches. Thus the composition and texture of the soil is not maintained unless by artificial means. Also, lawn grasses greedily devour much available water and essential nutrients before they reach the roots of any tree.

---

[*] Weeds, Trees and Turf (May, 1969).

As a result of insufficient nutrients trees may grow slowly, exhibit weak color, dead branches, few new buds, and be slow to produce healing calluses over wounds.

The safest course of action then becomes the "wait and see" technique. If you wish, drop a dead fish into the planting pit and then add the tree. However, it is definitely best to avoid adding *any* kind of fertilizer at the time of planting. Too often an overabundance will actually "burn" the roots, thereby killing the tree before it has had a chance to grow. Even manure may inhibit a young tree's chance of survival, by preventing the tiny rootlets from gaining access to soil moisture and oxygen or by releasing toxic substances during decomposition.

So, after planting, wait a few weeks or months before fertilizing. If the tree does well, leave it alone. If not, and any or all of the signs of illness appear, it is time to fertilize, assuming all other planting instructions have been accurately followed.

While the elements necessary for tree growth are contained in good soils, those that are most rapidly utilized and exhausted are *nitrogen, phosphorous*, and *potassium*. Trees (and other plants) require more of these elements than of the others in the soil.

Nitrogen influences cellular growth and thereby promotes production of healthy twigs, wood, and green leaves. This element also helps in the synthesis of chlorophyll, a deficiency of which results in undersized, yellow leaves. (An excess of nitrogen will often cause injury to roots.) In good soils, most nitrogen originates from dead plants and animals, as they decay.

Phosphorous aids development of roots, while strengthening the tree against adverse conditions. In forests, this element enters the soil from decaying bones and those rocks that naturally contain deposits of phosphorous.

Potassium or potash plays a role in the production of sugars, starches, and cellulose. It thereby promotes a tough stem while contributing toward the development of healthy foliage.

While the merits of fertilization cannot be argued, where natural conditions are not adequate the question of chemical (or inorganic) versus natural (or organic) fertilizers deserves consideration.

The natural fertilizers are derived from plant or animal remains. This organic matter adds humus to the soil and benefits the tree, but is much slower acting than chemicals. Natural fertilizers, it should be remembered, last much longer than the inorganic varieties.

Some natural, organic fertilizers are as follows:

By-products of slaughter houses
{
Animal manures
Dried blood
Raw bonemeal
Tankage
}

Cottonseed meal

Peat: from decayed vegetation in swampy habitats

Milorganite: a by-product of sewage treatment

Compost ("artificial manure"): may be rich in nitrogen, but usually a poor source of phosphorous and potassium

Hardwood ashes, unleached: a rich source (2 to 8%) of potash, or potassium

Chemical, or inorganic, fertilizers contain the three essential plant nutrients in concentrated form. They each deliver twenty units of these elements in combinations such as 10-6-4, 10-10-10, 7-8-6, or 10-5-5. The first number denotes the percentage of nitrogen; the second, the phosphoric acid; and the third, the potash. Some also contain small amounts of boron, magnesium, and manganese, but these elements are usually listed as "minor elements" on the package, their percentage usually not noted.

There is little agreement on a "perfect" inorganic fertilizer formula for shade trees. Dr. P. P. Pirone, of New York Botanical Garden, states that well-rotted stable manure is "one of the best materials for small trees."

The Threat of Chemical Fertilizers

While organic fertilizers used on the land infrequently contribute an overabundance of nitrates to adjacent streams, lakes, or rivers, chemical fertilizers may have ruinous effects on the drinking water of areas in which they are heavily utilized.

Barry Commoner, in his book *The Closing Circle*, traces the destruction of drinking water in Decatur, Illinois (a farm community of 100,000 people), to the great amounts of inorganic nitrogen fertilizers used on the surrounding farmlands. As the use of fertilizer nitrogen increased, it was found, nitrate levels of surrounding rivers also increased. These nitrates also appeared in shallow wells.

When nitrates are converted to nitrites by intestinal bacteria (this occurs more frequently in infants than adults) oxygen transport is inhibited and asphyxiation often results.

Excessive nitrate in the water has alarmed public health authorities in Decatur as well as in Missouri, Czechoslovakia, France, Germany, and Israel. All have noted an increase in infant methemoglobinemia.

While flourishing trees are desirable (why else was this book written?) we must consider the effects of

Similarly, we cannot use *any* means available (such as massive applications of inorganic fertilizers) to promote the growth of shade trees. It must be remembered that while we are attempting to correct an environmental problem by increasing the numbers of trees in America we must be careful to avoid damaging another

How to Fertilize. Holes 15-18 inches deep should be made with a crow-bar or other sharp instrument. Make holes 3 ft. apart in concentric circles 3 ft. apart. Starting 3 or 4 ft. from the trunk and extending just beyond the edge of the foliage.

fertilization on the environment before buying a bag of inorganic compounds. It is no longer possible to treat all aspects of the living world as separate entities.

An analogy of the "separation approach" to a biological problem can be seen in dentistry. Fluoride in concentrated form, such as tablets, may definitely decrease the incidence of tooth decay but what effects do massive doses of this chemical have on other systems of the organism? Can a dentist just "take care of his end of the body" without considering the body as a whole?

part of the environment (our waters) in the process.

Therefore, greater efforts must be made to secure organic fertilizers for the growth of shade trees.

Such fertilizers are becoming increasingly available at garden-supply centers. Slaughterhouses will often sell their by-products, which are excellent organic fertilizers, directly to consumers who order them in advance.

How to Apply

Under no circumstances must dry chemical fertilizer

be applied within one foot of the trunk, since injury may result.

Where possible, fertilizer should be put into the ground at a depth of fifteen to eighteen inches. By punching holes in the soil, using a crowbar, or other similar device, the fertilizer is put where it is readily available to the tree roots. Surface fertilization encourages surface feeding roots, which are not desirable. Further, on lawns, broadcasting fertilizer often feeds only the grass. If enough is scattered to feed both the tree and the grass, it will probably burn the grass and ruin the lawn.

A handy method for producing a ready supply of liquid fertilizer is obtained by placing well-rotted cow manure or other organic fertilizer into a pail of water for a few hours, stirring occasionally with a stick. This rich solution may be poured directly into the soil (away from the trunk) and is especially handy during dry spells because both watering and fertilization are combined into one operation.

Parasites and Their Control

The tragic decline of the American elm is caused by a fungus transmitted by elm bark beetles, which bore their way into the bark. This is one key example of the reality of the damage done to trees by harmful insects. There are other tree problems caused by parasites; the list is too long to enumerate—observation being the best teacher. However, all insects that live on trees are not *necessarily* harmful. Do most people fear "bugs" of any kind ("entomophobia") and automatically want to kill them? Certainly advertisements reinforce this attitude toward the insect world.

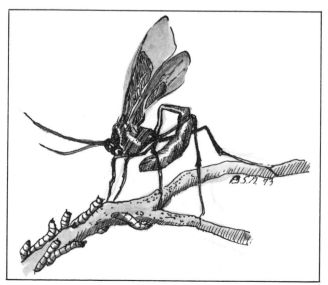

Predatory Wasp eating larvae of destructive insects.

Further, the reflex to spray every tree with pesticides is in no small way encouraged by manufacturers of such poisons and the tree-care industry. A recent article, "Tree Insects: The Commercial Arborist's Money Crop," even pointed out how lucrative the spraying of trees can be to people in the business.*

Woodpeckers may eat destructive insects such as beetles.

Therefore, "pests" on trees, except in obvious cases of destruction, may not be dangerous. The question of spraying every ornamental and shade tree automatically, for "controlling pests," must be reexamined.

To begin with, we might examine the origin of pest problems on trees. Forest trees are able to live with pests they are host to simply because in a natural setting life forms are maintained through the "checks and balances" of nature. For example, robins eat a good part of the insect populations in Illinois woodlands, while three species of woodpeckers are the primary control of the Engelmann spruce beetle in Colorado. Ants, wasps, and bees eat many insects that

---

* Arborist's News *Vol. 38, No. 2, (February 1973), pp. 49–52.*

may parasitize trees, while lady bugs feed on aphids, scale insects, mealybugs and spider mites. Life eats life and innumerable organisms are in continuous battle with one another, which in the overall scheme is how trees (and all organisms, for that matter) survive.

Urban areas are unnatural environments for trees. Herbivorous pests denied an abundance of vegetation in such environments voraciously feed on trees and whichever other plants dare show themselves in urban areas. The problem is further increased when exotic trees are introduced. Insect species may also be brought in with these trees but *without* their natural enemies! While native predators often attack these invading insects, they do not usually manage to control the new populations.

The best way to approach the entire question is to select pest-resistant species. In the "Tree-Profiles" section those trees that are noted as especially hardy for "urban conditions" are generally resistant to most pests.

Of course, we must also maintain those trees that are presently growing, which may be susceptible to pest problems.

Lady Beetle feeding upon an aphid.

Dr. William Olkowski, of the Division of Biological Control, University of California, at Berkeley, devised a system for managing tree pests on the 30,000 street trees (of 123 species) in the city of Berkeley. The city used to spend over $7,000 yearly to control insects, mainly by spraying more than 106 gallons of synthetic pesticides and applying over 200 pounds of lead arsenate. Today it is costing Berkeley only $2,500 yearly to control tree pests, and the use of pesticides has been reduced to less than 25 gallons, while lead arsenate has been completely phased out.

Dr. Olkowski and others achieved this remarkable goal by rethinking the entire question of pests and plants.

Early in their research the entomologists at Berkeley

A Preying Mantis.

realized that synthetic pesticides did not halt invasions by insect pests but only *temporarily* slowed them down. Biological control methods were seen as possibly yielding *permanent* control over tree pests. This and strategies other than chemical tools were implemented and successfully limited pests.

The first major new concept was in the area of bio-aesthetic judgments. Dr. Olkowski stresses that we must learn to "tolerate slight to moderate insect damage" on trees. Urban man must accept aesthetic damage to trees caused by the plant's "wildlife companions" because, he realized, "there can be no herbivoral life without some plant damage."

Wholesale use of sprays for entire *stands* of trees when only *individual* plants were affected by pests was also seen as a misconception. Each tree was managed individually, greatly *decreasing* expenditures of time and costly chemicals. Many trees that were automatically treated in the past were now untreated, their insect problems deemed "tolerable."

Next, the feasibility of employing biological predators was evaluated.

TABLE I

THE STATUS OF STREET TREE INSECT PROBLEMS IN BERKELEY ACCORDING TO THE ECOSYSTEM MANAGEMENT MODEL
(From "A Model Ecosystem Management Program" by William Olkowski)

Herbivorous Insects   Final Status 1972

HOMOPTERA
  APHIDIDAE
    Aphis spiraecola   Water sprays
    Calaphis sp.   Water sprays
    Drepanaphis acerifolia   Tolerable
    Drepanosiphum zimmermanni   Water sprays
    Eucallipterus tiliae   Evaluation of B.C.
    Euceraphis betulae   Water sprays
    Hyalopterus pruni   Water sprays
    Myzocallis castanicola   Evaluation of B.C.
    Periphyllus californica   Tolerable
    Phyllaphis fagi   Water sprays
    Prociphilus sp.   Pruning, water sprays
    Tinocallis plantani   Evaluation of B.C.
  COCCIDAE
    Saissetia oleae   Tolerable
  CICADELLIDAE
    Hordnia circellata   Tolerable
HEMIPTERA
  COREIDAE
    Leptocorris trivitattus   Tolerable
  MIRIDAE
    Neoborus sp.   Water sprays
LEPIDOPTERA
  DIOPTIDAE
    Phryganidia californica   *Bacillus thuringiensis*

TABLE II

"SOFT" (BUT EFFECTIVE) PESTICIDES

Agent	Preparation and Application	Used Against
Bordeaux mixture	Stir prepared mixture in water. Or, make a fresh solution, which is more effective, as follows: To make 25 gallons—to 16 gals. of water in a sprayer, slowly add 2 lbs. of copper sulfate ("snow form") while shaking the container. Add 2 lbs. of fresh lime, which has been turned into a paste with a little water. Fill the sprayer to the 25-gal. mark with water. Continuously agitate and use immediately	Fungous infections
Kerosene	Daub on infested areas with a mop attached to a pole	Many insects and their eggs; also used to burn off tent or web caterpillars
Kerosene emulsion	As a spray	Scales and soft-bodied insects
Lime sulfur	To make 1 gal. add 20–30 tablespoonfuls if used when trees are dormant. For use when trees are active, as in summer, add 7.5 to 11 teaspoonfuls to 1 gal. water. Used as a spray, or painted on	Armored-scale insects
Nicotine sulfate, 40%	Dilute as directed on label; add 1 oz. of soap to each gal. of spray as a spreader and sticking agent	Leaf miners
Pyrethrum	Comes as a spray. Good for "knocking down" insects from trees	All insects
Rotenone	Comes as a spray. A potent natural insecticide	All insects
Soap	For summer use dissolve 1 lb. of laundry soap in 3–4 gals. water. For winter use dissolve 2 lbs. soap per gal. Mix thoroughly (heat may help). Use solution in a sprayer. Acts by clogging breathing pores	Aphids and other sucking insects

Before and during the release of biological predators nontoxic control procedures were used; some new and some quite ancient.

Where trees were partly destroyed by insects, diseased branches were pruned away and burned. Ashes and elms were pruned in the inner canopies, near the trunk, particularly where new branches were growing. This ancient method effectively controls large populations of aphids, a serious pest.

High-pressure water streams were used to kill aphids on birches, plums, scarlet oaks, big leaf maples, and white ash. A remarkable 85 percent mortality of aphids resulted when small trees were treated with this method! Here a perfectly nontoxic liquid (water) was found to be capable of controlling harmful insects by applying it in a new way.

To keep ants off weakened trees a barrier of sticky material ("Stickem," available from Michael and Pelton, Emeryville, California) was placed around their trunks.

When it was feasible, predators were introduced to control problem insects.

Linden aphids on Berkeley's trees were successfully limited in numbers after Dr. Robert Van den Bosch introduced *Trioxys curvicaudus,* a tiny wasp from Europe. Oak worms were controlled by introducing *Bacillus thuringiensis,* a potent insect parasite.* (Table I shows street tree insect problems in Berkeley and the final method of treating them, as of 1972.)

Of course, the apparently successful management of tree pests through nontoxic means in Berkeley, California, does not mean that *all* the parasitic diseases of *all* ornamental and shade trees in America can be solved by parallel means. Nevertheless, Berkeley's success indicates that other than toxic chemical tools *can* be employed elsewhere. For those trees that are *obviously* under heavy siege by parasites and *obviously* being heavily damaged other controls may be required.

The first step in maintaining diseased trees is to increase the supply of water (unless, of course, the problem is too much water!) and give them a healthy dose of a good organic fertilizer.

After all the steps discussed above have been tried and the tree is *still* being damaged, its life apparently threatened, "soft" chemicals such as outlined in Table II are to be used. Many of these have been in use since

_____
* Available from Abbott Laboratories, North Chicago, Illinois; International Mineral and Chemical, Skokie, Illinois; and Thompson-Hayward Chemical, Kansas City, Kansas.

the early 1900's; some, such as pyrethrum and rotenones, are fairly recent.

In this age of ecological awareness, and I mean of the true environmental impacts of many of these compounds, there is almost no excuse for using the "hard" or synthetic insecticides. (For an excellent discussion of some of the problems generated by using such pesticides, see *The Closing Circle* by Barry Commoner.)

The problems with synthetic pesticides can be simplified into two categories. One, they are generally harmful to other life forms besides the target pest; and two, they are not *permanent* controls, only temporary. Further, such substances may actually harm *the treated tree,* in the long run, by reducing the number of predators and parasites that attack the host pests. As put by Barry Commoner, "By killing off the beneficial insects that previously kept insect pests in check, the new insecticides deprive us of the natural, freely available competitor to the new technological product."

Mechanical Treatments

In addition to parasitic diseases various mechanical injuries will have to be treated from time to time. While advanced tree-maintenance procedures can be studied and mastered by reading other books, major problems might best be evaluated by a commercial tree company. If the estimated cost of treatment exceeds the planter's budget it will have to be decided whether the tree is worth saving at all. Sometimes removal of a *seriously* diseased tree is the best choice, especially where falling branches become a hazard, or when the disease may spread to other trees.

Any tree-planting group should include at least one individual who can perform the following functions, which may be considered routine maintenance.

Pruning

It is best to prune trees within a few years after planting, while the tree is still young and pruning wounds are small and heal quite easily. Also, less labor is required to prune a young tree because the small branches can be removed with a knife or pruning shears. Older trees generally require large saws, ladders, and a roped off area.

In nature, trees prune themselves, or prune each other by the action of growing branches competing with other growing branches.

In "civilization," trees need man to prune them.

Young trees are generally pruned for two reasons. To remove broken branches, and to remove low-growing branches that will ultimately interfere with street and sidewalk traffic if left to grow to full size.

Older trees are often pruned to remove dead or dis-

First, saw an *undercut* about eight or ten inches from the base of the limb being removed. Saw only *halfway* through.

1.

2.

3.

4.

STEPS IN PRUNING A TREE

eased branches, branches that interfere with other branches or with other trees, wires, traffic signs, or buildings. Other reasons for pruning may include removal of too many branches for a reduced root system to support, eliminating a weak "V" crotch, and shaping.

One-cut pruning often leaves a raw patch of stripped bark, which increases the danger of infections that may be caused by parasites such as fungi or insects.

Three cuts are necessary to prune a branch without causing bark damage.

Second, saw outward from the first cut all the way through until the branch falls off.

Third, remove the stub by sawing as close to the trunk as possible.

Wound Dressings

Branches of trees often originate from the very center of the trunks. After a branch is removed the stub that remains is like a lifeless block of wood driven into the heart of the tree. New tissue must be formed over the outside of the stub to eliminate exposure to weather and parasites; or, with larger pruning wounds, a dressing must be applied. The function of dressings is to prevent stub decay while a new callus is formed. The same dressings should be applied to all surface wounds.

While commercial wound dressings are available in most gardening centers a wound can profitably be treated with other substances as well.

Orange shellac is a very mild wound dressing that is recommended by many experts. It is applied to the edges of exposed bark; after drying, the whole wound

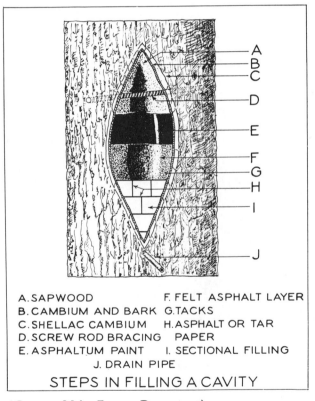

A. SAPWOOD　　　　　F. FELT ASPHALT LAYER
B. CAMBIUM AND BARK　G. TACKS
C. SHELLAC CAMBIUM　　H. ASPHALT OR TAR
D. SCREW ROD BRACING　　PAPER
E. ASPHALTUM PAINT　　I. SECTIONAL FILLING
　　　　　J. DRAIN PIPE

STEPS IN FILLING A CAVITY

(Courtesy, Maine Forestry Department)

is painted over with an asphalt base paint that acts as a sealant.

While asphalt applications are generally recommended they should be thin to avoid blistering. They will have to be reapplied at least once yearly (old peeling coats must be removed), and must *not* cover the callus as it forms, but only bare wood.

Asphalt mixtures containing the following ingredients must *not* be used: carbolineum, creosote, gasoline, or kerosene. Regular house paints must also be avoided. They may injure the tree.

STEPS IN FILLING A LARGE CAVITY:

1. On the outside the injury does not seem serious.
2. & 3. When the probing begins, it is found that the decay extends far into the tree. Many kinds of tools are used to clean the wound.

1.

4.

4. The cavity ready for filling.
5. An idea of the size of the cavity.
6. The tree restored. (After Solotaroff)

2.

3.

5.

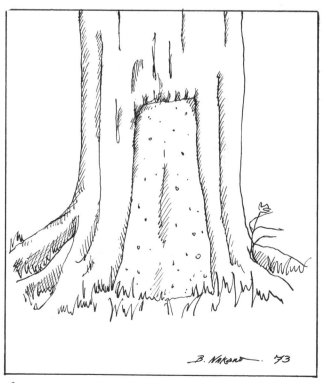

6.

Other pruning or wound dressings include:

Bordeaux paint—linseed oil is stirred into bordeaux powder to produce a thick paint

Lanolin paint—10 parts lanolin, 2 parts rosin, 2 parts crude pine gum—all melted together

Interestingly, tree wounds generally callus over more quickly when *no* dressings are applied. By natural means a tree will heal itself. However, a simple dressing such as orange shellac—which contains alcohol—acts to inhibit the growth of fungi, which can rot the tree.

Small wounds, one inch or less in diameter, need not be treated on hardwood trees. Small wounds on evergreens are best treated by spreading the natural resins of the tree around the cut. Large wounds on evergreens should be treated with the natural resins and then covered with a coat of asphalt dressing.

The repair of large cavities is *not* a job for an amateur. While other manuals describe the methods used for filling cavities, all trees will not withstand such work. A local "tree surgeon" should be called in to determine *if* the tree will withstand such repair and whether the work is worthwhile. Some of the major stages in such repair work are illustrated to give some idea of the complex of procedures involved.

2. It is removed with a chisel and hammer.

3. The tree now has a chance to survive. (By Maile)

GIRDLING ROOTS
1. The root has grown around the base of the trunk.

Girdling Roots

Trees sometimes "commit suicide" by strangling themselves with one of their own large roots. Psychological reasons are definitely not the problem. Girdling roots may be caused by improper planting. Too small a planting hole may encourage a root to seek the path of least resistance in its growth. Instead of growing outward from the tree the root follows around the outer trunk, primarily below the soil surface, increasing in size yearly. A boulder, a ledge of rock, or a sidewalk may also encourage a root to change its course and turn back around the trunk. In any case, in time the pressure of the root against the trunk will gradually reduce the flow of nutrients and kill the tree.

A tree that is suffering from root strangulation is easily recognized. The trunk is the same diameter at ground level as it is one foot above the ground, or is concave on one side. A normal tree is, of course, thickest at the base, flaring out into the soil.

A girdling root is simply removed with a sharpened wood chisel. After "surgery" the exposed root ends are treated with dressing and the soil replaced. If the tree has been seriously weakened radical pruning of some branches is recommended.

Cables and Braces

Heavy, overhanging limbs, or weakened "V" crotches must *not* be supported by chains or cables placed *around* the branches. Such encircling constrictors will choke the tree and inhibit the flow of nutrients and water very much like girdling roots. Cables and braces are secured through the tree, as illustrated. Generally, cables are secured about two-thirds of the distance between the base of the "V" crotch and the ends of the top branch. Rust-resistant material is always preferred. However, a rust-resistant application on some supporting material may be adequate. Screw hooks are not to be used because they frequently open under stress.

Wetwood and Slime Flux

Elms, maples, birches, and other hardwood trees may develop a condition known as *wetwood*. Bacteria in the diseased sap produce gases that force the fermented sap out of the tree through cuts, wounds, or weak crotches. This clear sap turns brown on exposure to air and eventually becomes a foul-smelling slime flux. In time, this flux on the bark may kill the internal cambium layer. Dried fluxing sap turns the covered bark light gray to whitish in color.

Wetwood can be treated by inserting a drain pipe or plastic tubing into a hole drilled to the *side* of and one foot *below* the top of the origin of the dripping

(Courtesy, Maine Forestry Department)

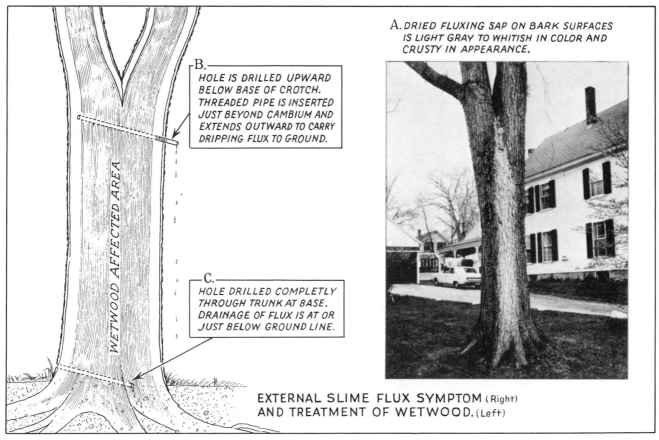

B.——
HOLE IS DRILLED UPWARD BELOW BASE OF CROTCH. THREADED PIPE IS INSERTED JUST BEYOND CAMBIUM AND EXTENDS OUTWARD TO CARRY DRIPPING FLUX TO GROUND.

WETWOOD AFFECTED AREA

C.——
HOLE DRILLED COMPLETLY THROUGH TRUNK AT BASE. DRAINAGE OF FLUX IS AT OR JUST BELOW GROUND LINE.

A. DRIED FLUXING SAP ON BARK SURFACES IS LIGHT GRAY TO WHITISH IN COLOR AND CRUSTY IN APPEARANCE.

EXTERNAL SLIME FLUX SYMPTOM (Right) AND TREATMENT OF WETWOOD. (Left)

flux. The hole must slant *upward*, to promote drainage, and pass through the heartwood of the tree and enter the cambium on the other side. Several holes may have to be bored to effect proper drainage. Be certain the drainage tubes or pipes project far enough out from the tree so the flux falls directly on the ground without running down over the bark.

Safety Precautions for Tree Climbers

An early pamphlet issued by the Brooklyn and Queens Parks Department offered the following "Hints to Tree-Climbers." The same precautions still apply and might be considered before *any* tree work is undertaken:

1. Before starting out on a tree, judge its general condition. The trunk of a tree that shows age, disease, or wood-destroying insects generally has its branches in an equally unhealthy condition. Greater precautions should, therefore, be taken with a tree in this condition than with a young, vigorous tree.

2. The different kinds of wood differ naturally in their strength and pliability. The soft and brash woods need greater precautions than the strong and pliable ones. All the poplars, the ailanthus, the silver maple, the chestnut, catalpa, and willow are either too soft or brittle to depend on without special care. The elm, hickory, and oak have strong, flexible woods and are, therefore, safer than any others. The red oak is weaker than the other oaks. The sycamore and beech have a tough cross-grained wood and are, therefore, fairly strong. The linden has a soft wood, while the ash and gum, though strong and flexible, are apt to split.

3. Look out for a limb that shows fungous growths. Every fungus sends out a lot of fibers into the main body of the limb which draw out its sap. The interior of the *branch then loses all strength and becomes like powder. Outside appearances sometimes do not show the interior condition, but one can be sure that every time he sees a fungus popping out, there is trouble behind it, and the limb is not altogether safe.*

4. When a limb is full of holes or knots, it generally indicates that borers have been working all kinds of galleries through it, making it unsafe. The silver maple and sycamore maple are especially full of borers, which in many cases work on the under side of the branch, so that the man in the tree looking down cannot see its dangerous condition.

5. A dead limb with bark falling off indicates that it died at least three months before and is, therefore, less safe than one with its bark tightly adhering to it.

6. Branches are more apt to snap on a frosty day when they are covered with an icy coating than on a warm, summer day.

7. A rainy or drizzly day causes the branches of a tree to be slippery, and greater precautions are then necessary.

8. Always use the pole-saw and pole-shear on the tips of long branches, and use the pole-hook in removing dead branches of the ailanthus and other brittle trees where it would be too dangerous to reach them otherwise.

9. Examine your ladder before using it.

10. Be sure of the strength of your branch before tying an extension-ladder to it.

11. Do not slant the extension-ladder too much.

12. Always watch the upper end of your ladder.

13. Do not forget to use the "danger sign" on streets where falling branches are apt to injure careless passersby.

It might be added that spiked shoes injure the tree and soft-bottomed footwear is desirable when climbing trees.

DIAGNOSIS OF PRINCIPAL CAUSES OF INJURY TO TREES*

Agent	Symptoms	Cause	Remedy or Treatment
Insects Foliage feeders	Devouring of foliage, or skeletonizing leaf surfaces	Feeding by various caterpillars, sawfly larvae, beetles or their grubs	1. Try to live with the insects 2. Try water sprays, pruning, and organic fertilizers
"	Two surfaces of leaf split apart and tissues mined out with insect inside	Leaf-mining insects	3. Locate a biological predator (see text) 4. Use "soft" pesticides (see text)
"	Somewhat angular-spotted mining and small holes in leaves, small insects bearing cases over them	Case-bearing insects	5. Resort to "hard" pesticides as a last resort to save a tree (see text)

* Adapted from Maine Forestry Department, Bulletin #22. (Courtesy of State Entomologist)

Agent	Symptoms	Cause	Remedy or Treatment
Wood feeders	Small holes in trunk or limbs from which sap and frass is being forced out	Bark beetles just beneath the bark and borers working in wood	
"	Honeycombing of interior wood of trees	Carpenter ants	
"	Numerous twigs of oak lying on ground with the pith eaten out, grubs inside	Oak twig pruning beetle	
Sap feeders	Slowing of growth and death of twigs, limbs or trees with (1) raised scale-like material or white woolly masses over the bark or foliage; (2) frail insects winged or wingless clustered on the foliage of twigs and with or without white cottony masses attached to them, or giving off secretions appearing shiny or dark in color on foliage and twigs below; (3) white cottony masses on trunks, twigs, and buds as on fir and pine	1. Scale insects 2. Aphids or plant lice 3. Woolly aphids Pierce tissues and suck juices	See steps 1–5 above
Gall formers	Gall-like swellings of various forms on buds, leaves, twigs, and branches	Various forms of insects feed on and stimulate local areas to form galls. The spruce twig galls are an example	
Mites	Globular or upright swellings or sugarlike erineums on hardwood foliage. Flower galls on ash. Splotchy, rusty appearance of foliage of evergreens and hardwoods	Stimulation to cause galls on some hardwoods. Feeding by numerous, very tiny mites	
Bacteria	Leaf and twig blights, and limb galls of a woody, rough-surfaced nature	Clogging and interruption of normal processes in the plant. Some bacteria stimulate growth	Cutting out and burning of diseased parts. Prevention of wounds in bark of trees. Sterilize the tools used and wounds made when pruning

Agent	Symptoms	Cause	Remedy or Treatment

Fungi
    Leaf spots,
    blights, scabs,
    anthracnose,
    needle
    blights
	Formation in leaf tissues or variously shaped dead areas of yellow to brown and black color often with zoned areas. Minute fruiting bodies of fungus may appear on dead tissues	Various species of fungi living on and killing the infected areas of lead tissue	Raking and burning of leaves in fall. If twigs are infected, prune and burn these

Powdery mildews	Blanched areas in leaf often with a whitish powdery growth of dense white masses on leaf surface	Growth and effect on foliage of vegetative strands of the fungus	Rake and burn infected leaves in the fall
Wilts	Foliage browns, suddenly wilts, and wrinkles on single branches on one or all sides of a tree. Discoloration in sapwood of involved branches	Growth of fungus in and clogging of conducting vessels of branches stopping sap flow	Removal and burning of involved branches. Disinfect pruning implements. Prevention of wounds in tree. Sample elms for Dutch elm disease symptoms
Rusts	Various symptoms principally dying of needles, twigs, branches or trees plus blistered pustules on involved areas and swellings on woody parts of evergreens; foliage spots or deformed fruits with blistered pustules on deciduous plants. Witches broom or balsam	Growth and effect of rust fungi on host plants to rupture and kill cells. Blisters formed containing reproductive spores, which are released as blisters rupture	Rusts usually require the presence of two host plants to complete their life; hence, keep apart by several hundred feet the involved plants by eradication of the undesired host plant
Cankers	Depressed, discolored, or dead areas of bark often around wounds; or open wounds with concentric areas of dead callus rolls —either with pustules on or around diseased areas	Toxic effect and growth of fungus in involved areas. Various fungi cause cankers	Protect pruning wounds with dressings. Prevent other wounds on tree. Removal and burning of cankered areas and dead limbs well back into healthy tissue. Fertilize trees

Root rots—
    the shoe-
    string fungus
	General decline in health. Poor foliage and growth. Finally, death of trees alone or in patches. Dark strands like shoestrings beneath bark and through soil. White fans beneath bark	Shoestring fungus strands run through soil and penetrate roots spreading from one tree to another. Also lives on dead stumps and roots in ground. Other species of fungi also attack roots	Remove diseased trees and any old roots that may serve as sources for the fungus. Drill holes 18 in. apart in infected area and fumigate by injecting 2 oz. carbon disulfide in each hole

Agent	Symptoms	Cause	Remedy or Treatment
Dog urine	General decline in health. Roots killed	Soluble salts enter the soil killing roots	Entire planting area must be screened off. Metal collar on trunk merely protects bark, not the roots
Wood decay	Wood checking, discoloring, becoming soft and punky, and breaking apart easily. External conks	Various fungi living on the wood cells. Composition of the wood is changed, leaving it weak and soft	Prevention of wounds in trees. Treatment of all pruning or other wounds immediately with wound dressings. Treatment of cavities to remove decayed wood, and repair damage before decay gets extensive
False or dwarf mistletoe	Excessive branching or witches brooms formed on larch and spruce. Small false mistletoe plants on involved branches	Growth on host plant by the mistletoe and stimulation of excessive branching of host	Removal and burning of infected trees or parts thereof except in Sept. and Oct., when seeds are disseminated
Birds	(a) Numerous shallow holes through bark around trees. (b) Small, deep, roughly rectangular holes chipped from trunk of tree	(a) Sap-suckers (b) Woodpeckers after ants or other insects	(a) Apply lime-sulfur to trunk of tree (b) Eliminate ants as recommended above (c) Apply tree paint to wounded areas in both cases
Mammals	Elm twigs with seeds; fir, and spruce twigs with flower buds on the ground	Squirrels—food	Leave food around for the squirrels
	Small to large patches of bark eaten from trees and shrubs	Porcupines, squirrels, and field mice (winter)	Trapping. Placing of wire around base in fall to prevent mice
Shade	Spindly growth and death of lower limbs and those on inner parts of clumps, or inner twigs, and of light-loving trees under heavy shade of larger trees	Lack of sunlight	Keep trees, especially evergreens, well spaced when transplanting. Plant shade-tolerant trees in areas shaded by larger trees. Prune out inner limbs of heavy shade species, e.g., Norway maple
Sun scorch	Yellowing, browning, and withering of leaves on one side of or the whole tree. Starts on tips and margins of leaves	High temperature and drought, injured or diseased roots so that all or parts of tree are not supplied with sufficient moisture	Keep tree watered in dry times, do not disturb roots. Prune tree if roots are disturbed to balance the two

Agent	Symptoms	Cause	Remedy or Treatment
Sun scald	Bark tissues dry, crack, and curl on limbs and trunks usually where bark was smooth or previously shaded	Bark accustomed to protection suddenly exposed to drying and heat from wind or sun by cutting or thinning operations or on young trees planted in open areas	Do not expose valued trees. Young trees can be protected on the south exposure by a vertical board or by winding with burlap or special wrapping tape
Winter injury or drying	Usually shows in late winter and spring as browning and withering of foliage and twigs. Common on evergreens	Dry winds in late winter, or early spring removing moisture, while roots and soil water are still frozen. Reflection of sun from buildings and pavement	Mulch about base in early fall. Water thoroughly. Protect with burlap screens or spray with latex or wax emulsions
Frosts or cold	(1) New growth in spring killed (2) Parts killed which resumed growth in late autumn due to warm moist spells (3) Parts of trees injured which have been stimulated by feeding late in the growing season (4) Twigs or branches killed on weak or exotic trees	(1) Late frost after growth has started (2 & 3) Parts of trees stimulated late in the season cannot mature and harden for the winter cold (4) Severe winter cold	Do not stimulate trees to grow earlier than normal in the spring or late in the growing season. Plant native or known hardy trees. Protect valuable and small exotics with shelters in the winter
Frost cracks	Longitudinal splits in trunk, tending to form successive layers of callus until a large "frost rib" protrudes from the trunk	Severe cold and sudden changes in winter temperatures. Formation of ice plus natural preponderance of tangential strain in tree. Occurs particularly in fall or early winter, after late-autumn rainfall has caused late growth, and thus immaturity of bark and sapwood	Proper drainage to prevent excess moisture about base. Dead bark can be cut away from the edges, and a disinfectant plus a wound dressing applied
Girdling roots	General weakening to death of parts of, or whole of, tree	A root growing around and choking another root or base of a tree. Poor planting practices generally involved	Spread roots properly when transplanting. Cut the girdling roots and remove
Starvation	Poor foliage and twig growth, lichens on bark, general weakening	Planting in poor soil, exhaustion of soil food, lack of water, extensive paving, or packing of surface soil	Fertilizing and watering. Leave space between paving and trees. Cultivation or aeration of root-soil area

Agent	Symptoms	Cause	Remedy or Treatment
Grading work	Same as starvation	See text. Very important today in this era of building in wooded areas	See text
Change in water level	General weakening of tree, slow growth, early discoloration of foliage, and death	Suffocation by flooding soil with water to exclude air. Drying out when draining areas. Feeding rootlets very sensitive to changes in water level	For valuable trees make fills (see text) and after feeding roots have become established at a level higher than the water will be, then flood area. When draining make provisions for sufficient water
Oil, salt, calcium chloride, soap	Gradual loss of healthy foliage color, slowing of growth, and death	Leakage and drainage from auto-service stations, ice cream plants, calcium chloride on tennis courts and walks, soap from laundries—suffocate or poison roots	Care where dumping refuse
Gases, dusts, and smoke	Discoloration and browning of foliage especially on evergreens—often mottling of hardwood foliage and browning between veins	Brick kilns, cement plants, factories, smelters, wood dires, etc. Smoke and gases given off contain arsenic and forms of sulfur poisonous to leaves. Dust given off coats foliage to smother it	Dust collectors. Removal of operations near valuable stands. Use of resistant trees. In general, hardwoods most resistant
Illuminating gas	Yellowing of foliage, slow growth, and death. Blue or brown streaks in wood of roots and trunk. Other plants nearby affected. Odor in soil. Tomato seedlings give a positive test by drooping of foliage	Leakage from service mains permeates soil and poisons tree. Strong concentrations in air are also injurious	Remedy the source. Trench on side of gas leak or all around tree, then aerate soil thoroughly by compressed air; next, water heavily. Do this also if replacing dead with new trees
High-intensity sodium street lights	Unexpected death due to a sudden cold spell; increased damage due to pollution. London plane-trees are particularly susceptible	Lights make trees grow faster—increasing their vulnerability to air pollution; increase vulnerability of young trees to frost damage by keeping them growing longer into autumn than normal	Plant dormant trees in the fall; choose more resistant trees such as ginkgo; eliminate these lights

Agent	Symptoms	Cause	Remedy or Treatment
Alternating and direct currents of electricity	(1) Localized, rough open wounds varying in size where wires contact trees. (2) Same plus death of limbs or whole trees or injury to base of trunk	(1) Alternating current and (2) direct current service wires. A short circuiting of current and raising of temperature to lethal points in tender tissue of the tree. Wet weather is an important factor in causing the short circuiting. Wires of both cause mechanical injury by chafing. Direct current is much more apt to cause injury, especially when the positive charge is carried in the ground and the negative charge is carried aerially	Keep wires away from trees or limbs either by location or by judiciously pruning involved branches. Thoroughly insulate wires that are close to a tree
Lightning	Wilting of foliage with or without trunk abrasions	Direct strike or roots in area of tree hit	Trace wound—stimulate growth by fertilizing, watering. Installation of lightning rods may help those trees likely to be hit.
Weedkiller, e.g. 2–4 D injury	Curling of twig tips— distortion of leaves	Direct application of material or drift of fumes	Wash soil with water thoroughly. Exercise caution in use of weed killers around trees

Trees
and the
Law

With the exception of a few mental patients and several city politicians such as the former mayoral aide in New York City who declared, "I hate trees . . . I love the feel of pavement beneath my feet," most everyone agrees that trees are desirable. Who would argue that the cooling shade, the reduction of heat and glare, the softening of background noise, and the favorable exchange of gases are harmful?

And so we all agree it would be positive to plant trees in all the towns and cities of America.

But how are we to preserve those trees that we plant and those that already exist? How are we going to save those great giants that were planted by our fathers and their fathers from the hot and eager developer who needs access to a construction site, or from the power saws in the hands of the weekend maulers?

Must we chain ourselves to these friendly giants each time they are threatened? This method has worked in the past. In Chicago a group of women chained themselves to an entire grove of trees on the day the bulldozers came to push them down. The ladies refused to budge until city officials agreed to reroute the planned expressway and to commit themselves to this through new legislation. The expressway *was* rerouted and the trees saved for future generations. However, not every citizen can expect the same fine results. We must remember that these ladies happened to be married to the very same city officials who agreed to meet their reasonable demands.

And yet the ladies did point the way. What is required is tough, new legislation as well as a defiant citizenry.

Laws are needed that go to favor the public's desire for *living* trees. We must be careful to include the word "living" in any new laws we may write lest a future salesman of plastic foliage interpret our legislative efforts in his own self-interests.

A Standard Municipal Tree Ordinance prepared by the publications committee of the International Shade Tree Conference is a good *model* for preparing a street-tree ordinance in any municipality. Its provisions regarding the planting and maintenance of street trees are reasonable. However, I disagree with the ISTC recommendation that "municipalities should assume complete control over all public tree planting, maintenance and removal." Too often, this means hands off to the citizen who wants to take up the initiative and plant trees by himself or with a community group. Certainly, a municipality should *supervise* tree projects

and offer assistance wherever possible (advising on species difficult to grow or troublesome, providing advice on how to plant, cutting concrete, providing watering and maintenance services, etc.). However, citizens must *not* be prohibited or discouraged from planting trees on public or private property.

The best immediate hope for replanting America lies with *private* parties. Governmental policies are apparently too strongly influenced by commercial interests to be counted on for any sincere support.

"PATIENCE, SIRE."

(Lillian Scalzo drawing, from an early Arbor Day Manual)

Similarly, if we allow *only* municipalities to maintain trees how will some of the newer (and less expensive) methods of, for example, controlling insects be objectively analyzed? While the city of Berkeley, California, has had success with biological and other natural insect controls, few other cities have had the opportunity or the interest to undertake similar controls. Pesticides have become the instant answer and are used year after year in most cities with little "gain" over the causative organisms. Would the concept of "total municipal control" over tree maintenance allow an individual to try some of the nonpolluting methods (described under "Maintenance") instead of using synthetic pesticides and fungicides?

How would citizens know if a municipality had been convinced to employ a certain tree species, variety, or cultivar by less-than-objective influences? If we allow a municipality to dictate which trees can be planted we could foreseeably end up with too few species, and the pet varieties of a few salesmen who stand to profit by their acceptance in the "approved tree" list. Obviously, some trees are "villains" for certain sites and must not be planted where they might do some damage or fail to grow. Those with weak wood break up easily and must be discouraged in cities and towns, as must those trees that buckle sidewalks with surface-feeding roots. Certainly, a municipal tree department should *inform* its citizens of these problems and strongly advise *against* the planting of problem trees. Any rational citizen (anyone who wants to plant a tree at his or her own expense would by definition be rational!) would follow such advice when it would be provided by an informed tree department.

Total municipal control over a tree program should be evaluated by asking one simple question: Will these laws *encourage* or *discourage* people from planting and caring for trees in this town? If the answer is negative, then the laws should not be passed. It is trees we are all after, after all, not arguments.

Yet we must not be too optimistic about replanting our cities and towns through individual efforts alone. Man is by nature lazy. We need merely look around those cities which have left the planting of trees up to the individual to see what true apathy accomplishes. Long stretches are completely unplanted. Those streets which have been planted often bear many different species, of all shapes and sizes, set either too closely or too far apart. In some cases the trees are not pruned regularly and the limbs collide with pedestrians and autos. In other cases trees are pruned too often, and are misshapen. Many trees are planted without stakes or guards and are knocked over by the wind, through vandalism, or by accident. Finally, too often people simply plant trees and "leave them to nature." Not being in their natural environment the trees wilt, decay, and die. Control of insects and other pests is often

"TOYS WHICH SURPASS ANYTHING YOU HAVE KNOWN BEFORE."

(Lillian Scalzo)

not treated at all, or treated by overkill methods that may harm the tree and the surrounding environment.

What is required in a street tree program is municipal *direction* with individual support. The people and the tree departments must work together. Neither can work alone.

The laws suggested by the ISTC are also too flexible with regard to the *removal* of trees. I think the time has come in America where trees might be deemed sacred objects (like the cow in India) and their removal effectively prohibited for *any* reason! If an old tree begins to drop its huge branches on passersby, we can rope the area off and let the tree die in peace. After a lifetime of giving shade and rendering peace to countless humans, the least we can do is allow the tree its right to die in its own time. The sad experience of death might be more easily understood if we allowed ourselves to see it occurring around us—through objects other than man, including plants.

Too many municipalities allow the removal of trees for any "reason" and merely collect funds for a "replacement" specimen. Can anyone replace a planetree such as the one illustrated in "Tree Profiles" with an equally commanding specimen? If a building, driveway, supermarket, or road is planned, why not build *around* our sacred trees? Wouldn't the result be a less mechanical, more humanized construction? I know of one pharmacy, smack in the middle of an asphalt shopping center, that was built around a huge banyan tree. The trunk system is enclosed within handsome paneling (why not expose the trunk, too?) behind the drug counter and the owner has the benefits of a clear conscience as well as lowered air-conditioning costs.

Who Shall Own the Trees?

While most municipal ordinances concern those trees planted on *public* property, none that I know of makes any provision that prohibits an individual from cutting down a tree that grows on *private* property. We have all at some time seen a lunatic cutting down beautiful trees for some "reason" of his own. Something in us tells us he is wrong and that we should stop him, and yet we are reminded that the tree "belongs" to him and he can legally do with it as he pleases. But our biological wisdom tells us he is violating us all.

Should people continue to "own" trees? Certainly those planted primarily for produce (apples, oranges, pecans, etc.—tree groves) will be maintained by their "owners." But what about shade or ornamental trees that grow on nonpublic lands? Are they, in fact, to be cut down as the property holder sees fit?

The general principles that govern ownership of boundary trees are based on early Greek and Roman codes. Boundary trees that have limbs that overhang both properties are considered the common property of both landowners.

This relationship generally serves to limit the total destruction of trees. A single owner often undertakes tree removal, or "trimming," for no apparent reason—except a letting of hostilities against a defenseless object, or the desire to continue to make noise after his power lawnmower has done its job—with a power saw pitted against some gracious limbs. With boundary trees such tree barbers must legally have their neighbor's permission for removal, and this is the germ of an idea for preserving *all* trees that are threatened by the owners of property on which they grow.

Insofar as the laws of the land are enforceable against violators, a stream or waterway cannot be polluted by individuals (or corporations) owning adjacent property. This law was enacted because, in a very real sense, the waters are *common* property, shared by all who live along its shores or banks. What is done to destroy the water quality in one part of a stream, river, lake, pond, or ocean invariably affects the *overall* water quality and so threatens the biological rights of others.

So too with trees. While they may grow up from one section of private property, they penetrate the *air space* of a neighborhood and are thus members of common property—the air! Why should any one individual, corporation, city, state, or federal agency continue to have the right to destroy an object of beauty that serves to purify the air while screening out harsh sounds? Aren't trees, by nature's laws, living bodies that deserve the right to life? Wouldn't any group of rational citizens vote to preserve a tree threatened by destruction if they were given a choice in the matter? We must remember that we are not just talking aesthetics (though this point of view is sorely neglected in modern landscape design, as well) but biologics as well. The communal tree not only purifies the air but may also provide shade for many houses beneath its canopy, while binding the soil and maintaining a healthy water table.

Of course, we could also solve the problem of preserving and planting trees by electing a "tree czar" in each state, whose responsibility would be to *protect* his charges at all costs, the way present-day admirals and generals protect their ships and tanks.

Dictators seem to like trees and generally treat anyone who threatens the beauty and order of their domain with characteristic rewards. During the Batista regime in Cuba it was illegal to remove a royal palm so long as it exhibited at least two live fronds. Further, for every one of these princely palms removed by an individual no fewer than *five* had to be planted.

Spare Those Trees

Tehran, Iran—Anyone who uproots a tree which has a diameter of more than 10 centimeters—about four inches—will go to jail for three years, the Iranian parliament decreed.

Who knows what a benevolent, nature-loving tyrant might do for the retreeing of America?

PART

·VI·
Tree
Profiles

The following tree profiles give pertinent data for over 170 different trees that may be grown in regions of the United States and Canada, including Alaska and Hawaii.

Obviously, these tree profiles do not represent *all* the kinds of trees that may be grown. The list is based upon the tree lists of the International Shade Tree Conference, the United States Department of Agriculture list *Shade Trees for the Home,* and the recent American Horticultural Society survey of extremely hardy urban trees.

While a few additional trees have been added for their special qualities, the list is quite limited in scope. It would be useless to profile thousands of trees. By reading through the following pages, while absorbing the visual impact of the photographs, it should be possible to select at least one or two desirable trees worth planting in your neighborhood. More extensive local lists can be reviewed in the chapter "Selecting a Tree," or by contacting agricultural experiment stations, directors of arboreta, park and recreation commissions, forestry services, and departments of horticulture at universities or colleges.

In the profiles, anecdotal information was excluded or kept to a brief sentence or two. While stories about trees are often fascinating and entire books have been devoted to telling these tales, it is my intent to transmit a maximum amount of useful data through an easily absorbed format in a minimum number of pages. At a glance you can see for each tree the zone of growth, the average height, growth rate, life expectancy, and soil requirements. If fruits and flowers appear, this is indicated, as is the autumn color, if any. The "Miscellaneous" section generally highlights the particular suitability of the tree—whether it is recommended as a street tree, for parks, lawns, the seashore, or as a windbreak or shelterbelt.

The zone of growth is based upon the Plant Hardiness Zone Map of the U.S.D.A. While soil and water needs can usually be adjusted, the temperature in which the tree is to be grown is not a manageable phenomenon. It therefore becomes necessary to know the average annual *minimum* temperatures for the area in which the tree will be expected to survive. After finding this information by looking at the map on page 109, the "zone of growth" numeral becomes a key to which trees may be grown in a particular area.

It should be borne in mind that the zone of growth is the *northernmost* zone in which the listed tree can

be grown. Many trees can also be grown in zones *south* of (*higher* in number) the zones indicated on the profiles. As one example, flowering dogwood, which is native to New England (Zone 5), will also thrive in the southeastern states. It is best to check with local tree people before automatically eliminating an interesting tree that has a more northern zone of growth than the one in which your site is located.

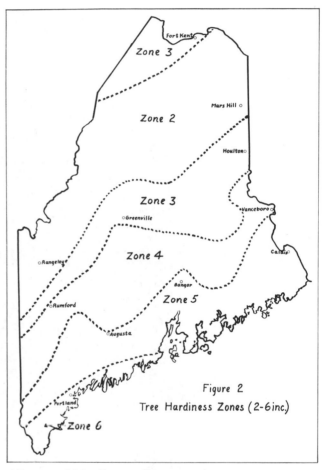

Figure 2
Tree Hardiness Zones (2-6 inc.)

(Courtesy, Maine Forestry Department)

References to the letters "A" and "B" on zones refer to the northern and southern portions of a zone.

The cold hardiness of trees not included in the "profiles" may be obtained from nurserymen, arborists, colleges of agriculture, and experiment stations. Also, more detailed hardiness zone maps are available for certain states and localities (see Maine map, as an example). These include zone numbers that correlate with the U.S.D.A. map but are more useful because they reflect additional factors affecting plant growth such as winds, altitude, rainfall, and variation in soil conditions. Check with your experiment station for a local plant-hardiness zone map.

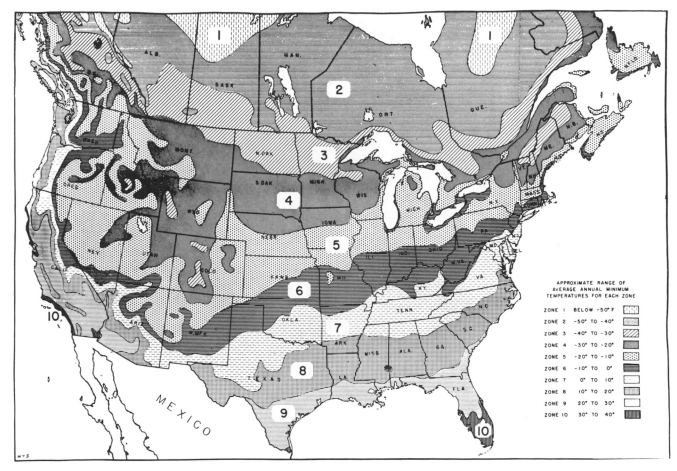

Plant hardiness zone map.

COMMON NAME:	**AFRICAN TULIP TREE** (Bell Flambeau)
LATIN NAME:	*Spathodea campanulata*
NORTHERNMOST ZONE OF GROWTH:	10
NATIVE TO:	Tropical Africa
TYPE OF TREE: Deciduous or Evergreen?	Evergreen (deciduous in parts of Zone 9)
Leaves (shape, size, color, autumn color)	Glossy, dark green leaves are 1–2 feet long and subdivided into oval leaflets
Type of Shade?	Irregular canopy
HEIGHT:	70 feet
GROWTH RATE:	Fast
FRUIT & FLOWERS:	Canoe-shaped pods contain winged, shiny seeds; fiery orange-red flowers yellow-edged. Blooms best in mid-winter, however some flowers visible during all seasons
SOIL:	Well-drained, rich soils
PROPAGATION:	Cuttings are easily propagated
MISCELLANEOUS:	A showy, ornamental quick-growing tree recommended for yards, parks, and broad streets in the subtropics

COMMON NAME:	**AILANTHUS** (Tree of Heaven)
LATIN NAME:	*Ailanthus altissima*
NORTHERNMOST ZONE OF GROWTH:	5
NATIVE TO:	China, introduced in 1784
TYPE OF TREE: Deciduous or Evergreen?	Deciduous
Bark (color & texture)	Gray, shallow, coarsely fissured
Type of Shade?	Round to irregular canopy
HEIGHT:	60–80 feet
LIFE EXPECTANCY:	75 years
GROWTH RATE:	Fast
FRUIT & FLOWERS:	Plant females only. Males produce foul-smelling yellow flowers. Females produce maplelike winged seeds
SOIL:	Will grow in the poorest urban soils. Does best in pH range 6.5–7.5
PROPAGATION:	Seeds stratified when ripe for 2 months at 40° F., and then planted. Can also be stored. Root cuttings easily grown
MISCELLANEOUS:	A quick-growing "weed tree," common in many cities. Withstands no care, wet or dry soil; not susceptible to parasitic or other diseases, and can even stand submergence in salt water! Recommended for alleyways, dirty streets, and urban yards inhospitable to most other plant life. Weak wood, breaks easily

COMMON NAME:	ANGELICA-TREE, JAPANESE
LATIN NAME:	*Aralia elata*
NORTHERNMOST ZONE OF GROWTH:	3B
NATIVE TO:	Northeastern Asia
TYPE OF TREE: Deciduous or Evergreen?	Deciduous
Kind of Trunk?	Several
Leaves (shape, size, color, autumn color)	Broadleaf; large, 2½ inches long, dark glossy green; autumn color reddish orange
Type of Foliage?	Coarse
HEIGHT:	45 feet
FRUIT & FLOWERS:	Small white flowers in large (18 inches) terminal clusters are produced in August. Produces small black berries that birds love to eat
SOIL:	Grows well in any good soil
PROPAGATION:	Stratify at room temperature for 3–5 months, then at 40° F. for 3 months; then sow
MISCELLANEOUS:	This small, spiny tree with large doubly compound leaves is planted for its white flowers and tropical appearance in northern gardens. Hardy under city conditions. Variety 'variegata' — leaflets bordered in white. Variety 'aureo-variegata' — leaflets bordered in yellow

COMMON NAME:	APRICOT
LATIN NAME:	*Prunus armeniaca*
NORTHERNMOST ZONE OF GROWTH:	6
NATIVE TO:	Western Asia
TYPE OF TREE: Deciduous or Evergreen?	Deciduous
Leaves (shape, size, color, autumn color)	Some varieties of apricot display a brilliant red autumn color
Type of Foliage?	Open
HEIGHT:	30 feet
GROWTH RATE:	Fast
FRUIT & FLOWERS:	White or pinkish flowers appear late April, or earlier; 1¼-inch yellowish red fruits
SOIL:	Tolerates a wide range of soils, but requires much fertilization and a consistent supply of water
PROPAGATION:	Stratify seeds as soon as ripe for 4 months at 40° F. (Seeds may be preserved for up to one year in airtight containers that are stored in a cool, dry place.) Softwood cuttings easily rooted
MISCELLANEOUS:	This species is commonly grown on the West Coast for its fruit and ornamental qualities. In orchards are planted 20–30 feet apart and pruned regularly to renew the fruit spurs. Variety 'Ansu'—pink flowers. Variety 'Charles Abraham'—double, deep-pink flowers

APRICOT

COMMON NAME:	**ARBORVITAE, GIANT**	COMMON NAME:	**ARBORVITAE, ORIENTAL**
LATIN NAME:	*Thuja plicata*	LATIN NAME:	*Thuja orientalis*
NORTHERNMOST ZONE OF GROWTH:	6	NORTHERNMOST ZONE OF GROWTH:	6B
NATIVE TO:	Northern California to Alaska	NATIVE TO:	Korea, northern China
TYPE OF TREE: Deciduous or Evergreen?	Evergreen	TYPE OF TREE: Deciduous or Evergreen?	Evergreen
Leaves (shape, size, color, autumn color)	Leaves are scalelike glossy green, which are bronze through the winter	Leaves (shape, size, color, autumn color)	Some varieties have blue or yellow leaves
Type of Shade?	Dense	Type of Shade?	Open, pyramid-shaped tree, affording good shade
Type of Foliage?	Dense	Type of Foliage?	Open
HEIGHT:	To 180 feet!	HEIGHT:	To 50 feet
LIFE EXPECTANCY:	75 years	LIFE EXPECTANCY:	100 years
GROWTH RATE:	Moderately fast	GROWTH RATE:	Moderate
FRUIT & FLOWERS:	Small, dired capsules	FRUIT & FLOWERS:	Small cones have curved hooks; a characteristic of this species
SOIL:	Requires well-drained soil with a pH of 6.5–7.5	SOIL:	Requires well-drained soils. Will tolerate mildly alkaline soils, but prefers pH 6.5–7.5
PROPAGATION:	Seeds. (Only the seeds collected in the mountains of Utah and Montana yield seedlings capable of growth in the northeast)		
MISCELLANEOUS:	A massive giant that remains green year-round. Recommended for parks, large gardens. Often clipped and shaped	MISCELLANEOUS:	Most popular in the South, the tree is not well adapted to the northern zones. This species of arborvitae is more resistant to many of the pests that plague the white cedar. A symmetrical evergreen often used in gardens

ORIENTAL ARBORVITAE

COMMON NAME:	**ASH, GREEN**	COMMON NAME:	**ASH, KOREAN MOUNTAIN**
LATIN NAME:	*Fraxinus pennsylvanica*	LATIN NAME:	*Sorbus alnifolia*
NORTHERNMOST ZONE OF GROWTH:	2	NORTHERNMOST ZONE OF GROWTH:	5
NATIVE TO:	North America (eastern to central states)	NATIVE TO:	Japan, China, and Korea
TYPE OF TREE: Deciduous or Evergreen?	Deciduous	TYPE OF TREE: Deciduous or Evergreen?	Deciduous
Leaves (shape, size, color, autumn color)	Bright green leaves, yellow in autumn	Bark (color & texture)	Smooth, gray
Type of Shade?	Round to pyramidal canopy, affording good shade	Leaves (shape, size, color, autumn color)	Bright green. Orange to scarlet in autumn
Type of Foliage?	Dense	Type of Shade?	Dense
HEIGHT:	60 feet	Type of Foliage?	Pyramid shape when young, round and spreading when mature
GROWTH RATE:	Moderately fast	HEIGHT:	60 feet
FRUIT & FLOWERS:	'Marshall's Seedless' variety preferred (males with excellent growth characteristics)	GROWTH RATE:	Fast
SOIL:	Easily grown on dry soil, while in the Plains states does best in moist soil; tolerates alkaline conditions. Prefers pH 6.0–7.5	FRUIT & FLOWERS:	Beautiful ⅜-inch berries, orange to scarlet in the fall. Small, white flowers in clusters appear in late May
PROPAGATION:	Budding and grafting, often using the European ash as understock	SOIL:	No special requirements
MISCELLANEOUS:	'Marshall's Seedless' is a widely popular tree, commonly used for planting streets and roadsides. The green ash is official state tree of North Dakota	PROPAGATION:	Stratify seeds at 40° F. for 3 months, then sow. May require an additional 3 months of cold to germinate. Also grown by grafting on other mountain ash stock
		MISCELLANEOUS:	This ash requires little attention, has bark like the beech, flowers profusely, produces dense shade, and is more resistant to the borers than any other mountain ash. An easy to grow, beautiful shade tree

KOREAN MOUNTAIN ASH

COMMON NAME:	**ASH, MODESTO** (Arizona Ash)
LATIN NAME:	*Fraxinus velutina*
NORTHERNMOST ZONE OF GROWTH:	6
NATIVE TO:	Southwestern United States
TYPE OF TREE: Deciduous or Evergreen?	Deciduous
Leaves (shape, size, color, autumn color)	Glossy foliage with leaves turning yellow in the autumn
Type of Foliage?	Open
HEIGHT:	20–45 feet
GROWTH RATE:	Fast
SOIL:	Will grow in alkaline soil. Prefers pH 6.0–7.5. Does well in the deserts
PROPAGATION:	Stratify seed for 3–5 months in a warm atmosphere, and then for another 3 months at 40° F. Sow immediately thereafter
MISCELLANEOUS:	The modesto ash is becoming a popular street tree in the Southwest. Also thrives in seashore plantings, owing to its ability to withstand saltwater spray year after year

COMMON NAME:	**ASH, WHITE**
LATIN NAME:	*Fraxinus americana*
NORTHERNMOST ZONE OF GROWTH:	3B
NATIVE TO:	Eastern United States
TYPE OF TREE: Deciduous or Evergreen?	Deciduous
Kind of Trunk?	Straight
Bark (color & texture)	Ridged, ash-gray bark
Leaves (shape, size, color, autumn color)	Leaves appear late in spring and become yellow or purple in the fall
Type of Shade?	Varies
Type of Foliage?	Dense
HEIGHT:	To 120 feet
LIFE EXPECTANCY:	75–100 years
GROWTH RATE:	Fast
FRUIT & FLOWERS:	Winged fruit; small flowers
SOIL:	Grows well on moist soils. Prefers pH 6.0–7.5, but has no special soil requirements
PROPAGATION:	The tree often seeds itself (for this reason some consider it to be a weed); otherwise seeds can be stratified for 3 months at 40° F., then sown immediately. Transplants easily
MISCELLANEOUS:	This hardwood is used to make baseball bats, tool handles, oars, furniture, etc. Is very hardy tree and widely recommended for city plantings owing to abilities to withstand tough conditions. Also planted as windbreak (in areas other than Great Plains)

COMMON NAME:	**ASPEN, EUROPEAN**
LATIN NAME:	*Populas tremula* 'Erecta'
NORTHERNMOST ZONE OF GROWTH:	2
NATIVE TO:	Sweden
TYPE OF TREE: Deciduous or Evergreen?	Deciduous
Leaves (shape, size, color, autumn color)	Broadleaf; small leaves tremble in breeze; a narrow tree shape
HEIGHT:	50 feet
GROWTH RATE:	Fast
SOIL:	Grows well in a variety of soil conditions. Prefers pH 6.5–7.5
MISCELLANEOUS:	An extremely hardy tree for urban conditions, according to a recent survey by the American Horticultural Society

COMMON NAME:	**ASPEN, QUAKING**
LATIN NAME:	*Populus tremuloides*
NORTHERNMOST ZONE OF GROWTH:	1
NATIVE TO:	North America
TYPE OF TREE: Deciduous or Evergreen?	Deciduous
Bark (color & texture)	Smooth, grayish white
Leaves (shape, size, color, autumn color)	Leaves tremble in the slightest wind motion and are a gorgeous yellow in autumn
Type of Shade?	Fair
Type of Foliage?	Loose and open; oval to round canopy
HEIGHT:	90 feet
LIFE EXPECTANCY:	To 50 years
GROWTH RATE:	Fast
SOIL:	Tolerant of most except very dry regions. Quaking aspen is one of first trees to grow in land burned over by fire. Prefers pH 6.5–7.5
PROPAGATION:	Seeds must be sown as soon as ripe; keep them moist and planted shallow. Will root well from hardwood cuttings
MISCELLANEOUS:	Very popular American tree, widely planted. Is hardy in the coldest habitable regions of North America. Is the official state tree of Nevada.

QUAKING ASPEN

COMMON NAME:	**BALDCYPRESS**
LATIN NAME:	*Taxodium distichum*
NORTHERNMOST ZONE OF GROWTH:	5
NATIVE TO:	Swampy regions in south-eastern and south-central United States
TYPE OF TREE: Deciduous or Evergreen?	Deciduous conifer
Bark (color & texture)	Scaly
Leaves (shape, size, color, autumn color)	Comblike needles
Type of Shade?	Poor
Type of Foliage?	Very open
HEIGHT:	To 150 feet
LIFE EXPECTANCY:	To 100 years
GROWTH RATE:	Moderate
SOIL:	Tolerates well-drained as well as preferred wet-soil habitat, but needs great space to truly expand into the beauty that it is. Prefers pH range 6.5–7.5
PROPAGATION:	Stratify seeds for 30 days at 32° to 50° F. Sow them in the springtime
MISCELLANEOUS:	Wood highly resistant to decay even when submerged in water for long periods of time. Used to make shingles and for constructing greenhouse platforms. A large, pyramidal tree (may be columnar at maturity), requires lots of space, and often planted in parks and large estates. Cypress "knees" grow up from roots to obtain air when in swamps

COMMON NAME:	**BEECH, AMERICAN**
LATIN NAME:	*Fagus grandifolia*
NORTHERNMOST ZONE OF GROWTH:	3B
NATIVE TO:	Eastern North America
TYPE OF TREE: Deciduous or Evergreen?	Deciduous
Bark (color & texture)	Silvery light gray, satin smooth
Leaves (shape, size, color, autumn color)	Round to conically shaped leaves with serrated edges. Golden-bronze autumn color
Type of Shade?	Good
Type of Foliage?	Dense
HEIGHT:	90 feet
LIFE EXPECTANCY:	75–100 years
GROWTH RATE:	Moderate
FRUIT & FLOWERS:	The nuts a favorite food of squirrels, deer, and birds
SOIL:	Grows on many soils, and prefers pH 6.5–7.5
PROPAGATION:	Seeds should be mixed with sand and placed in cool storage for spring planting. Young trees that have been cut back in their first year or two may be transplanted
MISCELLANEOUS:	Wood is used for making furniture and tool handles. American beech does not tolerate city conditions well. A stand of these trees forms good windbreak in areas other than Great Plains. A very beautiful ornamental year-round

BALDCYPRESS

AMERICAN BEECH

COMMON NAME:	**BEECH, EUROPEAN**	COMMON NAME:	**BIRCH, PAPER** (**Canoe Birch**)
LATIN NAME:	*Fagus sylvatica*	LATIN NAME:	*Betula papyrifera*
NORTHERNMOST ZONE OF GROWTH:	5	NORTHERNMOST ZONE OF GROWTH:	2
NATIVE TO:	Central and southern Europe	NATIVE TO:	North-central and northeastern United States
TYPE OF TREE: Deciduous or Evergreen?	Deciduous	TYPE OF TREE: Deciduous or Evergreen?	Deciduous
Kind of Trunk?	Solid, round trunk	Kind of Trunk?	Multiple trunks
Bark (color & texture)	Gray, smooth bark	Bark (color & texture)	White, peels off in thin sheets
Leaves (shape, size, color, autumn color)	Broad leaves of a glossy, dark green color turning bronze in autumn	Leaves (shape, size, color, autumn color)	Yellow autumn color
Type of Shade?	Thick shade	Type of Shade?	Fair
Type of Foliage?	Dense	Type of Foliage?	Loosely pyramidal in shape
HEIGHT:	90 feet	HEIGHT:	90 feet
LIFE EXPECTANCY:	100 years +	LIFE EXPECTANCY:	75 years
GROWTH RATE:	Moderate	GROWTH RATE:	Fast
SOIL:	Adaptable to many soils. Preferred pH range 6.5–7.5	FRUIT & FLOWERS:	Small, winged nut
		SOIL:	Prefers moist soil
PROPAGATION:	Mix seeds with sand and store in a cool place. Plant in the springtime. Transplants easily after professional root-pruning	PROPAGATION:	Stratify seeds at 32° F.–40° F. for 5 or 6 months. Plant in seedbeds in early spring
MISCELLANEOUS:	One of best ornamental trees, comes in varieties such as purple beech (purple leaves), weeping beech (drooping branches), variety tricolor beech (leaves white with green spots and pink margins), and many others. Does well when planted as windbreaks in areas other than Great Plains. A very handsome, large shade tree. Beautiful year-round	MISCELLANEOUS:	The bark of this beautiful native American tree was used by the Indians to cover canoes and wigwams. Waterproof and pliable, it peels from tree naturally. Highly resistant to bronze-birch borer, which plagues the European birch, these trees are beautiful on lawns, especially when planted with single trunk. The official state tree of New Hampshire

EUROPEAN BEECH

COMMON NAME:	**BOX ELDER**
LATIN NAME:	*Acer negundo*
NORTHERNMOST ZONE OF GROWTH:	2
NATIVE TO:	Eastern and central North America
TYPE OF TREE: Deciduous or Evergreen?	Deciduous
Leaves (shape, size, color, autumn color)	Twigs are reddish compound, 3–5 leaflets bright green, yellow in fall; the only maple with compound leaves
Type of Foliage?	Open—a broad, deep crown
HEIGHT:	60 feet
LIFE EXPECTANCY:	Short-lived
GROWTH RATE:	Fast
FRUIT & FLOWERS:	Yellowish green flowers appear in April, before the leaves. Winged fruits or "keys" appear later in the year
SOIL:	Tolerates most any soil, including dry
PROPAGATION:	Seeds must be sown or stratified when ripe. Stratify at 40° F. for 4 months, or plant directly in ground
MISCELLANEOUS:	Highly recommended for regions of Great Plains where drought and cold make it difficult to grow other trees. Much used in shelterbelts to protect slower-growing but longer-lived trees. (Sap makes excellent syrup and sugar while several birds favor the seeds.) Is sometimes used for quick, dense growth, but breaks easily in storms. Many municipalities prohibit its planting

COMMON NAME:	**BO TREE**
LATIN NAME:	*Ficus religiosa*
NORTHERNMOST ZONE OF GROWTH:	10
NATIVE TO:	India
TYPE OF TREE: Deciduous or Evergreen?	Semideciduous
Kind of Trunk?	Few aerial roots
Bark (color & texture)	Smooth, gray
Leaves (shape, size, color, autumn color)	Heart-shaped, broadleaf; green at first, turning yellow. Long flexible stems on leaves
Type of Shade?	Dense
Type of Foliage?	Dense
HEIGHT:	75 feet
LIFE EXPECTANCY:	Thousands of years, in some cases
FRUIT & FLOWERS:	Fruits are yellowish red
MISCELLANEOUS:	Bo trees are planted beside every Buddhist temple because of association with divinity Buddha. Juice of bark is used medicinally for toothaches and strengthening of gums. There may be a bo tree 3,000 years old in Bombay, India. Even largest-growing *Ficus* species can be grown in limited spaces, provided prop roots are trimmed and spreading roots are inhibited in growth by being encased in tub

BOX ELDER

BO TREE (FIG)

COMMON NAME:	BUCKTHORN, DAHURIAN
LATIN NAME:	*Rhamnus davurica*
NORTHERNMOST ZONE OF GROWTH:	2
NATIVE TO:	North China, Manchuria, and Korea
TYPE OF TREE: Deciduous or Evergreen?	Deciduous or evergreen
Leaves (shape, size, color, autumn color)	Lustrous leaves; irregular tree shape
Type of Foliage?	Dense
HEIGHT:	30 feet
GROWTH RATE:	Fast
FRUIT & FLOWERS:	Fruits are small, shiny, black berries that attract many kinds of birds
SOIL:	Grows vigorously in almost any kind of soil
PROPAGATION:	Stratify seeds at 40° F. for 3 months, then sow extremely hardily
MISCELLANEOUS:	An extremely hardy, rugged, fast-growing, small tree useful for attracting birds

COMMON NAME:	CAJEPUT
LATIN NAME:	*Melaleuca leucadendron*
NORTHERNMOST ZONE OF GROWTH:	10
NATIVE TO:	Australia
TYPE OF TREE: Deciduous or Evergreen?	Evergreen
Leaves (shape, size, color, autumn color)	Pale green, long broadleaf
Type of Foliage?	Drooping branches
HEIGHT:	40 feet
LIFE EXPECTANCY:	50–75 years
GROWTH RATE:	Moderate
FRUIT & FLOWERS:	Flowers are 6 inches long, creamy white to purplish in color. Tree flowers from June to October
SOIL:	Well tolerated in both southern California and Florida, but grows well in a wide range of soil conditions
MISCELLANEOUS:	Cajeput trees are resistant to grass fires and saltwater spray. In moist soils may vigorously reseed itself

CAJEPUT

DAHURIAN BUCKTHORN

COMMON NAME:	**CAMELLIA, COMMON**	COMMON NAME:	**CAMPHOR TREE**
LATIN NAME:	*Camellia japonica*	LATIN NAME:	*Cinnamomum camphora*
NORTHERNMOST ZONE OF GROWTH:	7B	NORTHERNMOST ZONE OF GROWTH:	9
NATIVE TO:	China and Japan	NATIVE TO:	China and Japan
TYPE OF TREE: Deciduous or Evergreen?	Evergreen	TYPE OF TREE: Deciduous or Evergreen?	Evergreen
Leaves (shape, size, color, autumn color)	Broadleaf; very dark green, thick and leathery, 4 inches long; rounded tree shape	Kind of Trunk?	Enlarged at base
Type of Shade?	Good	Leaves (shape, size, color, autumn color)	Glossy green leaves, grayish white on the undersides
Type of Foliage?	Glossy, coarse, large	Type of Shade?	Excellent deep shade
		Type of Foliage?	Very dense
HEIGHT:	45 feet	HEIGHT:	40 feet
FRUIT & FLOWERS:	Flowers late fall to spring, the blossoms are large, waxy, white to red in color, 2–5 inches wide	LIFE EXPECTANCY:	75 years +
		GROWTH RATE:	Slow
SOIL:	Will grow in most soil; full sun or shade	FRUIT & FLOWERS:	Small black berries; yellow flowers
PROPAGATION:	25 varieties available. May be attacked by flower blight	SOIL:	Prefers coastal and warmer areas with sandy loam, and will tolerate dry soil, as has very competitive root structure
MISCELLANEOUS:	An extremely hardy, small tree for urban areas, according to a recent survey by the American Horticultural Society. Frequently chosen as an ornamental planting because of its lovely flowers. Many forms available	PROPAGATION:	Wash the seeds thoroughly when ripe and plant in fall. Difficult to transplant
		MISCELLANEOUS:	Commercial camphor is derived from leaves, trunk, and twigs. An excellent shade tree, noted for aromatic qualities. Frequently grows twice as wide as it is tall

CAMPHOR TREE

COMMON NAME:	**CAROB** (St. John's Bread)
LATIN NAME:	*Ceratonia siliqua*
NORTHERNMOST ZONE OF GROWTH:	10
NATIVE TO:	Eastern Mediterranean region
TYPE OF TREE: Deciduous or Evergreen?	Evergreen
Leaves (shape, size, color, autumn color)	Leaves are broad, shiny dark green, and have wavy edges
Type of Shade?	Thick
Type of Foliage?	Dense
HEIGHT:	50 feet
LIFE EXPECTANCY:	75 years
GROWTH RATE:	Slow
FRUIT & FLOWERS:	Small red flowers. The fruits are 1-foot-long pods
SOIL:	Will not grow in clay soils, but may be grown in dry soils (desert)
PROPAGATION:	Soak seeds in water several days before planting. Difficult to transplant bare-root, should always be balled and burlapped
MISCELLANEOUS:	Well suited for shade-tree plantings. Carob pods are edible, and constitute an economic crop of livestock feed. Carob powder, made from seeds inside pod, is eaten by humans as alternative to chocolate. The seeds, about as round as a nickel and about 1/4-inch thick, are called carats, and became the standard in jewel industry for determining weight of precious stones

COMMON NAME:	**CASUARINA** (Horsetail Beefwood; Ironwood)
LATIN NAME:	*Casuarina equisetifolia*
NORTHERNMOST ZONE OF GROWTH:	10
NATIVE TO:	Australia
TYPE OF TREE: Deciduous or Evergreen?	Evergreen
Kind of Trunk?	Large
Bark (color & texture)	Gray, furrowed
Leaves (shape, size, color, autumn color)	Long, drooping, scaly green needles resembling those of the pines
Type of Shade?	Poor
Type of Foliage?	Profuse
HEIGHT:	70 feet
GROWTH RATE:	Fast
FRUIT & FLOWERS:	Produces hard, conelike fruit
SOIL:	Tolerates many soils, even brackish
PROPAGATION:	Seeds sown in springtime 1/8-inch deep
MISCELLANEOUS:	Red wood used for making tools, while bark is highly medicinal and used in folk medicine in South Pacific. A very successful tree for the seashore. Tolerates salt spray and brackish water. Also used as windbreaks. Along avenues of subtropics, produces a dramatic, intimate effect

CASUARINA

COMMON NAME:	**CATALPA, NORTHERN**	COMMON NAME:	**CATALPA, SOUTHERN**
LATIN NAME:	*Catalpa speciosa*	LATIN NAME:	*Catalpa bignonioides*
NORTHERNMOST ZONE OF GROWTH:	5	NORTHERNMOST ZONE OF GROWTH:	5
NATIVE TO:	Indiana to northern Arkansas	NATIVE TO:	Georgia, Florida, and Mississippi
TYPE OF TREE: Deciduous or Evergreen?	Deciduous	TYPE OF TREE: Deciduous or Evergreen?	Deciduous
Kind of Trunk?	Tall, strong	Kind of Trunk?	Strong
Bark (color & texture)	Red-brown, coarse	Bark (color & texture)	Light brown with thin scales
Leaves (shape, size, color, autumn color)	Broadleaf; heart-shaped leaves may be up to 1 foot long; no autumn color	Leaves (shape, size, color, autumn color)	Broadleaf; leaves are 4 inches long; no autumn color
Type of Shade?	Dense	Type of Shade?	Dense
Type of Foliage?	Large thick leaves, flowers, pods	Type of Foliage?	Thick with leaves, flowers, seed pods
HEIGHT:	75 feet	HEIGHT:	45 feet
LIFE EXPECTANCY:	50 years and more	LIFE EXPECTANCY:	50 years or more
GROWTH RATE:	Fast	GROWTH RATE:	Fast
FRUIT & FLOWERS:	Fragrant white flowers in summer; long, brown seed pods called "Indian beans" appear into winter	FRUIT & FLOWERS:	White summer flowers; seed pods as long as 16 inches
SOIL:	Grows on wide range of soils but does best on pH range of 6.5–7.5. Needs great space to grow properly. Withstands poor soil, drought, or salt air	SOIL:	Prefers moist soil and shaded areas. Most favorable pH range 6.5–7.5
PROPAGATION:	Easily and quickly grown from seed; sow in spring. Stratify seeds in winter so that they will not dry out	PROPAGATION:	Easily grown from seed; also easily grafted
MISCELLANEOUS:	Withstands drought and heat. Wood is often used for fence posts because does not deteriorate quickly when placed in soil. In winter, seed pods hang like hair, giving tree a distinctive silhouette. A useful shade tree	MISCELLANEOUS:	Similar to northern catalpa, but smaller. Wood used for fence posts because resists decay in soil and water. A good shade tree, especially hardy in urban areas

NORTHERN CATALPA

NORTHERN CATALPA

COMMON NAME:	**CEDAR, ATLAS**
LATIN NAME:	*Cedrus atlantica*
NORTHERNMOST ZONE OF GROWTH:	6B
NATIVE TO:	Northern Africa
TYPE OF TREE:	
Deciduous or Evergreen?	Evergreen, member of pine family
Kind of Trunk?	Very tall, straight
Leaves (shape, size, color, autumn color)	Needleleaf; broadly conical tree in shape
Type of Shade?	Heavy
Type of Foliage?	Needlelike in bunches, silvery to light green
HEIGHT:	120 feet
LIFE EXPECTANCY:	75 years or more
GROWTH RATE:	Moderately fast
FRUIT & FLOWERS:	Cones appear on upper side of branches, 3 inches long and 2 inches in diameter; takes cones two years to mature. Both sexes of flower appear on one tree
SOIL:	Grows best on well-drained soil
PROPAGATION:	Stratify seeds at 40° F. for 60 days. Sow as soon as seeds are ripe (or after stratification). Stratification unifies germination
MISCELLANEOUS:	This tall tree from the Atlas Mountains of Algeria and Morocco is flat-topped like cedar of Lebanon at maturity, but easily distinguished by its silvery to light green foliage. A dramatic tree for large lawns and parks

COMMON NAME:	**CEDAR, EASTERN RED** (Juniper)
LATIN NAME:	*Juniperus virginiana*
NORTHERNMOST ZONE OF GROWTH:	2
NATIVE TO:	Eastern United States
TYPE OF TREE:	
Bark (color & texture)	Red, shreds in long strips
Leaves (shape, size, color, autumn color)	Needleleaf; conical tree shape; leaves vary in shape
Type of Shade?	Branches form close to the ground; dense
Type of Foliage?	Soft, needlelike and scaly; may vary in appearance on the same tree
HEIGHT:	90 feet
LIFE EXPECTANCY:	75–100 years
GROWTH RATE:	Slow
FRUIT & FLOWERS:	Female trees have blue berries that ripen in first season; sexes of flowers are on separate trees; flowers are minute
SOIL:	Grows best on well-drained soil; hardy. Prefers alkaline soil in pH range of 6.0–6.5
PROPAGATION:	Free seeds from pulp. Stratify for 30–60 days at 32°–50° F. Germination may take up to 2 years
MISCELLANEOUS:	Wood very much desired for its fragrance and beauty and is used in lead pencils, cedar chests and home construction. Dark evergreens add needed contrast in shape and texture to deciduous trees, especially in winter. Excellent as shelterbelts on Great Plains. Available in many varieties

ATLAS CEDAR

EASTERN RED CEDAR

COMMON NAME:	**CEDAR, INCENSE**
LATIN NAME:	*Libocedrus decurrens*
NORTHERNMOST ZONE OF GROWTH:	6
NATIVE TO:	Oregon, northern California
TYPE OF TREE: Deciduous or Evergreen?	Evergreen
Bark (color & texture)	Cinnamon-red and scaly
Leaves (shape, size, color, autumn color)	Needleleaf; conical tree. Leaves are aromatic when crushed and are bright green and scalelike
Type of Shade?	Branches to base of tree need dense shade
Type of Foliage?	Dense and bright green, scaly foliage
HEIGHT:	135 feet
LIFE EXPECTANCY:	100 years or more
GROWTH RATE:	Moderate
FRUIT & FLOWERS:	Cones consist of 5 or 6 woody scales, ¾ inches long at the tips of branches
SOIL:	Grows best in moist soil
PROPAGATION:	Sow seeds in spring; stratify at 40° F. for 90 days
MISCELLANEOUS:	Wood has been used in construction, mothproofing, and for making cedar chests and cigar boxes. An excellent, tall-growing aromatic evergreen, suitable for homesites and formal gardens

COMMON NAME:	**CEDAR OF LEBANON**
LATIN NAME:	*Cedrus libani*
NORTHERNMOST ZONE OF GROWTH:	6
NATIVE TO:	Asia Minor
TYPE OF TREE: Deciduous or Evergreen?	Evergreen
Kind of Trunk?	Very wide at base
Bark (color & texture)	Dark gray
Leaves (shape, size, color, autumn color)	Needleleaf; conical-shaped tree; dark green. The stiffness of tree's silhouette is appealing
Type of Shade?	Sparse
Type of Foliage?	Branches are stiffly horizontal
HEIGHT:	120 feet
LIFE EXPECTANCY:	100 years
GROWTH RATE:	Moderate
FRUIT & FLOWERS:	Large cones on upper sides of branches. Sexes are on different trees
SOIL:	Prefers well-drained soil
PROPAGATION:	Seeds are short-lived; sow in spring
MISCELLANEOUS:	Cedar oil has been used to discourage book worms and for embalming by Egyptians. Ancient cedar of the Bible reputedly used in the construction of King Solomon's temples. A grand tree that requires lots of space to spread properly with age. Variety *stenocoma* hardier in cold climates and will grow in northeastern states

CEDAR OF LEBANON

COMMON NAME:	**CEDAR, WHITE** (Arborvitae, American)	COMMON NAME:	**CHERRY, BLACK** (Rum Cherry)
LATIN NAME:	*Thuja occidentalis*	LATIN NAME:	*Prunus serotina*
NORTHERNMOST ZONE OF GROWTH:	2	NORTHERNMOST ZONE OF GROWTH:	3B
NATIVE TO:	Eastern North America	NATIVE TO:	Eastern and central North America
TYPE OF TREE: Deciduous or Evergreen?	Evergreen	TYPE OF TREE: Deciduous or Evergreen?	Deciduous
Leaves (shape, size, color, autumn color)	Soft, scalelike leaves	Leaves (shape, size, color, autumn color)	Broadleaf; round tree shape; lustrous, peach-shaped leaves; no autumn color
Type of Shade?	Sparse	Type of Shade?	Dense
		Type of Foliage?	Dense
HEIGHT:	To 60 feet	HEIGHT:	90 feet
LIFE EXPECTANCY:	75–100 years	LIFE EXPECTANCY:	75 years
GROWTH RATE:	Slow	GROWTH RATE:	Moderately fast
FRUIT & FLOWERS:	Small dried capsules	FRUIT & FLOWERS:	Flowers in late May; single, small, white flowers profusely. Cherry fruit immature when red, mature when black
SOIL:	Moist; neutral to low-acid soils. Prefers pH range 6.5–7.5	SOIL:	Prefers cold climates and highlands. Prefers pH range 6.5–7.5
PROPAGATION:	Mainly from cuttings but also from seeds that are stratified at 40° F. for 2 months	PROPAGATION:	Stratify seeds at 40° F. for 120 days; sow when ripe
MISCELLANEOUS:	White cedar often not green in winter, turning brown especially in northern climates. Branches of older specimens frequently break easily and are subject to bagworms, leaf minor worms, weevils, juniper scale, and spruce mite. Is still popular choice as ornamental, but more recent introductions such as Oriental arborvitae are easier to grow. About 127 forms available. Pyramidal shape	MISCELLANEOUS:	Cherries are edible and loved by birds. Wood has been popular for furniture making since the seventeenth century. One of the best flowering shade trees available in the eastern states

COMMON NAME:	**CHERRY, EUROPEAN BIRD**
LATIN NAME:	*Prunus padus*
NORTHERNMOST ZONE OF GROWTH:	3B
TYPE OF TREE: Deciduous or Evergreen?	Deciduous
Leaves (shape, size, color, autumn color)	Broadleaf
Type of Shade?	Fair
Type of Foliage?	Open
HEIGHT:	45 feet
FRUIT & FLOWERS:	Flowers—small, white, fragrant in racemes; fruit—small, black cherries
SOIL:	Best pH range 6.5–7.5
PROPAGATION:	Stratify seed at 40° F. for 4 months, then sow
MISCELLANEOUS:	Early to leaf in spring and quite resistant to tent caterpillars. An extremely hardy tree for urban conditions, according to recent survey by American Horticultural Society

COMMON NAME:	**CHERRY, ORIENTAL**
LATIN NAME:	*Prunus serrulata*
NORTHERNMOST ZONE OF GROWTH:	6
NATIVE TO:	Japan
TYPE OF TREE: Deciduous or Evergreen?	Deciduous
Bark (color & texture)	Smooth, dark chestnut-brown
Leaves (shape, size, color, autumn color)	Ovate, saw-toothed; greenish brown, gray beneath
HEIGHT:	Most varieties are under 30 feet, but this species reaches 75 feet
FRUIT & FLOWERS:	White, nonfragrant flowers
PROPAGATION:	Often grown by grafting or budding. Seeds may be sown when ripe or stratified at 40° F. for 4 months
MISCELLANEOUS:	The species from which most of cultivated varieties of flowering Oriental cherry trees have been developed. Variety 'Kwanzan' is most popular of all double pink-flowering varieties. The cherries are grown on both coasts for fabulous blooms

ORIENTAL CHERRY

COMMON NAME:	**CHERRY, WILD, RED** **(Pin)**
LATIN NAME:	*Prunus pennsylvanica*
NORTHERNMOST ZONE OF GROWTH:	2
NATIVE TO:	Eastern and central North America
TYPE OF TREE: Deciduous or Evergreen?	Deciduous
Bark (color & texture)	Red, shining
Leaves (shape, size, color, autumn color)	Broadleaf; 3–5½ inches long, autumn color red
Type of Shade?	Good
Type of Foliage?	Open
HEIGHT:	30–40 feet
LIFE EXPECTANCY:	Not long
GROWTH RATE:	Rapid
FRUIT & FLOWERS:	Small white flowers. Small, bright red fruits, ⅓-inch wide, make good bird food
SOIL:	Prefers pH range 6.5–7.5
PROPAGATION:	Stratify seed at 40° F. for 4 months, then sow
MISCELLANEOUS:	Excellent wildlife tree; birds very attracted to fruit. An extremely hardy tree for urban conditions, according to recent survey by American Horticultural Society. Also highly useful for rural plantings for its flowering and fruiting qualities as well as its shade

COMMON NAME:	**CHESTNUT, CHINESE**
LATIN NAME:	*Castanea mollissima*
NORTHERNMOST ZONE OF GROWTH:	5
NATIVE TO:	China and Korea
TYPE OF TREE: Deciduous or Evergreen?	Deciduous
Leaves (shape, size, color, autumn color)	Lustrous, dark green leaves, yellow to bronze in fall
Type of Shade?	Dense
Type of Foliage?	Rounded canopy
HEIGHT:	60 feet
FRUIT & FLOWERS:	Male flowers in the form of catkins; chestnuts are the fruits
PROPAGATION:	Sow chestnuts when ripe under screens to keep them from hungry rats and squirrels, or store them in sand over winter and sow in springtime
MISCELLANEOUS:	Since the native chestnut forests were blighted, this chestnut has been planted in profusion for its edible nuts and ornamental qualities. Is most resistant to bark disease. The U.S.D.A. has been encouraging the planting of this species to regenerate the chestnut industry. To produce nuts, more than one tree is necessary, as they are self-sterile. Two or more seedlings should be planted to ensure an abundance of nuts. Interestingly, a strong reddish brown dye can be produced from bark, nut shells, and male flowers of chestnut trees

CHINESE CHESTNUT

COMMON NAME:	**CHESTNUT, JAPANESE**
LATIN NAME:	*Castanea crenata*
NORTHERNMOST ZONE OF GROWTH:	6B
NATIVE TO:	Japan
TYPE OF TREE: Deciduous or Evergreen?	Deciduous
Leaves (shape, size, color, autumn color)	Lustrous green foliage, yellow to bronze in autumn
Type of Shade?	Dense
HEIGHT:	30 feet
FRUIT & FLOWERS:	Large nuts
PROPAGATION:	See "Chinese Chestnut"
MISCELLANEOUS:	Less resistant than the Chinese chestnut to bark disease, it is still grown for its large nuts. More of a shrub or small tree than the Chinese chestnut, this species is less highly recommended

COMMON NAME:	**CHINABERRY** (Umbrella Tree)
LATIN NAME:	*Melia azedarach*
NORTHERNMOST ZONE OF GROWTH:	7B
NATIVE TO:	Himalayas
TYPE OF TREE: Deciduous or Evergreen?	Deciduous
Leaves (shape, size, color, autumn color)	Broadleaf; round-shaped tree with flattened head
Type of Shade?	Thick, dense shade gives it the name "umbrella tree"
Type of Foliage?	Dense
HEIGHT:	45 feet
LIFE EXPECTANCY:	50 years
GROWTH RATE:	Fast
FRUIT & FLOWERS:	Produces fragrant lilac flowers April to May; produces ½-inch yellow berries in the fall that remain until winter
SOIL:	Does well in hot, dry soils
PROPAGATION:	Sow seeds when ripe. Grows easily and quickly
MISCELLANEOUS:	An excellent flowering shade tree that attracts birds which eat the fruit. Well known in the southern states, where it has been planted since colonial times. Grows quickly, blooms early in life and provides dense shade; however, is short-lived

JAPANESE CHESTNUT

COMMON NAME:	**CHINESE TALLOW TREE**
LATIN NAME:	*Sapium sebiferum*
NORTHERNMOST ZONE OF GROWTH:	9
NATIVE TO:	China and Japan
TYPE OF TREE: Deciduous or Evergreen?	Deciduous
Kind of Trunk?	Spreading, branching
Leaves (shape, size, color, autumn color)	Broadleaf; lustrous, light green leaves with red stalks; autumn colors red or yellow
Type of Shade?	Moderate
Type of Foliage?	Spreading
HEIGHT:	40 feet
LIFE EXPECTANCY:	50 years
GROWTH RATE:	Moderate
FRUIT & FLOWERS:	Fruit in the form of a capsule containing milk-white seeds
SOIL:	Does well in wide range of soils
MISCELLANEOUS:	Chinese use waxy coating around seeds for making soap and candles. Resistant to insects or other parasites. Now being planted in southern regions of Gulf states and in southern California. A fine ornamental tree. (Milky juice reportedly *poisonous*)

COMMON NAME:	**CHINESE TOON**
LATIN NAME:	*Cedrela sinensis*
NORTHERNMOST ZONE OF GROWTH:	6
NATIVE TO:	China
TYPE OF TREE: Deciduous or Evergreen?	Deciduous
Bark (color & texture)	Loose, shredding
Leaves (shape, size, color, autumn color)	Broadleaf; compound leaflets 10–20 inches long; no autumn color
Type of Shade?	Dense
Type of Foliage?	Coarse, dense
HEIGHT:	70 feet
FRUIT & FLOWERS:	Greenish-yellow to white fruit in 12-inch long, hanging clusters in June; flowers do not have color; fruits are leathery capsules containing winged seeds
PROPAGATION:	Sow as soon as ripe
MISCELLANEOUS:	The Chinese toon has been grown in the past for its wood, which is beautiful in color and used for making boxes and furniture. A hardy urban street tree, of same order as tree of heaven (ailanthus). Flowers do not emit a disagreeable odor, but it takes many years before they first appear

CHINESE TALLOW TREE

CHINESE TOON

COMMON NAME:	**CORK TREE, AMUR**
LATIN NAME:	*Phellodendron amurense*
NORTHERNMOST ZONE OF GROWTH:	3B
NATIVE TO:	Northern China and Manchuria
TYPE OF TREE: Deciduous or Evergreen?	Deciduous
Kind of Trunk?	Large, wide branching
Bark (color & texture)	Light gray, deeply fissured, corklike
Leaves (shape, size, color, autumn color)	Broadleaf; wide-spreading shape; leaves yellow in autumn but drop quickly
Type of Shade?	Loose, open foliage makes nice shade
Type of Foliage?	Wide-spreading massive branches; loose, open foliage
HEIGHT:	30 feet
LIFE EXPECTANCY:	75 years or more
GROWTH RATE:	Moderately fast
FRUIT & FLOWERS:	Small, white flowers; small black fruit on female trees in fall emits odor of turpentine
SOIL:	Grows on wide range of soils
PROPAGATION:	Sow seeds when ripe (in fall); grows easily and quickly; transplants easily
MISCELLANEOUS:	Though leafless in winter, its bark is so textured as to be very interesting and attractive. Recommended as small but massive shade tree. Extremely hardy in urban areas

COMMON NAME:	**COTTONWOOD** (Eastern Poplar)
LATIN NAME:	*Populus deltoides*
NORTHERNMOST ZONE OF GROWTH:	2
NATIVE TO:	Central North America
TYPE OF TREE: Deciduous or Evergreen?	Deciduous
Leaves (shape, size, color, autumn color)	Broadleaf; glossy dark green above; light, fuzzy below
Type of Foliage?	Coarse
HEIGHT:	90 feet
GROWTH RATE:	Fast
SOIL:	Will tolerate high temperatures, drought, poor soil; needs lots of space to mature. Prefers pH 6.5–7.5
PROPAGATION:	Sow seed as soon as ripe
MISCELLANEOUS:	The value of this tree is well known in areas with difficult growing conditions. An extremely hardy tree for urban conditions, according to recent survey by American Horticultural Society. Official state tree of South Dakota

COMMON NAME:	**COTTONWOOD, PLAINS** (Plains Poplar)
LATIN NAME:	*Populus sargentii*
NORTHERNMOST ZONE OF GROWTH:	3
TYPE OF TREE: Deciduous or Evergreen?	Deciduous
Leaves (shape, size, color, autumn color)	Broadleaf; egg-shaped tree
HEIGHT:	60–100 feet
LIFE EXPECTANCY:	40 years
GROWTH RATE:	Fast
SOIL:	Grows best in sandy soil. Prefers pH 6.5–7.5
PROPAGATION:	Sow seeds as soon as ripe at shallow depth; keep moist
MISCELLANEOUS:	May be only tree capable of growing in driest areas of Plains states. Official state tree of Wyoming and Kansas

COMMON NAME:	**CRABAPPLE**
LATIN NAME:	*Malus* spp. and *Malus* cultivars
NORTHERNMOST ZONE OF GROWTH:	Varieties exist for Zones 2–6
NATIVE TO:	Many temperate locales
TYPE OF TREE: Deciduous or Evergreen?	Deciduous
Leaves (shape, size, color, autumn color)	Broadleaf; rounded habit
HEIGHT:	15–50 feet
FRUIT & FLOWERS:	Small rosaceous flowers, followed by edible fruits the size of a pea to 2–4 inches in diameter
SOIL:	Does best in pH range 6.5–7.5
PROPAGATION:	Stratify seed at 40° F. for 3 months, then sow. Varieties resistant to fire blight and apple-scab disease should be chosen. American varieties have green fruit; Oriental varieties have fruit red, yellow, or purplish
MISCELLANEOUS:	These trees are chosen for many good reasons, not the least of which is their hardiness. Flowers are white to purple, dense, fragrant; fruit is ornamental as well as edible. There is considerable choice among varieties. Birds can eat the fruit of some varieties late in winter when food is scarce. Economic uses include jellies, jams, preserves. In very cold country crabapples may be only fruit available. They are also very effective, fast-growing windbreaks in areas other than Great Plains

COMMON NAME:	**CRAPE MYRTLE**	COMMON NAME:	**CRYPTOMERIA**
LATIN NAME:	*Lagerstroemia indica*	LATIN NAME:	*Cryptomeria japonica*
NORTHERNMOST ZONE OF GROWTH:	7B	NORTHERNMOST ZONE OF GROWTH:	6
NATIVE TO:	China, tropical and subtropical countries	NATIVE TO:	Japan
TYPE OF TREE: Deciduous or Evergreen?	Deciduous	TYPE OF TREE: Deciduous or Evergreen?	Evergreen
Bark (color & texture)	Shredding in winter; smooth, brown	Bark (color & texture)	Reddish; shreds off in strips
Leaves (shape, size, color, autumn color)	Broadleaf; rounded tree shape; privetlike leaves	Leaves (shape, size, color, autumn color)	Needleleaf; pyramidal tree shape; spreading branches
Type of Shade?	Moderate	Type of Shade?	Poor
Type of Foliage?	Fairly dense	Type of Foliage?	Green
HEIGHT:	21 feet	HEIGHT:	150 feet
GROWTH RATE:	Moderate	LIFE EXPECTANCY:	75 years or more
		GROWTH RATE:	Fast
FRUIT & FLOWERS:	Flowers are like crepe paper and so profuse that tree looks like a bouquet—pink, purple, white, or red	FRUIT & FLOWERS:	Produces small cones
SOIL:	Grows on wide range of soils	SOIL:	Grows best on moist, well-drained soil; needs room to develop properly
PROPAGATION:	Sow seeds when ripe. A difficult transplant	PROPAGATION:	Sow seed as soon as ripe
MISCELLANEOUS:	Seeds or plant cuttings sold by color because profuse blossoming is greatest asset of tree. This variety is really a *shrub*. Very hardy in urban areas. Another variety, giant crape myrtle, native to India, becomes magnificient tree. Its red timber and medicinal bark are highly valued, while white to pink flowers are true ornaments in any subtropical landscape (Florida, California, or Hawaii) [*L. speciosa* Zone 10]	MISCELLANEOUS:	Japanese use it for timber and bark for roof shingles. With foliage similar to giant sequoia, this easy-to-grow, large tree is popular as far north as Boston. Hardy in seashore areas

COMMON NAME:	CUCUMBER TREE (Cucumber Magnolia)
LATIN NAME:	*Magnolia acuminata*
NORTHERNMOST ZONE OF GROWTH:	5
NATIVE TO:	Eastern United States
TYPE OF TREE: Deciduous or Evergreen?	Deciduous
Kind of Trunk?	
Bark (color & texture)	Gray-brown, rough, vertically ridged
Leaves (shape, size, color, autumn color)	Broadleaf; perfectly oval tree shape; wide-reaching branches; soft, thin, hairy, light green leaves
Type of Shade?	Dense
Type of Foliage?	Very nice, dense foliage
HEIGHT:	90 feet
LIFE EXPECTANCY:	15 years
GROWTH RATE:	Moderately fast
FRUIT & FLOWERS:	Greenish-yellow flowers; pink to red fruit that resemble a cucumber
SOIL:	Grows best on moist, well-drained soil; pH range 4.0–7.0
PROPAGATION:	Stratify seed at 40° F. for 120 days, then sow. Needs plenty of room to develop. Difficult to transplant
MISCELLANEOUS:	A handsome flowering shade tree often selected for its perfectly oval shape. Tall growing, develops massive trunk and branches

COMMON NAME:	CYPRESS, ARIZONA
LATIN NAME:	*Cupressus arizonica*
NORTHERNMOST ZONE OF GROWTH:	7B
NATIVE TO:	Southern Arizona
TYPE OF TREE: Deciduous or Evergreen?	Evergreen
Bark (color & texture)	Reddish brown; in flakes and shreds
Leaves (shape, size, color, autumn color)	Scalelike, flattened leaves are sharp and contain dots of resin
HEIGHT:	50 feet
GROWTH RATE:	Fast
FRUIT & FLOWERS:	Small cones
SOIL:	Tolerates drought, prefers a dry, light soil
PROPAGATION:	Sow seeds in springtime in a cool greenhouse. Also grown by grafting
MISCELLANEOUS:	Variety 'Bonita' most frequently available of this species but has a weak root system and is difficult to plant successfully. For this reason, tree is often grown by grafting onto sturdier understock, such as Oriental arborvitae. As its name indicates, it is Arizona's official state tree. Pyramidal to columnar in shape

ARIZONA CYPRESS

COMMON NAME:	**CYPRESS, ITALIAN**
LATIN NAME:	*Cupressus sempervirens*
NORTHERNMOST ZONE OF GROWTH:	7B
NATIVE TO:	Southern Europe and western Asia
TYPE OF TREE: Deciduous or Evergreen?	Evergreen
Kind of Trunk?	Straight, tall
Leaves (shape, size, color, autumn color)	Scalelike leaves; dark green; narrowly conical-shaped tree
Type of Shade?	None
Type of Foliage?	Dark, evergreen, scalelike, aromatic
HEIGHT:	75 feet
GROWTH RATE:	Fast
FRUIT & FLOWERS:	Flowers separate sexes, but both may be on the same tree; produces small cones
SOIL:	Grows in a wide range of soils
PROPAGATION:	Sow seeds in spring
MISCELLANEOUS:	Conspicuous because of tall, narrow shape. Wood has good, everlasting qualities. Egyptians used it for mummy cases. Doors of St. Peter's Cathedral in Rome made of wood, which lasted 1,100 years! The cypress of ancient Greeks and Romans frequently planted on southern European estates and gardens. This tall evergreen is popular in Pacific, Gulf, and South Atlantic states

COMMON NAME:	**DAWN REDWOOD**
LATIN NAME:	*Metasequoia glyptostroboides*
NORTHERNMOST ZONE OF GROWTH:	6
NATIVE TO:	China
TYPE OF TREE: Deciduous or Evergreen?	Deciduous conifer
Kind of Trunk?	Straight, single
Leaves (shape, size, color, autumn color)	Reddish brown autumn color
Type of Foliage?	Open
HEIGHT:	100 feet
GROWTH RATE:	Very fast
FRUIT & FLOWERS:	Small cones
SOIL:	Prefers moist soils (does best in soils preferred by Canada hemlocks)
PROPAGATION:	Softwood or hardwood cuttings. Sow seeds as soon as ripe (or store dry in airtight place for as long as one year)
MISCELLANEOUS:	An ancient species, at least 50 million years old. Related to the sequoia tree, needs lots of room to fully develop. Generally planted for its quick growth and ancient ties, has recently been introduced to streets of New York City with excellent results. Pyramidal shape

ITALIAN CYPRESS

COMMON NAME:	**DOGWOOD, GIANT**	COMMON NAME:	**DOGWOOD, PACIFIC**
LATIN NAME:	*Cornus controversa*	LATIN NAME:	*Cornus nuttallii*
NORTHERNMOST ZONE OF GROWTH:	6	NORTHERNMOST ZONE OF GROWTH:	7
NATIVE TO:	China and Japan	NATIVE TO:	British Columbia to southern California
TYPE OF TREE: Deciduous or Evergreen?	Deciduous	TYPE OF TREE: Deciduous or Evergreen?	Deciduous
Leaves (shape, size, color, autumn color)	Alternate leaves, appear on reddish stems. Red in autumn	Bark (color & texture)	Scales gray to red-brown
Type of Shade?	Dense	Leaves (shape, size, color, autumn color)	Broadleaf; lovely green leaves turn scarlet and yellow in autumn; pyramidal tree shape
HEIGHT:	60 feet	Type of Shade?	Moderate to dense
FRUIT & FLOWERS:	Small, white flowers appear in May or June. Clusters of bluish black berries	Type of Foliage?	Narrow habit compared with *C. controversa*
PROPAGATION:	Propagated from seed	HEIGHT:	75 feet
MISCELLANEOUS:	Not susceptible to the twig blight disease, which injures native dogwood (*C. alternifolia*), and of sufficient ornamental impact to warrant greater representation in America	GROWTH RATE:	Slow
		FRUIT & FLOWERS:	White flowers in spring; followed by red-orange berries in fall
		SOIL:	Enjoys moist soils
		PROPAGATION:	Stratify seeds at 41° F. for 145–165 days; then sow
		MISCELLANEOUS:	One of best ornamentals because of lovely summer flowers, and later, berries and lively autumn leaf colors. Silhouette of dogwood in winter lacy and delicate. A beautiful flowering tree that does not grow well in eastern states but is extremely popular on Pacific coast

GIANT DOGWOOD

COMMON NAME:	**DOUGLAS FIR**	COMMON NAME:	**ELM, AMERICAN**
LATIN NAME:	*Pseudotsuga menziesii* (taxifolia)	LATIN NAME:	*Ulmus americana*
NORTHERNMOST ZONE OF GROWTH:	5	NORTHERNMOST ZONE OF GROWTH:	2
NATIVE TO:	Rocky Mountains and Pacific coast	NATIVE TO:	Central and eastern North America
TYPE OF TREE: Deciduous or Evergreen?	Evergreen	TYPE OF TREE: Deciduous or Evergreen?	Deciduous
Kind of Trunk?	Straight and tall	Kind of Trunk?	Large (up to 25 feet in diameter)
Leaves (shape, size, color, autumn color)	Needleleaf; conical tree shape; soft needles, long pointed terminal end buds that have many scales	Bark (color & texture)	Light gray, scaly, and deeply fissured
		Leaves (shape, size, color, autumn color)	Broadleaf; tree shape may be "umbrella," "vase," or "plume"
Type of Shade?	Branches from the base	Type of Shade?	Dense
Type of Foliage?	Dense	Type of Foliage?	Thick, high
HEIGHT:	300 feet	HEIGHT:	120 feet
LIFE EXPECTANCY:	60 years	LIFE EXPECTANCY:	50–150 years
GROWTH RATE:	Fast	GROWTH RATE:	Fast
FRUIT & FLOWERS:	Pendulus cones 2–4½ inches long	FRUIT & FLOWERS:	Winged, notched hairy fruit
SOIL:	Grows in wide range of soil with good drainage. Prefers pH range 6.0–6.5	SOIL:	Prefers rich, moist soil. Does best in pH range 6.5–7.5
PROPAGATION:	Grows easily from seeds sown in spring	PROPAGATION:	Seeds ripen in May or June, are ready to germinate in July and August; broken branches regenerate new ones
MISCELLANEOUS:	Famous tree of the Northwest. Distinguished from other evergreens by pendulous cones, soft needles, and pointed, scaly buds. Variety *glauca* ('Rocky Mountain') hardy in Zone 5 and thrives in the eastern states. Variety *viridis,* deep green, is for Pacific coast and not hardy in Northeast. All are fast-growing, excellent ornamentals	MISCELLANEOUS:	In great demand for streets, shade, and ornament. Highly susceptible to Dutch elm disease. Wood used for flooring and boat building. Official state tree of Massachusetts and Nebraska. Since Dutch elm disease continues to threaten American elms, planting of this tree should be put off for future time when no longer threatened

AMERICAN ELM

COMMON NAME:	**ELM, CHINESE**	COMMON NAME:	**ELM, ENGLISH**
LATIN NAME:	*Ulmus parvifolia*	LATIN NAME:	*Ulmus procera*
NORTHERNMOST ZONE OF GROWTH:	6	NORTHERNMOST ZONE OF GROWTH:	6
NATIVE TO:	China, Korea, and Japan	NATIVE TO:	England and Western Europe
TYPE OF TREE: Deciduous or Evergreen?	Deciduous	TYPE OF TREE: Bark (color & texture)	Dark reddish brown; firm bark, smooth
Bark (color & texture)	Mottled and very interesting	Leaves (shape, size, color, autumn color)	Broadleaf; oval or oblong head, wide-spreading tree shape
Leaves (shape, size, color, autumn color)	Broadleaf; small, 1–2-inch long, green until fall; fall colors red to purple	Type of Shade?	Very dense
Type of Shade?	Deep, rich shade	Type of Foliage?	Dense
Type of Foliage?	Wide, spreading branches and dense foliage	HEIGHT:	120 feet
HEIGHT:	50 feet	LIFE EXPECTANCY:	100 years
LIFE EXPECTANCY:	50–75 years	GROWTH RATE:	Moderately fast
GROWTH RATE:	Fast	FRUIT & FLOWERS:	"Buds are smoky and smoothish" (Hotles)
FRUIT & FLOWERS:	Flowers in *autumn*	SOIL:	Will grow in a variety of soil conditions. Best pH range 6.5–7.5
SOIL:	Will grow on a wide range of soils, but does best in pH range 6.5–7.5	PROPAGATION:	Seeds ripen in May and June and are ready to germinate in July and August
PROPAGATION:	Seeds ripen in the fall and should be planted immediately. Root system at or near soil surface and prohibits much planting under the tree	MISCELLANEOUS:	Moderately susceptible to Dutch elm disease. Wood useful for timber to be used underwater, such as for ship hulls, docks, and pumps. Shade of this tree less interesting than that of American elm, but it is nonetheless a desirable shade tree
MISCELLANEOUS:	This is one of best elms and is highly resistant to Dutch elm disease. (Should not be confused with *U. pumila,* which is frequently sold as "Chinese elm" by nurseries.) Medium-sized, with round top and interesting exfoliating bark. Recommended for lawns and streets as well as for shelterbelts		

ENGLISH ELM

COMMON NAME:	**ELM, EUROPEAN FIELD**	COMMON NAME:	**ELM, SIBERIAN**
LATIN NAME:	*Ulmus carpinifolia*	LATIN NAME:	*Ulmus pumila*
NORTHERNMOST ZONE OF GROWTH:	5	NORTHERNMOST ZONE OF GROWTH	5
NATIVE TO:	Europe and western Asia	NATIVE TO:	Eastern Siberia and northern China
TYPE OF TREE: Deciduous or Evergreen?	Deciduous	TYPE OF TREE: Deciduous or Evergreen?	Deciduous
Kind of Trunk?	Single, narrow	Bark (color & texture)	Rough
Leaves (shape, size, color, autumn color)	Broadleaf; smooth-leaved, bright green; tree form varies with variety	Leaves (shape, size, color, autumn color)	Broadleaf; dark green and smooth; heart-shaped leaves
Type of Shade?	Fair	Type of Shade?	Dense
Type of Foliage?	Oval shape	Type of Foliage?	Rounded top
HEIGHT:	90 feet	HEIGHT:	75 feet
LIFE EXPECTANCY:	75 years	LIFE EXPECTANCY:	50–75 years
GROWTH RATE:	Moderately fast	GROWTH RATE:	Fast
SOIL:	Will grow on a wide range of soils; best pH range 6.5–7.5	SOIL:	Will grow on a wide range of soil, including alkaline soil. Best pH range 6.5–7.5
PROPAGATION:	Seeds ripen in May or June and will germinate in July and August	PROPAGATION:	Seeds ripen in May or June and are ready to germinate in July and August
MISCELLANEOUS:	This elm comes in various shapes and is recommended for planting on narrow streets. Some resistance to Dutch elm disease claimed for Dutch variety 'Bea Schwarz.' The oval-shaped 'Christine Buisman' variety popular in America for many years owing to excellent resistance to the Dutch elm disease	MISCELLANEOUS:	This elm used by farmers as windbreaks and is resistant to Dutch elm disease. Especially useful in drought-affected areas of the Midwest because is one of few large trees that will tolerate the climate and soil conditions. This species and the variety 'Dropmore' highly successful under trying urban conditions. (May be weak-wooded and subject to cotton-root rot and canker disease. Select varieties carefully; 'Coolshade' variety has stronger wood, others may be disease resistant)

SIBERIAN ELM

COMMON NAME:	**EUCALYPTUS (Gum)**
LATIN NAME:	*Eucalyptus* spp.
NORTHERNMOST ZONE OF GROWTH:	9
NATIVE TO:	Australia
TYPE OF TREE: Deciduous or Evergreen?	Most are evergreen; a few deciduous
Bark (color & texture)	Shredding, colorful
Leaves (shape, size, color, autumn color)	Simple
HEIGHT:	From 15 to over 200 feet
FRUIT & FLOWERS:	Unusual flowers and woody capsules
SOIL:	Prefer pH range 6.5–7.5
PROPAGATION:	Sow seeds in sandy soil in early spring. Cover with leafmold; keep lightly shaded until seeds germinate. When 4–5 leaves appear transplant to boxes. Transplant into desired site in March or April
MISCELLANEOUS:	More than 80 species and varieties are available in U.S., varying in mature height from 15 to over 200 feet. Local nurserymen and extension services should be consulted regarding selection of appropriate species. Generally do well near seashore and as windbreaks in areas other than Great Plains. Strongly aromatic

COMMON NAME:	**FIG, BENJAMIN**
LATIN NAME:	*Ficus benjamina*
NORTHERNMOST ZONE OF GROWTH:	10
NATIVE TO:	India
TYPE OF TREE: Deciduous or Evergreen?	Deciduous
Leaves (shape, size, color, autumn color)	Broadleaf; spreading top and drooping branches; bright green leaves
Type of Shade?	Dense and wide shade
Type of Foliage?	Dense
HEIGHT:	50 feet
GROWTH RATE:	Fast
FRUIT & FLOWERS:	Red, pink, purple, or yellow fruits, ¾ inches in diameter (figs)
SOIL:	Prefers well-drained soil
PROPAGATION:	Mostly by cuttings made of 2- or 3-year-old shoots
MISCELLANEOUS:	Sometimes called "weeping fig." As with other fig trees, has extensive root system both above and below ground. If green lawn is not the desired quality in a backyard, this fig tree is grand companion

EUCALYPTUS

EUCALYPTUS

BENJAMIN FIG

COMMON NAME:	**FIG, CHINESE BANYAN**
LATIN NAME:	*Ficus retusa*
NORTHERNMOST ZONE OF GROWTH:	10
NATIVE TO:	Australia
TYPE OF TREE: Deciduous or Evergreen?	Evergreen
Kind of Trunk?	Many aerial roots create interesting trunk
Leaves (shape, size, color, autumn color)	Broadleaf; round tree shape, very wide; glossy evergreen leaves
Type of Shade?	Immense, dense shade
Type of Foliage?	Dense, wide-spreading
HEIGHT:	75 feet
LIFE EXPECTANCY:	50–75 years
GROWTH RATE:	Fast
FRUIT & FLOWERS:	Tiny fruit grow in pairs and are colored shades from yellow to purple
SOIL:	Adaptable to many soils; needs moisture
PROPAGATION:	Grown mostly from cuttings
MISCELLANEOUS:	The varieties *Lofty Fig* and *Moreton Bay Fig* may also be considered. Crown of these trees may be twice as broad as tree is tall, creating shade for hundreds of people. Extremely hardy, even in cities

COMMON NAME:	**FIR, BALSAM**
LATIN NAME:	*Abies balsamea*
NORTHERNMOST ZONE OF GROWTH:	3B
NATIVE TO:	Northeastern North America
TYPE OF TREE: Deciduous or Evergreen?	Evergreen
Kind of Trunk?	Single
Leaves (shape, size, color, autumn color)	Needleleaf
Type of Shade?	None
HEIGHT:	75 feet
FRUIT & FLOWERS:	Cones produced
SOIL:	Prefers moist, cool, high altitude. Does best in pH range 4.0–6.5
PROPAGATION:	Stratify seed at 40° F. for 3 months, then sow. Cannot tolerate hot, dry summer
MISCELLANEOUS:	Extremely hardy tree for urban conditions, according to recent survey by American Horticultural Society. Excellent permanent Christmas tree (when planted on a lawn) noted for fragrance

CHINESE BANYAN FIG

COMMON NAME:	FIR, SILVER	COMMON NAME:	FIR, WHITE
LATIN NAME:	*Abies alba*	LATIN NAME:	*Abies concolor*
NORTHERNMOST ZONE OF GROWTH:	5	NORTHERNMOST ZONE OF GROWTH:	5
NATIVE TO:	Central and southern Europe	NATIVE TO:	Western and southwestern United States
TYPE OF TREE: Deciduous or Evergreen?	Evergreen	TYPE OF TREE: Deciduous or Evergreen?	Evergreen
Kind of Trunk?	Single, straight	Kind of Trunk?	Straight, single
Bark (color & texture)	Gray, smooth	Bark (color & texture)	Smooth, gray
Leaves (shape, size, color, autumn color)	Glossy, dark green with 2 silvery bands beneath	Leaves (shape, size, color, autumn color)	Needleleaf; bluish green 2-inch long needles
Type of Shade?	Sparse	Type of Shade?	Sparse
Type of Foliage?	Open		
HEIGHT:	150 feet	HEIGHT:	120 feet
LIFE EXPECTANCY:	75 years or more	LIFE EXPECTANCY:	75 years or more
GROWTH RATE:	Slow	GROWTH RATE:	Moderately fast
FRUIT & FLOWERS:	4–6-inch cones upright on branches; shattering completely as they ripen in fall	FRUIT & FLOWERS:	Grayish green cones, 3–5 inches long
SOIL:	Requires moist soil. Will grow in soils with pH range 4.0–6.5	SOIL:	Tolerates a wide range of soil conditions, pH 4.0–6.5. (Does not tolerate wet soils)
PROPAGATION:	Stratify ripe seeds for 3 months at 40° F., then sow. Requires cool, moist climate; will not do well where summers are hot and dry	PROPAGATION:	Tolerates heat and drought better than most firs. Stratify seeds at 40° F. for 120 days, then sow
MISCELLANEOUS:	Another popular fir, frequently planted on lawns and public places. A large, graceful tree that needs much space to develop properly. Not recommended for eastern states.	MISCELLANEOUS:	This fir can withstand city growing conditions better than any other variety. Particularly hardy in the East. Very attractive when planted to contrast with other evergreens such as hemlocks and pines

COMMON NAME:	**FRINGETREE**	COMMON NAME:	**GINKGO** (Maidenhair Tree)
LATIN NAME:	*Chionanthus virginicus*		
		LATIN NAME:	*Ginkgo biloba*
NORTHERNMOST ZONE OF GROWTH:	5		
		NORTHERNMOST ZONE OF GROWTH:	5
NATIVE TO:	Southeastern United States		
		NATIVE TO:	Eastern China
TYPE OF TREE: Deciduous or Evergreen?	Deciduous	TYPE OF TREE: Deciduous or Evergreen?	Deciduous
Leaves (shape, size, color, autumn color)	Broadleaf; 8 inches long; autumn color is bright yellow	Bark (color & texture)	Thick; longitudinal fissures, ashen gray
HEIGHT:	30 feet	Leaves (shape, size, color, autumn color)	Leaves shaped like duck feet; fan-shaped branching; autumn color clear yellow to brilliant gold
FRUIT & FLOWERS:	Long clusters (6-inch) of white flowers in June. Fruits—blue, grapelike clusters	Type of Shade?	Medium shade
		Type of Foliage?	Wide-spreading open
SOIL:	Does well in a wide range of soils, pH 4.0–6.0	HEIGHT:	120 feet
PROPAGATION:	Stratify for 3 months at room temperature, then for 3 months at 40° F., then sow	LIFE EXPECTANCY:	100 years or more
		GROWTH RATE:	Moderate
MISCELLANEOUS:	An extremely hardy, small tree or shrub for urban conditions, according to recent survey by American Horticultural Society. Produces leaves very late in the spring, but is still considered one of our best native trees	FRUIT & FLOWERS:	The 1-inch diameter fruit of female is plumlike and has a bad odor when ripe, but kernel is eaten by the Chinese. Flowers too small to be significant
		SOIL:	Grows on a wide variety of soils. Thrives in pH range of 6.0–6.5
		PROPAGATION:	Sow moist seeds in spring; transplant male trees. Softwood cuttings grow with some success
		MISCELLANEOUS:	Ginkgo has been growing on earth for 150 million years. One reason may be that it is not infested by any pest or disease. One of hardiest of all street trees. Only male trees planted because female trees drop strongly odored fruits

GINKGO

COMMON NAME:	**GOLDENRAIN TREE**
LATIN NAME:	*Koelreuteria paniculata*
NORTHERNMOST ZONE OF GROWTH:	6
NATIVE TO:	China, Korea, and Japan
TYPE OF TREE: Deciduous or Evergreen?	Deciduous
Kind of Trunk?	Never straight
Bark (color & texture)	Flat, gray ridges; orange-brown bark
Leaves (shape, size, color, autumn color)	Compound leaves, 7 to 15 oval, dark green leaflets; no autumn color
Type of Shade?	Medium
Type of Foliage?	Leaves coarse and open
HEIGHT:	30 feet
LIFE EXPECTANCY:	50 years or more
GROWTH RATE:	Moderate
FRUIT & FLOWERS:	Large, yellow flowers and yellow-brown, bladder-shaped fruits produced all summer into fall and winter
SOIL:	Grows well in wide range of soils; hardy to wind, frost and drought; grows up to 4,000 feet elevation
PROPAGATION:	Quickly and easily grown from seed. Spring best time for planting seedlings.
MISCELLANEOUS:	One of best small flowering trees for lawn and street planting because of wide tolerance of soil types. Unusually hardy under tough city conditions

COMMON NAME:	**HACKBERRY, EASTERN**
LATIN NAME:	*Celtis occidentalis*
NORTHERNMOST ZONE OF GROWTH:	3B
NATIVE TO:	Central and southeastern United States
TYPE OF TREE: Deciduous or Evergreen?	Deciduous
Bark (color & texture)	When young, ridges and warts light gray-brown
Leaves (shape, size, color, autumn color)	Broadleaf
Type of Shade?	Medium
Type of Foliage?	Round headed canopy
HEIGHT:	90 feet
LIFE EXPECTANCY:	75–100 years
GROWTH RATE:	Moderate
FRUIT & FLOWERS:	Inconspicuous flowering, orange to dark purple fruit smaller than a pea and edible
SOIL:	Prefers rich, moist soil but will grow in hot, dry areas. Tolerates a variety of conditions but does best in pH range 6.5–7.5
PROPAGATION:	Sow when seeds are ripe
MISCELLANEOUS:	This variety may be attacked by twig disease called "witches-broom." Used as street tree in the South, where it thrives even under difficult urban conditions. Birds eat hackberry fruit and insects, making the fruits less of a problem than usually proclaimed

GOLDENRAIN TREE

COMMON NAME:	**HACKBERRY, EUROPEAN**
LATIN NAME:	*Celtis australis*
NORTHERNMOST ZONE OF GROWTH:	6B
NATIVE TO:	Southern Europe
TYPE OF TREE: Deciduous or Evergreen?	Deciduous
Leaves (shape, size, color, autumn color)	Broadleaf
Type of Shade?	Good
Type of Foliage?	Round canopy, similar to elms
HEIGHT:	75 feet
FRUIT & FLOWERS:	Inconspicuous flowering; orange to dark purple fruit drupes, edible
SOIL:	Tolerates a variety of soil conditions including drought; pH range 6.5–7.5
PROPAGATION:	Sow seed as soon as ripe
MISCELLANEOUS:	An extremely hardy tree for urban sights, according to a recent survey by American Horticultural Society. Makes good street tree, and valued for highway plantings in dry regions of Southwest

COMMON NAME:	**HACKBERRY, WESTERN** (Sugar Berry)
LATIN NAME:	*Celtis laevigata*
NORTHERNMOST ZONE OF GROWTH:	6
NATIVE TO:	South-central and southeastern United States
TYPE OF TREE: Deciduous or Evergreen?	Deciduous
Bark (color & texture)	Light gray; covered with corky warts
Leaves (shape, size, color, autumn color)	Broadleaf; no autumn color
Type of Shade?	Good to medium shade
Type of Foliage?	Open
Misc:	
HEIGHT:	90 feet
LIFE EXPECTANCY:	100 years
GROWTH RATE:	Fast
FRUIT & FLOWERS:	Fruit is hard, black berry, ¼ inch wide
SOIL:	Will grow on wide range of soils but does best in pH range 6.5–7.5
PROPAGATION:	Sow seeds as soon as ripe
MISCELLANEOUS:	This variety resistant to twig disease and widely planted as a street tree in southern states

WESTERN HACKBERRY

COMMON NAME:	HAWTHORN, WASHINGTON
LATIN NAME:	*Crataegus phaenopyrum*
NORTHERNMOST ZONE OF GROWTH:	5
NATIVE TO:	Southeastern United States
TYPE OF TREE: Deciduous or Evergreen?	Deciduous
Leaves (shape, size, color, autumn color)	Broadleaf; lustrous, green; autumn color scarlet-orange
Type of Foliage?	Dense, thorny
HEIGHT:	30 feet
FRUIT & FLOWERS:	Produces small, white flowers in dense clusters in mid-June; followed by bright ¼-inch scarlet fruit that persists into winter
SOIL:	Will do well in pH range 6.0–7.5
PROPAGATION:	Stratify seed at room temperature for 3–5 months, then at 40° F. for 3 months, then sow
MISCELLANEOUS:	Excellent as a windbreak in areas other than Great Plains. Of ornamental interest through four seasons; dense, thorny foliage makes it good median strip highway choice

COMMON NAME:	HEMLOCK, CANADIAN
LATIN NAME:	*Tsuga canadensis*
NORTHERNMOST ZONE OF GROWTH:	3
NATIVE TO:	Northeastern North America
TYPE OF TREE: Deciduous or Evergreen?	Evergreen
Kind of Trunk?	Tapering, singular
Bark (color & texture)	Cinnamon-red, scaly
Leaves (shape, size, color, autumn color)	Needleleaf; conical tree shape; dark green with white lines beneath
Type of Shade?	Branches down to soil
Type of Foliage?	Dense, needlelike
HEIGHT:	90 feet
LIFE EXPECTANCY:	75 years
GROWTH RATE:	Slow
FRUIT & FLOWERS:	Cones produced
SOIL:	Grows best on moist, well-drained soil. Tolerates wide pH range, 4.0–6.5
PROPAGATION:	Sow seeds in spring. All varieties easily transplanted
MISCELLANEOUS:	Often pruned to make hedges; at least 40 varieties of hemlock available (Canadian hemlock being most adaptable). Valued as interesting ornamental trees when grown naturally, without clipping. Grows best in full sunlight. Not for windy areas. Official state tree for Pennsylvania

CANADIAN HEMLOCK

COMMON NAME:	**HEMLOCK, CAROLINA**
LATIN NAME:	*Tsuga caroliniana*
NORTHERNMOST ZONE OF GROWTH:	5
NATIVE TO:	Southwestern Virginia to Georgia
TYPE OF TREE: Deciduous or Evergreen?	Evergreen
Leaves (shape, size, color, autumn color)	Needleleaf; pendulous branches, dark green with white lines beneath
Type of Shade?	Branches to ground
Type of Foliage?	Dense, pyramidal shape
HEIGHT:	75 feet
LIFE EXPECTANCY:	75 years or more
GROWTH RATE:	Slow
FRUIT & FLOWERS:	Produces lovely, ornamental cones
SOIL:	Requires moist, well-drained soil with a pH range 4.0–5.0
PROPAGATION:	Sow seeds in spring
MISCELLANEOUS:	May be pruned to any shape. Tolerates city conditions. Better than Canadian hemlock, but grows slower in youth

COMMON NAME:	**HICKORY, BITTERNUT**
LATIN NAME:	*Carya cordiformis*
NORTHERNMOST ZONE OF GROWTH:	5
NATIVE TO:	Central and eastern United States
TYPE OF TREE: Deciduous or Evergreen?	Deciduous
Bark (color & texture)	Broken into thin scales
Leaves (shape, size, color, autumn color)	Broadleaf; autumn color yellow
Type of Shade?	Dense
Type of Foliage?	Dense, broadly rounded tree at maturity
HEIGHT:	90 feet
LIFE EXPECTANCY:	75 years
GROWTH RATE:	Moderate
FRUIT & FLOWERS:	Buds naked, bright yellow and dotted; produces an edible nut
SOIL:	Prefers light soil, but will tolerate wide range of soil conditions
PROPAGATION:	Sow seeds in spring. Large trees very difficult to transplant
MISCELLANEOUS:	Nuts are so bitter that squirrels will not eat them until all other food exhausted. Wood used in manufacture of baseball bats and shock-absorbing tool handles. An excellent lawn tree, noted for striking yellow autumn color and symmetrical form

BITTERNUT HICKORY

COMMON NAME:	**HICKORY, PIGNUT**
LATIN NAME:	*Carya glabra*
NORTHERNMOST ZONE OF GROWTH:	5
NATIVE TO:	Eastern United States
TYPE OF TREE: Deciduous or Evergreen?	Deciduous
Leaves (shape, size, color, autumn color)	Broadleaf; tall, handsome shape; yellow autumn color
Type of Shade?	Dense
Type of Foliage?	Dense
HEIGHT:	120 feet
LIFE EXPECTANCY:	100 years
GROWTH RATE:	Slow
FRUIT & FLOWERS:	Nuts small and difficult to crack open
SOIL:	Grows even in rocky and dry soils
PROPAGATION:	Stratify seeds at 40° F. for 4 months. Large trees of this species very difficult to transplant
MISCELLANEOUS:	Hogs will eat nuts, hence name. Slow growth makes it poor choice as street tree; nevertheless, is excellent, relatively long-lived lawn specimen

COMMON NAME:	**HICKORY, SHAGBARK**
LATIN NAME:	*Carya ovata*
NORTHERNMOST ZONE OF GROWTH:	5
NATIVE TO:	Eastern United States
TYPE OF TREE: Deciduous or Evergreen?	Deciduous
Bark (color & texture)	Light gray, flakes off in loose plates
Leaves (shape, size, color, autumn color)	Broadleaf; leaves fragrant when crushed; large leaves; narrow, upright, irregular tree shape; autumn color golden-brown
Type of Shade?	Medium shade
Type of Foliage?	Open branching habit; not too dense
HEIGHT:	120 feet
LIFE EXPECTANCY:	100 years
GROWTH RATE:	Very slow
FRUIT & FLOWERS:	Inconspicuous flowers; sweet nuts contained in thick husks that split
SOIL:	Grows on a variety of soils and does best in pH range 6.0–6.5
PROPAGATION:	Seeds may be sown in spring or fall; difficult to transplant
MISCELLANEOUS:	Nuts are preferred, next to pecans, over all other hickories. The wood, used for tool handles and light vehicles, is strong and elastic, but soon decays. Very popular as ornamental. A very hardy tree even in difficult urban conditions. Noted for its "shaggy" gray bark

SHAGBARK HICKORY

COMMON NAME:	**HOLLY, AMERICAN**	COMMON NAME:	**HOLLY, CHINESE**
LATIN NAME:	*Ilex opaca*	LATIN NAME:	*Ilex cornuta*
NORTHERNMOST ZONE OF GROWTH:	6	NORTHERNMOST ZONE OF GROWTH:	7
NATIVE TO:	Eastern United States	NATIVE TO:	Northern China
TYPE OF TREE: Deciduous or Evergreen?	Evergreen	TYPE OF TREE: Deciduous or Evergreen?	Evergreen
Bark (color & texture)	Smooth, light gray	Leaves (shape, size, color, autumn color)	Broadleaf; large, dark green, spiny, oblong leaves
Leaves (shape, size, color, autumn color)	Broadleaf; spiny leaves; pyramidal tree shape; dull green	Type of Shade?	Dense
Type of Shade?	Dense	Type of Foliage?	Dense
Type of Foliage?	Mostly dense	HEIGHT:	15 feet
HEIGHT:	45 feet	LIFE EXPECTANCY:	75 years or more
LIFE EXPECTANCY:	75 years or more	GROWTH RATE:	Slow
GROWTH RATE:	Slow	FRUIT & FLOWERS:	Sexes separate; large clusters of shining red fruit on female plants, without the aid of pollination
FRUIT & FLOWERS:	Sexes separate; bright red berries on female plants. Females must be pollinated to bear fruit	SOIL:	Grows best on moist, well-drained soil
SOIL:	Grows best on moist, well-drained soil, pH range 4.0–6.0	PROPAGATION:	Seeds may take up to 18 months to germinate
PROPAGATION:	Easily transplanted from woods to a cultivated garden. Seed develops very slowly; may take up to 18 months after berry ripens for seed to germinate. Do not stratify. May be potted and will produce berries during first season. Nearly 300 varieties known	MISCELLANEOUS:	This shrub or small tree popular because it will fruit without pollination. Holly branches cut from tree commonly used as Christmas decorations
MISCELLANEOUS:	Much desired as Christmas decoration, while wood is used in cabinetmaking. A hardy tree for tough city conditions, American holly also does well planted near seashore. Official state tree of Delaware		

AMERICAN HOLLY

CHINESE HOLLY

COMMON NAME:	**HOLLY, ENGLISH**
LATIN NAME:	*Ilex aquifolium*
NORTHERNMOST ZONE OF GROWTH:	6B
NATIVE TO:	Southern Europe, northern Africa, and western Asia
TYPE OF TREE: Deciduous or Evergreen?	Evergreen
Leaves (shape, size, color, autumn color)	Broadleaf; lustrous, large, green leaves; generally conical tree shape
Type of Shade?	Dense
Type of Foliage?	Dense branching
HEIGHT:	70 feet
LIFE EXPECTANCY:	75 years or more
GROWTH RATE:	Moderate
FRUIT & FLOWERS:	Sexes separate; red, large berries are produced on female flowering plants that have been pollinated
SOIL:	Prefers moist, well-drained soil. Will not grow in hot, dry areas
PROPAGATION:	More than 200 varieties available; seed may take 18 months to germinate. May also be propagated from cuttings
MISCELLANEOUS:	Cut branches widely used as Christmas decorations; preferred to American holly because foliage and fruit are larger and more lustrous. Since female must be pollinated in order to bear fruit, both male and a female tree should be planted to guarantee berry production

COMMON NAME:	**HONEY LOCUST, COMMON**
LATIN NAME:	*Gleditsia triacanthos*
NORTHERNMOST ZONE OF GROWTH:	5
NATIVE TO:	Central United States
TYPE OF TREE: Deciduous or Evergreen?	Deciduous
Leaves (shape, size, color, autumn color)	Broadleaf; autumn color a clear yellow
Type of Shade?	Light
Type of Foliage?	Broad, open, slender branches
HEIGHT:	135 feet
LIFE EXPECTANCY:	75 years or more
GROWTH RATE:	Moderate
FRUIT & FLOWERS:	Fruit—brown, twisted pods up to 18 inches long remain on tree after leaves have fallen and are interesting
SOIL:	Will grow on a wide range of soils, including dry, alkaline ones. Is hardy up to 7,000 feet altitude
PROPAGATION:	Some varieties do not produce fruit. Sow seed in spring
MISCELLANEOUS:	Wood used for fence posts, rails. Splendid tree for withstanding city conditions. Variety called 'Moraine' widely used as substitute for American elm. 'Inermis,' 'Moraine,' and 'Shademaster' most widely used varieties. Thornless variety 'Inermis' widely planted along city streets. As good as these trees are, they are *not* pest free. Roots can grow as deep as 10–20 feet, and need comparatively little rainfall. Excellent in Midwest as shelterbelts

COMMON NAME:	**HORNBEAM, AMERICAN**
LATIN NAME:	*Carpinus caroliniana*
NORTHERNMOST ZONE OF GROWTH:	2
NATIVE TO:	Eastern North America
TYPE OF TREE: Deciduous or Evergreen?	Deciduous
Kind of Trunk?	Zigzag; several trunks
Bark (color & texture)	Smooth, bluish gray
Leaves (shape, size, color, autumn color)	Broadleaf; autumn color is scarlet to orange; delicate leaves
Type of Shade?	Good
Type of Foliage?	Dense
HEIGHT:	36 feet
LIFE EXPECTANCY:	75 years
GROWTH RATE:	Moderate
FRUIT & FLOWERS:	Produces pendulous clusters of hard, nutlike fruit
SOIL:	Will grow on a wide range of soil conditions and does best in pH range 6.5–7.5
PROPAGATION:	Difficult to transplant; sow seeds in fall, some germinate in spring
MISCELLANEOUS:	Wood very hard to chop. Considered good ornamental because is interesting throughout the year; i.e., good fall color, interesting bark in winter. Does well in urban environments

COMMON NAME:	**HORNBEAM, EUROPEAN**
LATIN NAME:	*Carpinus betulus*
NORTHERNMOST ZONE OF GROWTH:	6
NATIVE TO:	Europe and Persia
TYPE OF TREE: Deciduous or Evergreen?	Deciduous
Leaves (shape, size, color, autumn color)	Broadleaf; autumn color yellow; almost egg-shaped tree; retains foliage through winter
Type of Foliage?	Dense; columnar
HEIGHT:	60 feet
GROWTH RATE:	Slow
FRUIT & FLOWERS:	Bears nutlike fruit in clusters
SOIL:	Grows in a variety of soil conditions with preferred pH range 6.5–7.5
PROPAGATION:	Difficult to transplant. Sow seeds in fall, some germinate by spring
MISCELLANEOUS:	Primarily used as hedge because it stands shearing well, this extremely hardy species should be grown as a tree. When planted in row, form very effective windbreaks, in areas other than Great Plains

COMMON NAME:	**HORNBEAM, HOP**	COMMON NAME:	**HORSECHESTNUT**
LATIN NAME:	*Ostrya virginiana*	LATIN NAME:	*Aesculus hippocastanum*
NORTHERNMOST ZONE OF GROWTH:	5	NORTHERNMOST ZONE OF GROWTH:	3B
NATIVE TO:	Eastern North America	NATIVE TO:	Balkan peninsula
TYPE OF TREE: Deciduous or Evergreen?	Deciduous	TYPE OF TREE: Deciduous or Evergreen?	Deciduous
Bark (color & texture)	Brown; flaky	Bark (color & texture)	Light gray to grayish brown with fissures
Leaves (shape, size, color, autumn color)	Broadleaf; heart-shaped leaves turn yellow in fall	Leaves (shape, size, color, autumn color)	Broadleaf; palmate leaf structure; coarse
Type of Shade?	Good	Type of Shade?	Very good
Type of Foliage?	Dense; pyramidal shape	Type of Foliage?	Dense; oval-shaped tree
HEIGHT:	60 feet	HEIGHT:	75 feet
LIFE EXPECTANCY:	75–100 years	LIFE EXPECTANCY:	75 years
GROWTH RATE:	Slow	GROWTH RATE:	Moderate
FRUIT & FLOWERS:	Produces clusters of bladderlike fruit pods in summer	FRUIT & FLOWERS:	White with red-tinged flowers in clusters appear in early summer; large, rounded fruit with green husks containing 1 or 2 shiny brown nutlets. ('Baumann' has no fruit, and double flowers, which make it preferable)
SOIL:	Does best in gravelly, well-drained soil; withstands drought conditions; pH range 6.0–6.5	SOIL:	Likes well-drained soil with pH range 6.0–7.0
PROPAGATION:	Sow as soon as ripe; large trees hard to transplant	PROPAGATION:	Sow seeds as soon as ripe and do not allow to dry out
MISCELLANEOUS:	Fairly free from serious insect and disease pests. Good medium-sized shade tree. Withstands difficult city conditions	MISCELLANEOUS:	Has been used extensively as shade tree but is messy with flowers, husks, and nuts dropping. Leaves susceptible to a rust disease in dry summers. Has lovely winter silhouette because of large, elegant, compact, and curving branches. Also well adapted for seashore plantings

HORSECHESTNUT

COMMON NAME:	**HORSECHESTNUT, RED**	COMMON NAME:	**INDIA RUBBER TREE**
LATIN NAME:	*Aesculus carnea*	LATIN NAME:	*Ficus elastica*
NORTHERNMOST ZONE OF GROWTH:	3B	NORTHERNMOST ZONE OF GROWTH:	10
NATIVE TO:	Hybrid: *A. hippocastanum* x *A. pavia* (1858) Europe	NATIVE TO:	Tropical Asia
TYPE OF TREE: Deciduous or Evergreen?	Deciduous	TYPE OF TREE: Deciduous or Evergreen?	Evergreen
		Kind of Trunk?	Narrow
Leaves (shape, size, color, autumn color)	Broadleaf; dark green palmate; coarse; no autumn color	Leaves (shape, size, color, autumn color)	Broadleaf; large, leathery, lustrous, alternate, green leaves
Type of Shade?	Adequate	Type of Foliage?	Large, coarse leaves, spreading at top of tree
Type of Foliage?	Coarse; round in form		
HEIGHT:	75 feet	HEIGHT:	100 feet
LIFE EXPECTANCY:	50–75 years	GROWTH RATE:	Fast
GROWTH RATE:	Fast	FRUIT & FLOWERS:	Produces yellowish, ½-inch long fruit
FRUIT & FLOWERS:	The 8-inch long flowers are flush to deep red, produced in upright panicles. Bloom in mid-May. Nutlike fruit follows	SOIL:	Prefers moist, tropical soil conditions
SOIL:	Will grow on a wide range of soils; is drought-, wind-, and cold-resistant	PROPAGATION:	Will grow from cuttings in pots or outdoors in soil
PROPAGATION:	Sow seeds as soon as ripe	MISCELLANEOUS:	Indoors, common household rubber plant seldom exceeds 10 feet in height. Outdoors, this fascinating tree reaches over 100 feet
MISCELLANEOUS:	Desired for its flowering and fast growth. Is very hardy, even under difficult city conditions		

COMMON NAME:	JACARANDA
LATIN NAME:	*Jacaranda acutifolia*
NORTHERNMOST ZONE OF GROWTH:	10
NATIVE TO:	Brazil
TYPE OF TREE: Deciduous or Evergreen?	Evergreen
Kind of Trunk?	Singular
Bark (color & texture)	Gray
Leaves (shape, size, color, autumn color)	Broadleaf
Type of Shade?	Good
Type of Foliage?	Fernlike and delicate; loses all foliage just before flowering
HEIGHT:	50 feet
GROWTH RATE:	Moderate
FRUIT & FLOWERS:	Abundant clusters of lavender-blue flowers in early summer; round, brown pods produced
SOIL:	Grows best on moist, well-drained soil
PROPAGATION:	Cuttings of half-ripe wood used for rootings
MISCELLANEOUS:	Excellent ornamental street tree but needs at least 40 feet of space. Profuse blossoming turns entire tree into lavender-blue bouquet!!

COMMON NAME:	JAPANESE PAGODA TREE
LATIN NAME:	*Sophora japonica*
NORTHERNMOST ZONE OF GROWTH:	5
NATIVE TO:	China, Korea
TYPE OF TREE: Deciduous or Evergreen?	Deciduous
Kind of Trunk?	Singular, smallish
Bark (color & texture)	Gray-brown
Leaves (shape, size, color, autumn color)	Broadleaf; dark green feather-formed leaves
Type of Shade?	Excellent
Type of Foliage?	Resembles American elm
HEIGHT:	75 feet
FRUIT & FLOWERS:	Yellow or white pealike clusters of upright flowers in August; seed pods produced—yellowish—often persist into winter
SOIL:	Tolerates wide range of soil conditions
PROPAGATION:	Seeds grow readily (when sown in spring, soak in hot water first). Transplants easily; is vigorous and strong
MISCELLANEOUS:	A dye is made by baking flowers and buds in an oven, then boiling them. A very good ornamental shade tree popularly planted around temples in Orient. Excellent foliage, late-blossoming, nice shape, and excellent tolerance of city conditions make it obvious choice for streets and parks

COMMON NAME:	JUNIPER, ROCKY MOUNTAIN (Western Red Cedar)
LATIN NAME:	*Juniperus scopulorum*
NORTHERNMOST ZONE OF GROWTH:	6
NATIVE TO:	Rocky Mountains from British Columbia to California
TYPE OF TREE: Deciduous or Evergreen?	Evergreen
Kind of Trunk?	Short, sometimes several
Leaves (shape, size, color, autumn color)	Needleleaf; green to light blue, pointed scalelike leaves
Type of Shade?	None
Type of Foliage?	Dense, columnar shape
HEIGHT:	36 feet
LIFE EXPECTANCY:	100 years
GROWTH RATE:	Moderate
FRUIT & FLOWERS:	Dark blue berries; sexes separate
SOIL:	Will grow on wide range of soils, including alkaline; will withstand drought conditions
PROPAGATION:	Free seeds from pulp; stratify during winter at 32°–50° F. for one or two months; may take 2 years to germinate
MISCELLANEOUS:	Lovely shape and color make this excellent ornamental tree. Very hardy in difficult city environments. (Related species, Utah juniper, is illustrated.) Both species make excellent windbreaks and shelterbelts

COMMON NAME:	KALOPANAX (Castor-aralia)
LATIN NAME:	*Kalopanax pictus*
NORTHERNMOST ZONE OF GROWTH:	5
NATIVE TO:	China, Korea, and Japan
TYPE OF TREE: Deciduous or Evergreen?	Deciduous
Kind of Trunk?	Straight
Leaves (shape, size, color, autumn color)	Ivylike leaves; glossy dark green on surface, light green on underside, autumn color reddish; maplelike leaves
Type of Shade?	Dappled shade
Type of Foliage?	Wide-spreading, open
HEIGHT:	90 feet
GROWTH RATE:	Moderate
FRUIT & FLOWERS:	Masses of small white flowers in July followed by small bluish black fruits in August
SOIL:	Likes moist, well-drained soil
PROPAGATION:	Seeds take 2 years to germinate; thorns appear on immature trees; stratify seeds when ripe at warm temperature for 6 months, then at 40° F. for 3 months, then sow (90% germinate by second spring)
MISCELLANEOUS:	Seeds quickly eaten by birds, making it good wildlife planting. White flowers in summer, black fruit in fall, stark and dramatic in winter, this shade tree highly recommended (highly resistant to pests)

ROCKY MOUNTAIN JUNIPER

COMMON NAME:	**KATSURA TREE**
LATIN NAME:	*Cercidiphyllum japonicum*
NORTHERNMOST ZONE OF GROWTH:	5
NATIVE TO:	Japan
TYPE OF TREE: Deciduous or Evergreen?	Deciduous
Kind of Trunk?	Several, narrow
Leaves (shape, size, color, autumn color)	Small, bluish green; autumn color yellow to scarlet; rounded leaves 4 inches long
Type of Shade?	Dappled shade
Type of Foliage?	Wide-spreading, open, fine texture
HEIGHT:	60–100 feet
LIFE EXPECTANCY:	50 years
GROWTH RATE:	Fast
FRUIT & FLOWERS:	Sexes separate; small fruit produced on female trees
SOIL:	Grows best on moist soils
PROPAGATION:	Soak ripe seed overnight in 190° F. water, stratify for 3 months at 40° F., then sow. Do not allow seeds to dry out.
MISCELLANEOUS:	A very graceful shade tree for parks; may be used as street tree if confined to one trunk. Very resistant to pests

COMMON NAME:	**KENTUCKY COFFEETREE**
LATIN NAME:	*Gymnocladus dioicus*
NORTHERNMOST ZONE OF GROWTH:	5
NATIVE TO:	Central United States
TYPE OF TREE: Deciduous or Evergreen?	Deciduous
Bark (color & texture)	Ridged, scaly gray
Leaves (shape, size, color, autumn color)	Broadleaf; leaves pink when unfolding, turn gold
Type of Shade?	Medium shade
Type of Foliage?	Open, coarse
HEIGHT:	90 feet
LIFE EXPECTANCY:	100 years
GROWTH RATE:	Moderate
FRUIT & FLOWERS:	Sexes separate; inconspicuous greenish white flowers followed by thick, flat, pulpy, brown pods that persist through winter on females
SOIL:	Grows best on well-drained to dry soil in pH range 6.5–7.5
PROPAGATION:	Sow seeds when ripe (self-sown in the wild)
MISCELLANEOUS:	Early settlers used seeds as coffee substitute. Unusual leaf color and winter pods make this good ornamental tree. Is leafless six months of the year, yet still quite ornamental, owing to rugged, dramatic form, and adds interest to landscape

KATSURA-TREE

COMMON NAME:	LARCH, EASTERN (Tamarack)	COMMON NAME:	LARCH, EUROPEAN
LATIN NAME:	*Larix laricina*	LATIN NAME:	*Larix decidua*
NORTHERNMOST ZONE OF GROWTH:	1	NORTHERNMOST ZONE OF GROWTH:	2
NATIVE TO:	Alaska, Canada, and United States	NATIVE TO:	Northern and central Europe
TYPE OF TREE: Deciduous or Evergreen?	Deciduous	TYPE OF TREE: Deciduous or Evergreen?	Deciduous conifer
		Kind of Trunk?	Straight
Bark (color & texture)	Thick, scaly, red-brown	Bark (color & texture)	Dark gray-brown
Leaves (shape, size, color, autumn color)	Needleleaf; blue-green, densely clustered 1–1½-inch long; autumn color yellow	Leaves (shape, size, color, autumn color)	Needleleaf; bright green, turning coppery in fall and spring
Type of Shade?	Sparse	Type of Shade?	Sparse
Type of Foliage?	Very open	Type of Foliage?	Open, needlelike horizontal branching, pyramidal shape
HEIGHT:	60 feet	HEIGHT:	100 feet
LIFE EXPECTANCY:	75 years or more	LIFE EXPECTANCY:	100 years
GROWTH RATE:	Moderate	GROWTH RATE:	Fast
FRUIT & FLOWERS:	Produces small cones ½-inch long	FRUIT & FLOWERS:	Bears large cones 2 inches long at about 20 years of age; cones remain on trees several years
SOIL:	Grows well on moist or wet soil; tolerates soggy conditions	SOIL:	Grows best in moist to wet soil, pH range 6.5–7.5
PROPAGATION:	Sow seeds in spring	PROPAGATION:	Seed can be stratified as soon as ripe (or first stored in airtight containers in a cool place for up to a year) at 40° F. for 3 months, then sown. Do not transplant in autumn or early spring, for it is almost fatal when the buds expand
MISCELLANEOUS:	Recommended for difficult urban conditions. Hardy in coldest habitable regions of North America	MISCELLANEOUS:	Susceptible to canker disease and larch case-bearer pest. Though they lose their leaves in winter, they are conifers. Able to survive urban conditions. Will grow further south than American larch

EASTERN LARCH

COMMON NAME:	**LARCH, SIBERIAN**
LATIN NAME:	*Larix sibirica*
NORTHERNMOST ZONE OF GROWTH:	3
NATIVE TO:	Siberia
TYPE OF TREE: Deciduous or Evergreen?	Deciduous
Leaves (shape, size, color, autumn color)	Needleleaf
Type of Shade?	Conical shape
HEIGHT:	60 feet
LIFE EXPECTANCY:	75 years
GROWTH RATE:	Fast
SOIL:	Does best in soils with a pH range 6.5–7.5
MISCELLANEOUS:	An extremely hardy tree for urban conditions, according to recent survey by American Horticultural Society

COMMON NAME:	**LAUREL, CALIFORNIA**
LATIN NAME:	*Umbellularia californica*
NORTHERNMOST ZONE OF GROWTH:	7B
NATIVE TO:	California to Oregon
TYPE OF TREE: Deciduous or Evergreen?	Evergreen
Leaves (shape, size, color, autumn color)	Broadleaf; dark green, lustrous, aromatic when crushed
Type of Shade?	Good
Type of Foliage?	Rounded head, widespread
HEIGHT:	75 feet
LIFE EXPECTANCY:	100 years or more
FRUIT & FLOWERS:	Flowers yellowish green in clusters; fruit is fleshy, egg-shaped, yellow-green drupe 1 inch long
SOIL:	Grows best in coastal areas; with additional water, will grow in interior valleys
MISCELLANEOUS:	Aromatic leaves have been used in flavoring soups. Wood is extremely strong. A good choice as ornamental for streets and parks

COMMON NAME:	**LAWSON FALSE CYPRESS**	COMMON NAME:	**LINDEN, AMERICAN** (Basswood)
LATIN NAME:	*Chamaecyparis lawsoniana*	LATIN NAME:	*Tilia americana*
NORTHERNMOST ZONE OF GROWTH:	6	NORTHERNMOST ZONE OF GROWTH:	2
NATIVE TO:	Southwestern Oregon to northwestern California	NATIVE TO:	From Canada to Virginia and Texas
TYPE OF TREE: Deciduous or Evergreen?	Evergreen	TYPE OF TREE: Deciduous or Evergreen?	Deciduous
Bark (color & texture)	Brownish red, shredding	Bark (color & texture)	Gray and firm
Leaves (shape, size, color, autumn color)	Scale leaf; conical; flat leaves in flat branches with white lines on underside; soft	Leaves (shape, size, color, autumn color)	Heart-shaped, coarse, large; turn brown in late summer
Type of Foliage?	Dense, soft	Type of Shade?	None
		Type of Foliage?	Coarse, narrow
HEIGHT:	120 feet	HEIGHT:	120 feet
LIFE EXPECTANCY:	75 years	LIFE EXPECTANCY:	75–100 years
GROWTH RATE:	Moderate	GROWTH RATE:	Fast
FRUIT & FLOWERS:	Cones less than ½ inch in diameter ripen in first year	FRUIT & FLOWERS:	Small, fragrant white flowers produced in late June; nutlike, pendulous fruit follow
SOIL:	Grows best on continually moist soil; does not like dry weather; tolerates wide pH range, 4.0–7.5	SOIL:	Will grow on a wide range of soils, but does best on fertile, moist, well-drained soil; pH range 6.5–7.5
PROPAGATION:	Seed may be stratified as soon as ripe for 3 months at 40° F., then sown	PROPAGATION:	Seeds develop slowly, may take a year or longer to germinate; stratify at warm temperature for 5 months, then for 4 months at 40° F., then sow
MISCELLANEOUS:	May be attacked by juniper scale and spruce mite, various bark beetles, and black vine weevil. Highly variable species; in colors of blue, silver, gray, green, etc., and many shapes	MISCELLANEOUS:	Not recommended as an ornamental because turns brown so early; however, this tree *is* very hardy in urban areas. (The illustrated species, European linden, no longer planted, owing to profuse suckering and susceptibility to plant lice)

COMMON NAME:	**LINDEN, LITTLELEAF**	COMMON NAME:	**LINDEN, SILVER**
LATIN NAME:	*Tilia cordata*	LATIN NAME:	*Tilia tomentosa*
NORTHERNMOST ZONE OF GROWTH:	3B	NORTHERNMOST ZONE OF GROWTH:	5
NATIVE TO:	Europe	NATIVE TO:	Southeastern Europe to western Asia
TYPE OF TREE: Deciduous or Evergreen?	Deciduous	TYPE OF TREE: Deciduous or Evergreen?	Deciduous
Leaves (shape, size, color, autumn color)	Broadleaf; small heart-shaped leaves, lustrous above, gray beneath	Leaves (shape, size, color, autumn color)	Broadleaf; leaves green above, white below; slightly sticky
Type of Shade?	Perfect shade tree	Type of Shade?	Good
Type of Foliage?	Dense, compact pyramidal shape	Type of Foliage?	Broad, compact, dense pyramidal shape
HEIGHT:	90 feet	HEIGHT:	90 feet
LIFE EXPECTANCY:	75 years	LIFE EXPECTANCY:	75 years or more
GROWTH RATE:	Slow	GROWTH RATE:	Moderate
FRUIT & FLOWERS:	Small white to cream, fragrant flowers produced in summer	FRUIT & FLOWERS:	Light cream, sweet-scented flowers open in midsummer, bloom all summer; followed by small warty fruits
SOIL:	Will grow on wide range of soils, including dry; pH range 6.5–7.5	SOIL:	Grows well on a variety of soils; pH range 6.5–7.5
PROPAGATION:	Seedlings develop slowly. Seeds may take more than year to germinate; stratify at warm temperatures for 5 months, then 4 months at 40° F., then sow.	PROPAGATION:	Stratify seed at warm temperatures for 5 months, then at 40° F. for 4 months, then sow. Seedlings slow to develop. Do not plant in areas where there is much dust and smoke, because particles will stick to underside of leaves and injure tree
MISCELLANEOUS:	Japanese beetle may attack and defoliate trees. Good choice for ornamental street and park planting; is slow growing but very tolerant of low temperatures and difficult city conditions	MISCELLANEOUS:	Beautiful ornamental tree because of interesting leaves. When the wind blows the entire tree appears silver white. Handsome linden, suitable for parks and estates.

LITTLELEAF LINDEN

COMMON NAME:	**LOCUST, BLACK**
LATIN NAME:	*Robinia pseudoacacia*
NORTHERNMOST ZONE OF GROWTH:	3B
NATIVE TO:	Eastern United States
TYPE OF TREE: Deciduous or Evergreen?	Deciduous
Bark (color & texture)	Brown, deeply furrowed
Leaves (shape, size, color, autumn color)	Broadleaf; featherlike, sharp-pointed leaves fold at night
Type of Shade?	Negligible
Type of Foliage?	Open
HEIGHT:	75 feet
LIFE EXPECTANCY:	75–100 years
GROWTH RATE:	Fast
FRUIT & FLOWERS:	White, fragrant flowers appear in spring, followed by dry pods
SOIL:	Grows on a variety of soils, pH range 5.0–7.5. Is storm-fast and resistant to decay
PROPAGATION:	Because seed coat is very hard, soak seed overnight in water at 90° F., or treat for a short period with concentrated sulfuric acid, then sow
MISCELLANEOUS:	Susceptible to cotton-root rot fungus and borer bees. Roots have sweet flavor of licorice; bark of young shoots poisonous when eaten, but flowers can be fried and eaten. A high-maintenance tree in areas where pests are problem

COMMON NAME:	**MAGNOLIA, BIGLEAF**
LATIN NAME:	*Magnolia macrophylla*
NORTHERNMOST ZONE OF GROWTH:	6
NATIVE TO:	Kentucky to Arkansas
TYPE OF TREE: Deciduous or Evergreen?	Deciduous
Leaves (shape, size, color, autumn color)	Broadleaf; largest leaves of any hardy native tree; 20–30 inches long, 10 inches wide
Type of Foliage?	Large, coarse
HEIGHT:	50 feet
FRUIT & FLOWERS:	Big, beautiful creamy white fragrant flowers 10–12 inches wide with 6 petals. Cucumber-like pods with red seeds
SOIL:	Tolerates a wide range of soils; pH range 4.0–7.0
PROPAGATION:	Stratify seeds for 4 months at 40° F., then sow
MISCELLANEOUS:	An extremely hardy tree for urban conditions, according to recent survey by American Horticultural Society. Not for windy locales, as the large leaves are easily shredded

COMMON NAME:	**MAGNOLIA, SAUCER**
LATIN NAME:	*Magnolia soulangeana*
NORTHERNMOST ZONE OF GROWTH:	6
NATIVE TO:	Hybrid
TYPE OF TREE: Kind of Trunk?	Multiple stems
Leaves (shape, size, color, autumn color)	6–8-inch long leaves, coarse; no autumn color
Type of Shade?	Sparse
Type of Foliage?	Open
HEIGHT:	25 feet
FRUIT & FLOWERS:	Cucumberlike pods contain red seeds. Large 5–10-inch-in-diameter white to purple flowers appear in May, before the leaves
MISCELLANEOUS:	Many varieties of this beautiful hybrid available in America. Originated by chance in garden in France over 100 years ago and is popular not only for its large flowers but also because it will bloom when barely 2–3 feet tall. Useful only as small, ornamental tree for gardens

COMMON NAME:	**MAGNOLIA, SOUTHERN**
LATIN NAME:	*Magnolia grandiflora*
NORTHERNMOST ZONE OF GROWTH:	7B
NATIVE TO:	Southeastern United States
TYPE OF TREE: Deciduous or Evergreen?	Evergreen
Bark (color & texture)	Gray-brown
Leaves (shape, size, color, autumn color)	Broadleaf; dark green lustrous above, rusty, hairy beneath; 5–8 inches long
Type of Shade?	Good
Type of Foliage?	Dense, evergreen
HEIGHT:	90 feet
LIFE EXPECTANCY:	100 years
FRUIT & FLOWERS:	Large, white, fragrant flowers from late May into summer; cucumberlike pods split open bearing red seeds in early fall
SOIL:	Grows best on fertile, well-drained soil; needs plenty of room to develop; pH range 4.0–7.0
PROPAGATION:	Stratify seed as soon as ripe at 40° F. for 4 months; then sow
MISCELLANEOUS:	The state tree of Louisiana and Mississippi. Beautiful ornamental with large, lovely, fragrant blossoms and lustrous, waxy evergreen leaves. Very hardy in urban areas

COMMON NAME:	**MAPLE, BIGLEAF**	COMMON NAME:	**MAPLE, NORWAY**
LATIN NAME:	*Acer macrophyllum*	LATIN NAME:	*Acer platanoides*
NORTHERNMOST ZONE OF GROWTH:	6B	NORTHERNMOST ZONE OF GROWTH:	3B
NATIVE TO:	Pacific coast from Alaska to California	NATIVE TO:	Europe, Caucasus
TYPE OF TREE: Deciduous or Evergreen?	Deciduous	TYPE OF TREE: Deciduous or Evergreen?	Deciduous
Leaves (shape, size, color, autumn color)	Broadleaf; large (6–12 inches), autumn color a good yellow to bright orange	Bark (color & texture)	Very dark
Type of Shade?	Dense	Leaves (shape, size, color, autumn color)	Broadleaf; bright green, lobed; milky sap; autumn color excellent yellow
Type of Foliage?	Abundant	Type of Shade?	Dense
HEIGHT:	90 feet	Type of Foliage?	Broadly rounded
LIFE EXPECTANCY:	75 years	HEIGHT:	90 feet
GROWTH RATE:	Fast	LIFE EXPECTANCY:	50–75 years
FRUIT & FLOWERS:	Flowers yellow, fragrant, in pendulous clusters in May; produces winged keys of fruit in pendulous clusters in early fall	GROWTH RATE:	Moderate
SOIL:	Will grow on a variety of soils provided it has large amount of space in which to develop	FRUIT & FLOWERS:	Small, yellow flower clusters appear before leaves in late April
PROPAGATION:	Seed ripens in September; sow in spring	SOIL:	Will grow on a wide range of soils
MISCELLANEOUS:	Has largest leaves of any maple —up to 1 foot across! A good choice for parks as an ornamental because of luxurious shade, lovely autumn colors, and fragrant flowers. Not for the northeastern states; a West Coast tree	PROPAGATION:	Sow seed as soon as ripe or else keep in cool storage, as they lose their vitality quickly. Transplants well in *large sizes* and is tolerant of city conditions. Plant 38–40 feet apart
		MISCELLANEOUS:	Owing to roots near surface and dense shade, grass unlikely to grow beneath this tree. Nevertheless, is an excellent ornamental and shade tree, very hardy in cities. Can be seen from great distances in spring when covered with flowers and in autumn when leaves turn yellow. Does well near seashore

SAUCER MAGNOLIA

COMMON NAME:	**MAPLE, RED (Swamp)**	COMMON NAME:	**MAPLE, SILVER**
LATIN NAME:	*Acer rubrum*	LATIN NAME:	*Acer saccharinum*
NORTHERNMOST ZONE OF GROWTH:	3B	NORTHERNMOST ZONE OF GROWTH:	3B
NATIVE TO:	Eastern and central North America	NATIVE TO:	Central and eastern North America
TYPE OF TREE: Deciduous or Evergreen?	Deciduous	TYPE OF TREE: Deciduous or Evergreen?	Deciduous
Kind of Trunk?	Short	Bark (color & texture)	Silver with flaky scales
Bark (color & texture)	Dark gray, shallow-ridged	Leaves (shape, size, color, autumn color)	Broadleaf; 5-lobed, bright green above, silvery white beneath; clear yellow in fall
Leaves (shape, size, color, autumn color)	Broadleaf; "maple"-shaped leaves turn brilliant red and orange in late spring, early fall	Type of Shade?	Dense
Type of Shade?	Dense	Type of Foliage?	Wide-spreading
Type of Foliage?	Dense	HEIGHT:	120 feet
HEIGHT:	120 feet	LIFE EXPECTANCY:	50 years
LIFE EXPECTANCY:	75 years	GROWTH RATE:	Fast
GROWTH RATE:	Moderate	SOIL:	Grows on a wide variety of soils, including slightly alkaline
FRUIT & FLOWERS:	Small, bright red flowers appear profusely in early April, before tree has leaves; small winged keys of red fruit appear in late spring	PROPAGATION:	Seeds lose vitality quickly; sow as soon as ripe; transplants easily
SOIL:	Grows best on fertile, well-drained soil; grows naturally in swamps and low spots; pH range 4.5–7.5	MISCELLANEOUS:	This maple breaks up easily in snow, wind, and ice storms, owing to weak wood. Is considered a villain by many cities because surface-growing roots often buckle sidewalks. Where better trees can be grown, this tree is better forgotten. Nevertheless, tall quick grower for cold, windy regions
PROPAGATION:	Because maple seeds lose vitality quickly, sow as soon as ripe		
MISCELLANEOUS:	A brilliant red maple when blooming, fruiting, and during autumn. A hardy urban tree; also serves well as windbreak in areas other than Great Plains		

RED MAPLE

SILVER MAPLE

COMMON NAME:	**MAPLE, SUGAR**	COMMON NAME:	**MAPLE, SYCAMORE**
LATIN NAME:	*Acer saccharum*	LATIN NAME:	*Acer pseudoplatanus*
NORTHERNMOST ZONE OF GROWTH:	3B	NORTHERNMOST ZONE OF GROWTH:	6
NATIVE TO:	Eastern North America	NATIVE TO:	Europe, western Asia
TYPE OF TREE: Deciduous or Evergreen?	Deciduous	TYPE OF TREE: Deciduous or Evergreen?	Deciduous
Bark (color & texture)	Gray, furrowed	Leaves (shape, size, color, autumn color)	Broadleaf; 5-lobed, dull green above, gray beneath; no autumn color
Leaves (shape, size, color, autumn color)	Broadleaf; 5-lobed, light green leaves turn yellow to orange and red	Type of Shade?	Good
Type of Shade?	Dense	Type of Foliage?	Wide-spreading
Type of Foliage?	Dense foliage, oval-shaped canopy	HEIGHT:	90 feet
HEIGHT:	120 feet	LIFE EXPECTANCY:	100 years
LIFE EXPECTANCY:	100 years	GROWTH RATE:	Moderate
GROWTH RATE:	Moderate	FRUIT & FLOWERS:	Flowers and seeds hang in panicles 5 inches long in summer
FRUIT & FLOWERS:	Sexes are separate; flowers on female trees are greenish yellow, borne in April in pendulous corymbs; winged keys of red fruit appear in summer	SOIL:	Grows on a wide variety of soils
SOIL:	Grows best on fertile, well-drained soil	PROPAGATION:	Seeds lose their vitality quickly; sow as soon as ripe
PROPAGATION:	As seeds lose vitality quickly, sow as soon as ripe. Transplants easily	MISCELLANEOUS:	The sycamore maple is often chosen for ability to withstand coastal climate and soil conditions. Also is quite useful where windbreaks are required, except on Great Plains
MISCELLANEOUS:	Very popular as shade tree. Is source of maple syrup. Wood desired for furniture. These are formal, symmetrical trees that do not tolerate city conditions well but are extremely successful as windbreaks and shelterbelts in all areas including windswept Great Plains		

SUGAR MAPLE

COMMON NAME:	**MESQUITE**		COMMON NAME:	MIMOSA (Silk Tree)
LATIN NAME:	*Prosopis* spp.		LATIN NAME:	*Albizia julibrissin*
NORTHERNMOST ZONE OF GROWTH:	9		NORTHERNMOST ZONE OF GROWTH:	7B
NATIVE TO:	Southwestern United States		NATIVE TO:	Persia to central China
TYPE OF TREE: Deciduous or Evergreen?	Deciduous		TYPE OF TREE: Deciduous or Evergreen?	Deciduous
Bark (color & texture)	Gray, hard		Bark (color & texture)	Gray-tan, smooth
Leaves (shape, size, color, autumn color)	Leaves are broadleaf, bright green, feathery; thorns on small branches and twigs		Leaves (shape, size, color, autumn color)	Fine, graceful leaves that curl on cool evenings. No autumn color
Type of Shade?	Good, small shade tree		Type of Shade?	Good
Type of Foliage?	Widespreading		Type of Foliage?	Dainty-leaved, flat-topped spreading tree shape
HEIGHT:	50 feet		HEIGHT:	36 feet
GROWTH RATE:	Moderate		LIFE EXPECTANCY:	30–40 years
FRUIT & FLOWERS:	Flowers are in racemes colored yellowish orange and are attractive to bees; produces pods (like yellow stringbeans)		GROWTH RATE:	Fast
			FRUIT & FLOWERS:	Light pink to dark pink flowers in spikes in summer, followed by flat, 6-inch-long papery, light brown pods
SOIL:	Requires well-drained soil; is drought-resistant		SOIL:	Will grow on both moist and well-drained soil and also tolerates poor, dry, gravelly soil
PROPAGATION:	Seeds grow readily. Will not withstand temperatures below zero		PROPAGATION:	Soak hard seeds in hot water for 2 hours before sowing in February or March
MISCELLANEOUS:	The sweetish pods are eaten by cattle. Also good bee tree. Wood is very tough. Excellent tree for windy, drought-stricken areas		MISCELLANEOUS:	May be attacked by webworm and fungus wilt. Blossoms from early summer to September. Extremely long flowering season in northern states makes it popular as ornamental

COMMON NAME:	**MULBERRY, PAPER** (Common)
LATIN NAME:	*Broussonetia papyrifera*
NORTHERNMOST ZONE OF GROWTH:	6B
NATIVE TO:	China and Japan
TYPE OF TREE: Deciduous or Evergreen?	Deciduous
Kind of Trunk?	Irregular-shaped
Leaves (shape, size, color, autumn color)	Heart-shaped, large, coarse broadleaves, hairy undersides
Type of Shade?	Good
Type of Foliage?	Dense
HEIGHT:	48 feet
LIFE EXPECTANCY:	More than 100 years
GROWTH RATE:	Moderate
FRUIT & FLOWERS:	Flowers in May; edible (but insipid) orange and red fruit produced in June and July
SOIL:	Tolerates poor soil and city conditions
PROPAGATION:	Sexes are separate; sow seeds when ripe. Has tendency to sucker
MISCELLANEOUS:	In China, paper is made from the bark; sap used as source of glue. In Hawaii and other Pacific islands, bark is used to make cloth. A tree that grows well even under difficult conditions

COMMON NAME:	**MULBERRY, RUSSIAN**
LATIN NAME:	*Morus alba forma tatarica*
NORTHERNMOST ZONE OF GROWTH:	5
NATIVE TO:	China
TYPE OF TREE: Deciduous or Evergreen?	Deciduous
Leaves (shape, size, color, autumn color)	Broadleaf; bright-green, irregular lobes. No autumn color
Type of Shade?	Quick
Type of Foliage?	Dense; sometimes drooping branches; round-topped tree shape
HEIGHT:	45 feet
GROWTH RATE:	Fast
FRUIT & FLOWERS:	Fruitless variety
SOIL:	Extremely hardy in any kind of soil, including gravel; pH range 6.5–7.5
PROPAGATION:	Seeds should be stratified at 40° F. for 3 months, then sown
MISCELLANEOUS:	Russian mulberry is a fruitless variety of mulberry, while fruits of true mulberry are quite edible (fresh or in jams and preserves), and are loved by birds and small children. This fruitless variety is desirable in street plantings to eliminate litter. Drought-resistant, tolerates seashore conditions

COMMON NAME:	**NORFOLK ISLAND PINE**
LATIN NAME:	*Araucaria excelsa*
NORTHERNMOST ZONE OF GROWTH:	10
NATIVE TO:	Norfolk Islands
TYPE OF TREE: Deciduous or Evergreen?	Evergreen
Bark (color & texture)	Furrowed, brown
Leaves (shape, size, color, autumn color)	Needleleaf; pyramidal tree shape
Type of Shade?	Poor
Type of Foliage?	Tender
HEIGHT:	160–200 feet
SOIL:	Grows on a wide variety of soils
PROPAGATION:	Usually grown from cuttings taken from the ripened tops of seedlings during winter or early spring. Allow cuttings to dry out for one day, then pot indoors at 60° F. for 3 weeks
MISCELLANEOUS:	Planted in pots by florists and used in Hawaii as a "Christmas tree," is not a pine, as name suggests, but a member of a strange group of trees including bunya-bunya and monkey-puzzle. Very hardy, even in tough urban conditions. Excellent street tree. Also does well along seashore

COMMON NAME:	**OAK, BLACK**
LATIN NAME:	*Quercus velutina*
NORTHERNMOST ZONE OF GROWTH:	5
NATIVE TO:	Eastern and central United States
TYPE OF TREE: Deciduous or Evergreen?	Deciduous
Leaves (shape, size, color, autumn color)	Broadleaf; lustrous green; red in autumn
Type of Shade?	Good, dense
Type of Foliage?	Shiny, dark green, dense, rounded tree shape
HEIGHT:	100–150 feet
GROWTH RATE:	Moderate
SOIL:	Will grow on a wide range of soils and needs plenty of room, as is one of the largest of oak varieties; pH range 6.0–6.5
PROPAGATION:	An oak difficult to transplant because of its deep roots
MISCELLANEOUS:	An extract made from inner bark is used in dyes of buff, gold, and orange. This tall growing oak is out of place on small property. A park or an estate tree

COMMON NAME:	**OAK, BURR**	COMMON NAME:	**OAK, ENGLISH**
LATIN NAME:	*Quercus macrocarpa*	LATIN NAME:	*Quercus robur*
NORTHERNMOST ZONE OF GROWTH:	3	NORTHERNMOST ZONE OF GROWTH:	6A
NATIVE TO:	Central and eastern North America	NATIVE TO:	Europe, northern Africa, and western Asia
TYPE OF TREE: Deciduous or Evergreen?	Deciduous	TYPE OF TREE: Deciduous or Evergreen?	Deciduous
Bark (color & texture)	Light brown, deeply furrowed, scaly	Kind of Trunk?	Short, thick
Leaves (shape, size, color, autumn color)	Large, glossy, dark green leaves turn reddish in fall	Bark (color & texture)	Deeply furrowed
Type of Shade?	Good	Leaves (shape, size, color, autumn color)	Broadleaf; green; no autumn color, as leaves drop in late fall; open, broad tree shape
Type of Foliage?	Wide-spreading, dense; broadly rounded tree	Type of Shade?	Good
HEIGHT:	75–100 feet	Type of Foliage?	Open, massive, spreading branches
LIFE EXPECTANCY:	100 years	HEIGHT:	75–150 feet
GROWTH RATE:	Slow	LIFE EXPECTANCY:	100 years or more
FRUIT & FLOWERS:	This sweetmeated acorn may be more than 1 inch long and has mossy cup	GROWTH RATE:	Slow
SOIL:	Prefers low, rich bottomlands but will grow on a variety of soils; pH range 4.0–5.0	FRUIT & FLOWERS:	Produces acorns
PROPAGATION:	Sow seeds (acorns) as soon as ripe; mulching is helpful to seedlings. Not a tree for small spaces	SOIL:	Will grow in a variety of soils; pH range 6.5–7.5
MISCELLANEOUS:	Wood is used for fences; acorns mature in one year. These trees chosen for fruit, wood, strength, and freedom from pests. A hardy urban street tree. State tree of Illinois	PROPAGATION:	Sow acorns as soon as ripe; mulch seedlings. Hard winters may kill or injure these trees
		MISCELLANEOUS:	A tall shade tree with massive branches that is good choice for large spaces. Varieties available with leaf colors from bright yellow to dark purple. (Variety *fastigiata* is an excellent columnar tree; grows 40–50 feet tall)

COMMON NAME:	**OAK, HOLLY**
LATIN NAME:	*Quercus ilex*
NORTHERNMOST ZONE OF GROWTH:	9
NATIVE TO:	Southern Europe
TYPE OF TREE: Deciduous or Evergreen?	Evergreen
Kind of Trunk?	Short, thick
Leaves (shape, size, color, autumn color)	Broadleaf; fine textured, hollylike
Type of Shade?	Excellent
Type of Foliage?	Dense, round top
HEIGHT:	60 feet
LIFE EXPECTANCY:	75 years or more
FRUIT & FLOWERS:	Edible acorns produced
SOIL:	Prefers well-drained soil and likes seashore
PROPAGATION:	Sow acorns as soon as ripe, mulch seedlings
MISCELLANEOUS:	Popular in southern Europe for hundreds of years. Will stand shearing; drops previous year's foliage each spring. Large, round, impressive tree, particularly suitable for parks and other large areas

COMMON NAME:	**OAK, LAUREL**
LATIN NAME:	*Quercus laurifolia*
NORTHERNMOST ZONE OF GROWTH:	9
NATIVE TO:	Southeastern United States
TYPE OF TREE: Deciduous or Evergreen?	Semievergreen
Leaves (shape, size, color, autumn color)	Broadleaf; lustrous, dark green leaves
Type of Shade?	Good
Type of Foliage?	Dense, round top
HEIGHT:	60 feet
LIFE EXPECTANCY:	50–100 years
GROWTH RATE:	Moderate
FRUIT & FLOWERS:	Produces acorns
SOIL:	Will grow in a variety of soil conditions
PROPAGATION:	Sow seed as soon as ripe
MISCELLANEOUS:	A popular street tree in southern United States. Withstands difficult urban demands, according to recent survey by American Horticultural Society

HOLLY OAK

COMMON NAME:	**OAK, LIVE**
LATIN NAME:	*Quercus virginiana*
NORTHERNMOST ZONE OF GROWTH:	7B
NATIVE TO:	Southeastern United States
TYPE OF TREE: Deciduous or Evergreen?	Evergreen
Kind of Trunk?	Massive
Leaves (shape, size, color, autumn color)	Broadleaf; shiny green leaves
Type of Shade?	Dense
Type of Foliage?	Wide-spreading, horizontal branching, densely rounded
HEIGHT:	60 feet
LIFE EXPECTANCY:	100 years or more
GROWTH RATE:	Moderate
FRUIT & FLOWERS:	Produces acorns
SOIL:	Will grow in a wide range of soils
PROPAGATION:	Small trees may be transplanted
MISCELLANEOUS:	Massive trunks and immense spread of branches (usually covered with Spanish moss) are familiar sight in southern states. Whereas most oaks shed leaves in fall, the live oak holds its leaves until *after* new leaves appear in spring. Once extensively grown for shipbuilding purposes the live oak is hardy tree that thrives in difficult urban situations. Official state tree of Georgia

COMMON NAME:	**OAK, PIN**
LATIN NAME:	*Quercus palustris*
NORTHERNMOST ZONE OF GROWTH:	5
NATIVE TO:	Central and mideastern United States
TYPE OF TREE: Deciduous or Evergreen?	Deciduous
Kind of Trunk?	Extends up through head
Bark (color & texture)	Gray-brown
Leaves (shape, size, color, autumn color)	Broadleaf; fine textured; turns scarlet in fall
Type of Shade?	Not the best, because of tree shape
Type of Foliage?	Pyramidal shape
HEIGHT:	75 feet
LIFE EXPECTANCY:	75 years
GROWTH RATE:	Fast
FRUIT & FLOWERS:	Produces acorns
SOIL:	Grows on a variety of soils, prefers moist bottom land. Alkalinity in soil turns tree yellow; pH range 5.5–6.5
PROPAGATION:	Sow seed as soon as ripe; tree withstands city smoke and makes lovely, formal street planting. Large trees can be transplanted successfully
MISCELLANEOUS:	An attractive, graceful, sweeping tree when allowed at least a 40-foot growing space. Adapts well to difficult city sites. Its leaves remain green for many months and their smooth leaf texture allows dust and soot to wash off easily. Tolerate dryness and alkaline soils and tough bark not easily peeled off

LIVE OAK

COMMON NAME:	**OAK, SOUTHERN RED**	COMMON NAME:	**OAK, WATER**
LATIN NAME:	*Quercus rubra*	LATIN NAME:	*Quercus nigra*
NORTHERNMOST ZONE OF GROWTH:	7	NORTHERNMOST ZONE OF GROWTH:	6B
NATIVE TO:	Northeastern and central North America	NATIVE TO:	Southeastern United States
TYPE OF TREE: Deciduous or Evergreen?	Deciduous	TYPE OF TREE: Deciduous or Evergreen?	Deciduous
Kind of Trunk?	Straight, massive, stout	Leaves (shape, size, color, autumn color)	Broadleaf; bluish green, small leaves; leaves turn yellow in fall in some regions
Bark (color & texture)	Dark brown, thick, broken	Type of Shade?	Good
Leaves (shape, size, color, autumn color)	Broadleaf; dull green with red midrib; autumn color red	Type of Foliage?	Dense; round to conical shape
Type of Shade?	Effective shade	HEIGHT:	75 feet
Type of Foliage?	Dense; shape pyramidal to round	LIFE EXPECTANCY:	75 years
HEIGHT:	75 feet	GROWTH RATE:	Fast
LIFE EXPECTANCY:	75–100 years	FRUIT & FLOWERS:	Produces small, nearly black acorns that are eaten by many birds and mammals including blue jays, wood ducks, and wild turkeys
GROWTH RATE:	Moderate	SOIL:	Grows on a wide range of soils, including wet
FRUIT & FLOWERS:	Produces acorns	PROPAGATION:	Sow seeds as soon as ripe; also easy to transplant
SOIL:	Prefers moist soil but will tolerate a variety of conditions, including those in cities; pH range 4.0–5.0	MISCELLANEOUS:	A good shade tree for street planting in Southeast.
PROPAGATION:	Sow seed as soon as ripe; transplants easily; the most rapid-growing variety of oak		
MISCELLANEOUS:	Wood used for furniture and interior decorating. This rugged oak planted as street tree throughout United States and quite often is wider than it is tall. The illustrated species, red oak, is excellent street tree for Northeast. Is easy to transplant, fast-growing, and withstands city conditions		

RED OAK

SOUTHERN RED OAK

COMMON NAME:	OAK, WHITE	COMMON NAME:	OAK, WILLOW
LATIN NAME:	*Quercus alba*	LATIN NAME:	*Quercus phellos*
NORTHERNMOST ZONE OF GROWTH:	5	NORTHERNMOST ZONE OF GROWTH:	6
NATIVE TO:	Eastern United States	NATIVE TO:	Eastern seaboard and Gulf states
TYPE OF TREE: Deciduous or Evergreen?	Deciduous	TYPE OF TREE: Deciduous or Evergreen?	Deciduous
Bark (color & texture)	Light gray; fissured, with scaly plates	Leaves (shape, size, color, autumn color)	Small, shiny leaves, willowlike, deep green, yellow autumn color
Leaves (shape, size, color, autumn color)	Broadleaf; 5–9 lobed; autumn color wine-red to violet-purple	Type of Shade?	Good
Type of Shade?	Excellent	Type of Foliage?	Round to conical shape; fine texture
Type of Foliage?	Dense, wide branching.		
HEIGHT:	90 feet	HEIGHT:	50 feet
LIFE EXPECTANCY:	100 years or more	LIFE EXPECTANCY:	75–100 years
GROWTH RATE:	Slow	GROWTH RATE:	Fast
FRUIT & FLOWERS:	Produces acorns	FRUIT & FLOWERS:	Produces acorns
SOIL:	Grows well on a variety of soils; pH range 6.5–7.5	SOIL:	Will grow on wide variety of soils; pH range 4.0–6.5
PROPAGATION:	Sow seeds as soon as ripe. Newly transplanted trees should be heavily pruned. Allow 60–100-foot growing space	PROPAGATION:	Sow seed as soon as ripe; easy to transplant because of shallow roots
MISCELLANEOUS:	The wood has wide variety of uses, including shipbuilding, baskets, and cabinetmaking. Excellent, stately, shade tree; majestic white oak needs 100 feet of space to grow in. Official state tree of Maryland and Connecticut	MISCELLANEOUS:	This tree may be a host of mistletoe. An ornamental choice because of lovely, fine-textured foliage and effective shape. Very hardy as a city street tree

WHITE OAK

COMMON NAME:	**OLIVE, COMMON**
LATIN NAME:	*Olea europaea*
NORTHERNMOST ZONE OF GROWTH:	9
NATIVE TO:	Mediterranean region
TYPE OF TREE: Deciduous or Evergreen?	Evergreen
Leaves (shape, size, color, autumn color)	Broadleaf; gray-green, silvery beneath
Type of Shade?	
Type of Foliage?	Dense
HEIGHT:	25 feet
GROWTH RATE:	Slow
FRUIT & FLOWERS:	Small, fragrant flowers borne in panicles; followed by purple olives (edible)
SOIL:	Does best in dry soil
MISCELLANEOUS:	Grown commercially in California for its fruit. The common olive is a very hardy tree that does well in cities

COMMON NAME:	**OLIVE, RUSSIAN**
LATIN NAME:	*Elaeagnus angustifolia*
NORTHERNMOST ZONE OF GROWTH:	2
NATIVE TO:	Southern Europe to west and central Asia
TYPE OF TREE: Deciduous or Evergreen?	Evergreen
Bark (color & texture)	Brown, exfoliates in long strips
Leaves (shape, size, color, autumn color)	Broadleaf; dull gray-green, long and narrow
Type of Shade?	Good
Type of Foliage?	Wide-spreading, open
HEIGHT:	20 feet
FRUIT & FLOWERS:	Small, fragrant yellow flowers produced in early June; yellow-coated berries with silvery scales produced in early fall
SOIL:	Grows easily in many kinds of soil; is drought-resistant
PROPAGATION:	Sow seeds when ripe; usually take 12 months to germinate
MISCELLANEOUS:	Fine, interesting ornamental choice noted for crooked, shredding trunk, lovely long desert-gray leaves, edible fruit, and shade. Adapts well to many parts of United States; is very hardy as street tree because of drought-resistant qualities. Also does well in seashore plantings, and has such a tenacious root system it is recommended for shelterbelts in Midwest

COMMON OLIVE

RUSSIAN OLIVE

COMMON NAME:	**PALM, CANARY DATE**
LATIN NAME:	*Phoenix canariensis*
NORTHERNMOST ZONE OF GROWTH:	9
NATIVE TO:	Africa
TYPE OF TREE: Deciduous or Evergreen?	Palm
Kind of Trunk?	Up to 3 feet in diameter, straight
Leaves (shape, size, color, autumn color)	Leaves 15–20 feet long, green arching gracefully
Type of Shade?	Dense
Type of Foliage?	Palm
HEIGHT:	60 feet
GROWTH RATE:	Fast
FRUIT & FLOWERS:	Sexes separate; flowering followed by clusters of orange egg-shaped fruits that hang from tree
SOIL:	Will grow well in variety of soils
PROPAGATION:	Easily propagated by seed
MISCELLANEOUS:	This variety fairly hardy and chosen as ornamental planting as far north as Yuba City, California. Other palms worthy of cultivation for ornamental purposes are Florida royal, Manila palm, and Senegal date; the last named an excellent street tree— well formed and a rapid grower

COMMON NAME:	**PALM, COCONUT (Niu)**
LATIN NAME:	*Cocos nucifera*
NORTHERNMOST ZONE OF GROWTH:	10
NATIVE TO:	Southern Florida and other tropical regions of the world
TYPE OF TREE: Deciduous or Evergreen?	Palm
Kind of Trunk?	Crooked, long
Leaves (shape, size, color, autumn color)	Evergreen, frondlike leaves 12–18 feet long; leaves only in globe-shaped mass
Type of Shade?	Not much
Type of Foliage?	Palm
HEIGHT:	80 feet
FRUIT & FLOWERS:	Produces coconut, which is edible, and all parts of the fruit may be used commercially. Sexes not separate
SOIL:	Adapts well to many soil conditions, including brackish soil
PROPAGATION:	Grown quickly and easily from seed
MISCELLANEOUS:	Considered world's most valuable fruiting tree. Thrives and forms groves in sandy soil along shores in tropical areas of world. Presently dying off in great numbers in Florida, where one-species planting has left many miles of streets treeless

CANARY DATE PALM

COCONUT PALM

DATE PALM

SENEGAL DATE PALM

LAWN PALM

COMMON NAME:	**PALM, CUBAN ROYAL**
LATIN NAME:	*Roystonea regia*
NORTHERNMOST ZONE OF GROWTH:	10
NATIVE TO:	Cuba and southern Florida
TYPE OF TREE: Deciduous or Evergreen?	Palm
Kind of Trunk?	Swollen slightly in center
Bark (color & texture)	Smooth, gray-white ringed
Leaves (shape, size, color, autumn color)	Palm leaves; bottom leaves droop, top leaves are upright; graceful, 15 feet long
Type of Shade?	Fair
Type of Foliage?	Palm
HEIGHT:	70 feet
FRUIT & FLOWERS:	Large, hanging flower clusters form at leaf sheath cylinder. Fruit small, ½-inch, and one-seeded
SOIL:	Grows well on moist, fertile soil
PROPAGATION:	Grown quickly from seed
MISCELLANEOUS:	Lovely, stately trees; appealing when planted along borders or roadways

COMMON NAME:	**PALM, MEXICAN FAN**
LATIN NAME:	*Washingtonia robusta*
NORTHERNMOST ZONE OF GROWTH:	9
NATIVE TO:	Mexico
TYPE OF TREE: Deciduous or Evergreen?	Monocotyledonous
Kind of Trunk?	Covered by dead leaves
Leaves (shape, size, color, autumn color)	Fan-shaped leaves at top of trunk
Type of Foliage?	Coarse
HEIGHT:	90 feet
LIFE EXPECTANCY:	75 years
SOIL:	Grows well on wet soil but tolerates dry conditions
PROPAGATION:	Grows easily from seed
MISCELLANEOUS:	Indians used fiber for cordage, leaves for houses and baskets, leaf buds and fruit pulp for food, and seeds for meal. A good choice as ornamental planting. The related California fan palm is native to United States and easily propagated from seeds

MEXICAN FAN PALM

COMMON NAME:	**PALMETTO, CABBAGE**	COMMON NAME:	**PEAR, CALLERY**
LATIN NAME:	*Sabal palmetto*	LATIN NAME:	*Pyrus calleryana* 'Bradford'
NORTHERNMOST ZONE OF GROWTH:	8	NORTHERNMOST ZONE OF GROWTH:	5
NATIVE TO:	North Carolina to Florida	NATIVE TO:	China
TYPE OF TREE: Deciduous or Evergreen?	Monocotyledonous	TYPE OF TREE: Deciduous or Evergreen?	Deciduous
Leaves (shape, size, color, autumn color)	7–8 feet long, 5–6 feet wide, smooth green leaves; heart-shaped; rounded mass at top of trunk	Leaves (shape, size, color, autumn color)	Broadleaf; autumn color is red to shiny scarlet
		Type of Shade?	Good
Type of Foliage?	Coarse	Type of Foliage?	Dense, broadly pyramidal shape
HEIGHT:	90 feet	HEIGHT:	30 feet
		GROWTH RATE:	Fast
FRUIT & FLOWERS:	Flower clusters; shiny black one-seeded fruit	FRUIT & FLOWERS:	Produces small, white flowers in early May followed by very small red pears
SOIL:	Grows well on a variety of soils; tolerates salt spray	SOIL:	Grows well on a wide range of soils
PROPAGATION:	Grows easily from seed	PROPAGATION:	Stratify seeds as soon as ripe for 3 months at 40° F., then sow
MISCELLANEOUS:	Being one of hardiest of palms, this is good choice for ornamental plantings. Useful: leaf buds and fruit are eaten, leaves make hats or house thatch, roots are source of tannin. (If bud is taken, tree dies.) Official state tree of Florida and South Carolina, it thrives on streets	MISCELLANEOUS:	'Bradford' variety less susceptible to blight than others, and is becoming extremely popular as street tree owing to ability to withstand difficult urban conditions

CABBAGE PALMETTO

CALLERY PEAR

COMMON NAME:	**PECAN**
LATIN NAME:	*Carya illinoinensis*
NORTHERNMOST ZONE OF GROWTH:	6
NATIVE TO:	South-central United States
TYPE OF TREE: Deciduous or Evergreen?	Deciduous
Bark (color & texture)	Deeply furrowed
Leaves (shape, size, color, autumn color)	Broadleaf; autumn color is yellow; massive branches
Type of Shade?	Good shade
Type of Foliage?	Medium density; round shape
HEIGHT:	150 feet
LIFE EXPECTANCY:	100 years
GROWTH RATE:	Fast
FRUIT & FLOWERS:	Produces edible pecans; buds yellow
SOIL:	Tolerates variety of soil conditions, but never dry soils
PROPAGATION:	Sow nuts in spring; difficult to transplant
MISCELLANEOUS:	This tall hickory considered good choice for ornamental use as well as for production of lovely, edible pecans (only in South). Quick-growing, eventually massive tree. Numerous forms available for local growing conditions. Official state tree of Texas.

COMMON NAME:	**PERSIMMON**
LATIN NAME:	*Diospyros virginiana*
NORTHERNMOST ZONE OF GROWTH:	5
NATIVE TO:	Eastern and southeastern United States
TYPE OF TREE: Deciduous or Evergreen?	Deciduous
Bark (color & texture)	Deeply cut into regular, small blocks
Leaves (shape, size, color, autumn color)	Glossy, dark green leaves; turn yellow to orange in autumn
HEIGHT:	75 feet
LIFE EXPECTANCY:	75 years
GROWTH RATE:	Moderate
FRUIT & FLOWERS:	Edible yellow-orange fruit produced on female trees
SOIL:	Grows best on moist, well-drained soil; tolerates salt spray and dry conditions
PROPAGATION:	Stratify seeds as soon as ripe at 40° F. for 3 months, then sow; suckers readily
MISCELLANEOUS:	Lovely, colorful, fruiting tree. Botanical name means "food for the gods," and fruit (when completely ripe) is delicious. The illustrated species, kaki persimmon (*D. kaki*), is native to China and Korea and is grown to some extent as shade tree. Is difficult to predict how many, if any, fruits will be borne, since sexes may or may not be separate. Generally, pollination required to gain satisfactory yield

PERSIMMON

COMMON NAME:	**PINE, AUSTRIAN**
LATIN NAME:	*Pinus nigra* var. *austriaca*
NORTHERNMOST ZONE OF GROWTH:	5
NATIVE TO:	Central and southern Europe, and Asia Minor
TYPE OF TREE: Deciduous or Evergreen?	Evergreen
Bark (color & texture)	Rough; deep reddish brown
Leaves (shape, size, color, autumn color)	Stiff, dark green needles in pairs
Type of Shade?	None
Type of Foliage?	Dense, compact; pyramidal shape
HEIGHT:	90 feet
LIFE EXPECTANCY:	60 years
GROWTH RATE:	Fast
FRUIT & FLOWERS:	Produces shiny, yellow cones, 3 inches long
SOIL:	Grows best in acid soil, but tolerates alkaline conditions and limestone soil
PROPAGATION:	Stratify seed when ripe at 40° F. for 3 months, then sow
MISCELLANEOUS:	Is very hardy, tolerating dust and smoke. Holds its needles for 3 years and frequently used as windbreak or screen

COMMON NAME:	**PINE, CANARY ISLAND**
LATIN NAME:	*Pinus canariensis*
NORTHERNMOST ZONE OF GROWTH:	8
NATIVE TO:	Canary Islands
TYPE OF TREE: Deciduous or Evergreen?	Evergreen
Leaves (shape, size, color, autumn color)	Needleleaf; 3 in a bundle, 9–12 inches long, shiny green
Type of Foliage?	Coarse, loose, open; round to pyramidal shape
HEIGHT:	80 feet
LIFE EXPECTANCY:	75 years
GROWTH RATE:	Fast
FRUIT & FLOWERS:	Produces cones 8–9 inches long
SOIL:	Grows well in dry, rocky soils
PROPAGATION:	Stratify ripe seed at 40° F. for 3 months, then sow. Grows shoots from its stump
MISCELLANEOUS:	This picturesque pine does especially well in dry, rocky soils of California and other southern regions

COMMON NAME:	**PINE, EASTERN WHITE**
LATIN NAME:	*Pinus strobus*
NORTHERNMOST ZONE OF GROWTH:	3B
NATIVE TO:	Eastern North America
TYPE OF TREE: Deciduous or Evergreen?	Evergreen
Bark (color & texture)	Thickly ridged; dark gray
Leaves (shape, size, color, autumn color)	5 needles in a bundle, 2–5½ inches long, blue-green, soft and flexible
Type of Shade?	Good
Type of Foliage?	Dense, irregular; round to pyramidal shape
HEIGHT:	100–150 feet
LIFE EXPECTANCY:	100 years
GROWTH RATE:	Moderate
FRUIT & FLOWERS:	Produces cones 4–6 inches long, which are small and green in the first year
SOIL:	Will tolerate any soil condition, except wet
PROPAGATION:	Stratify ripe seed at 40° F. for 3 months, then sow; transplants easily and tolerates proper shearing
MISCELLANEOUS:	A timber tree, valued for very white wood, as well as for ornamental plantings. Leaves are always lovely green. A stand of eastern white pine will form very effective windbreak. *Not* tolerant of city conditions

COMMON NAME:	**PINE, ITALIAN STONE**
LATIN NAME:	*Pinus pinea*
NORTHERNMOST ZONE OF GROWTH:	9
NATIVE TO:	Mediterranean area
TYPE OF TREE: Deciduous or Evergreen?	Evergreen
Leaves (shape, size, color, autumn color)	2 in a sheath, 4–8-inch-long needles
Type of Foliage?	Umbrella-shaped
HEIGHT:	60 feet
GROWTH RATE:	Slow
FRUIT & FLOWERS:	Cones are 5 inches long. Edible nuts have been eaten in Middle East for centuries
PROPAGATION:	Stratify seed for 3 months at 40° F.
MISCELLANEOUS:	Extremely hardy pine for urban conditions, according to recent survey by American Horticultural Society. (Frequent in countryside of Mediterranean)

EASTERN WHITE PINE

COMMON NAME:	**PINE, JACK**	COMMON NAME:	**PINE, LODGE POLE**
LATIN NAME:	*Pinus banksiana*	LATIN NAME:	*Pinus contorta latifolia*
NORTHERNMOST ZONE OF GROWTH:	2	NORTHERNMOST ZONE OF GROWTH:	6
NATIVE TO:	Northeastern United States	NATIVE TO:	Rocky Mountain area
TYPE OF TREE: Deciduous or Evergreen?	Evergreen	TYPE OF TREE: Deciduous or Evergreen?	Evergreen
Leaves (shape, size, color, autumn color)	Needleleaf; 1 inch long; yellow in winter	Leaves (shape, size, color, autumn color)	Short, twisted, paired needles
Type of Foliage?	Coarse, scrubby, open	Type of Foliage?	Dense head
HEIGHT:	75 feet	HEIGHT:	75 feet
SOIL:	Will tolerate loose, dry, sandy soils	FRUIT & FLOWERS:	Cones 3 inches long
PROPAGATION:	Stratify seeds for 3 months at 40° F.	SOIL:	Will grow in variety of soils
MISCELLANEOUS:	Not the best-looking pine, but very hardy tree that tolerates tough city conditions	MISCELLANEOUS:	Grows well in difficult urban conditions and is recommended as an urban tree in northern Rocky Mountain area

COMMON NAME:	**PINE, LONGLEAF**
LATIN NAME:	*Pinus palustris*
NORTHERNMOST ZONE OF GROWTH:	7B
NATIVE TO:	Southeastern United States
TYPE OF TREE: Deciduous or Evergreen?	Evergreen
Kind of Trunk?	Straight
Leaves (shape, size, color, autumn color)	Needleleaf; 3-bundled, 8–18 inches long
Type of Foliage?	Conical shape
HEIGHT:	100 feet
LIFE EXPECTANCY:	100 years
FRUIT & FLOWERS:	Produces cones 3–3½ inches long
SOIL:	Will grow in variety of soils, requires good drainage
PROPAGATION:	Stratify ripe seed at 40° F. for 3 months, then sow
MISCELLANEOUS:	This timber tree retains cones for up to 20 years. Liked by some for its long needles, straight trunk, and graceful habit

COMMON NAME:	**PINE, PONDEROSA**
LATIN NAME:	*Pinus ponderosa*
NORTHERNMOST ZONE OF GROWTH:	6
NATIVE TO:	Western North America
TYPE OF TREE: Deciduous or Evergreen?	Evergreen
Bark (color & texture)	Cinnamon to black; platelike
Leaves (shape, size, color, autumn color)	Needleleaf; 2–5 needles in a bundle, yellowish dark green, 5–10 inches long
Type of Foliage?	Open; conical shape
HEIGHT:	150 feet
LIFE EXPECTANCY:	100 years
GROWTH RATE:	Fast
FRUIT & FLOWERS:	Produces cones 6 inches long
SOIL:	Grows well in a variety of soils, including slightly alkaline soil, and even sand. Grows well at altitudes over 3,000 feet
PROPAGATION:	Stratify ripe seed at 40° F. for 3 months. Then sow. Allow ample room for this large tree to develop
MISCELLANEOUS:	Entire forests in western North America are made up of this species. Excellent as shelterbelts. Popular as ornamental for its rapid growth, colorful foliage, and eventually large size

NORFOLK ISLAND PINE

PONDEROSA PINE

COMMON NAME:	PINE, RED (Norway Pine)
LATIN NAME:	*Pinus resinosa*
NORTHERNMOST ZONE OF GROWTH:	2
NATIVE TO:	North-central and northeastern North America
TYPE OF TREE: Deciduous or Evergreen?	Evergreen
Bark (color & texture)	Reddish brown
Leaves (shape, size, color, autumn color)	2 needles to a bundle, soft, 5–6½ inches long, shiny, dark green
Type of Foliage?	Pyramidal shape
HEIGHT:	75 feet
LIFE EXPECTANCY:	100 years or more
GROWTH RATE:	Moderate
FRUIT & FLOWERS:	Produces cones 2 inches long
SOIL:	Grows well on a variety of well-drained soils; tolerates smoke
PROPAGATION:	Stratify ripe seed at 40° F. for 3 months, then sow
MISCELLANEOUS:	This variety grown for unique bark color and for hardiness under adverse soil conditions. An excellent pine for colder regions of northern states and Canada

COMMON NAME:	PINE, SCOTCH
LATIN NAME:	*Pinus sylvestris*
NORTHERNMOST ZONE OF GROWTH:	2
NATIVE TO:	Europe to Siberia
TYPE OF TREE: Deciduous or Evergreen?	Evergreen
Bark (color & texture)	Orange at maturity
Leaves (shape, size, color, autumn color)	Needleleaf; blue-green, 1–3 inches long, stiff needles
Type of Shade?	Poor
Type of Foliage?	Open, sparse; narrow tree shape
HEIGHT:	75 feet
FRUIT & FLOWERS:	Cones are 2 inches long
PROPAGATION:	Stratify at 40° F. for 3 months, then sow
MISCELLANEOUS:	Extremely hardy tree for urban conditions, according to recent survey by American Horticultural Society

COMMON NAME:	**PINE, SWISS STONE**	COMMON NAME:	**PISTACHE, CHINESE**
LATIN NAME:	*Pinus cembra*	LATIN NAME:	*Pistacia chinensis*
NORTHERNMOST ZONE OF GROWTH:	2	NORTHERNMOST ZONE OF GROWTH:	6B
NATIVE TO:	Central Europe and northern Asia	NATIVE TO:	China
TYPE OF TREE: Deciduous or Evergreen?	Evergreen	TYPE OF TREE: Deciduous or Evergreen?	Deciduous
		Kind of Trunk?	Broad, short
Leaves (shape, size, color, autumn color)	Soft-textured, dark green needles, 5 to sheath	Leaves (shape, size, color, autumn color)	Broadleaf; fine textured; autumn color is red-orange
Type of Foliage?	Dense; columnar or pyramidal shape	Type of Shade?	Good
		Type of Foliage?	Dense; broadly rounded shape
HEIGHT:	75 feet	HEIGHT:	50 feet
GROWTH RATE:	Very slow	LIFE EXPECTANCY:	50–75 years
SOIL:		GROWTH RATE:	Slow
PROPAGATION:	Stratify for 3 months at 40° F., then sow	FRUIT & FLOWERS:	Small red flowers in dense clusters, followed by seed pods
MISCELLANEOUS:	Another hardy tree for cities, according to American Horticultural Society	SOIL:	Does well in deep, dry soil; withstands heat and drought and coastal conditions; frost-resistant
		PROPAGATION:	Needs 6–8 feet for growth
		MISCELLANEOUS:	Both seeds and buds can be eaten. A good shade tree for small properties; tolerates heat, drought, frost, insects, and diseases

CHINESE PISTACHE

COMMON NAME:	**PLANETREE, AMERICAN** (Sycamore)	COMMON NAME:	**PLANETREE, LONDON**
LATIN NAME:	*Platanus occidentalis*	LATIN NAME:	*Platanus acerifolia*
NORTHERNMOST ZONE OF GROWTH:	6	NORTHERNMOST ZONE OF GROWTH:	6
NATIVE TO:	Eastern United States	NATIVE TO:	Hybrid origin: *P. occidentalis* x *P. orientalis*
TYPE OF TREE: Deciduous or Evergreen?	Deciduous	TYPE OF TREE: Deciduous or Evergreen?	Deciduous
Kind of Trunk?	Thick, sometimes several	Kind of Trunk?	Tall, straight
Bark (color & texture)	White, peeling in scabs	Bark (color & texture)	Under bark is light yellowish, scales off in pieces
Leaves (shape, size, color, autumn color)	Broadleaf; large, maplelike, coarse	Leaves (shape, size, color, autumn color)	Broadleaf; coarse, palmately veined, lobed, 5–10-inch-wide leaves; leaves often remain on tree into winter
Type of Shade?	Good		
Type of Foliage?	Dense	Type of Foliage?	Coarse; widespreading
HEIGHT:	120 feet	HEIGHT:	100 feet
LIFE EXPECTANCY:	75–100 years	LIFE EXPECTANCY:	75 years
GROWTH RATE:	Fast	GROWTH RATE:	Fast
FRUIT & FLOWERS:	Inconspicuous tiny flowers; fruit is ball hanging from tree on long threads (only one fruit ball)	FRUIT & FLOWERS:	Inconspicuous flowers; two or more fruit balls in fall and winter
SOIL:	Will grow in variety of soil conditions; withstands smoke, soot, and dust	SOIL:	Will grow on a wide range of soils, pH range 6.5–7.5
PROPAGATION:	Sow seeds in fall and expose them to freezing	PROPAGATION:	Seeds germinate as soon as sown if collected from trees in late winter. If collected in autumn, stratify the seeds for 2 months at 40° F.
MISCELLANEOUS:	This massive tree tolerates urban conditions but is quite susceptible to twig blight disease. For this reason London planetree (hybrid between sycamore and Oriental planetree) is preferred as street tree	MISCELLANEOUS:	Tolerates smoke, drought, severe pruning; widely planted in eastern United States

LONDON PLANETREE

AMERICAN PLANETREE

COMMON NAME:	**PLANETREE, ORIENTAL**
LATIN NAME:	*Platanus orientalis*
NORTHERNMOST ZONE OF GROWTH:	6
NATIVE TO:	Southeastern Europe and Asia Minor
TYPE OF TREE: Deciduous or Evergreen?	Deciduous
Kind of Trunk?	Straight, tall
Bark (color & texture)	Flakes off in large pieces
Leaves (shape, size, color, autumn color)	Large, maplelike leaves
Type of Foliage?	Coarse
HEIGHT:	90 feet
LIFE EXPECTANCY:	75–100 years (some in England are 300–400 years old)
GROWTH RATE:	Fast
FRUIT & FLOWERS:	Three balls of fruit in each cluster
SOIL:	Adapts to a wide range of soils, pH range 6.5–7.5
PROPAGATION:	See Planetree, London
MISCELLANEOUS:	A highly desirable, large street tree that has been planted in America since colonial times. In the eastern United States the London planetree is preferred

COMMON NAME:	**POPLAR, BOLLEANA** (White Poplar)
LATIN NAME:	*Populus alba*
NORTHERNMOST ZONE OF GROWTH:	3B
NATIVE TO:	Europe and Western Siberia
TYPE OF TREE: Deciduous or Evergreen?	Deciduous
Bark (color & texture)	Whitish-gray, smooth
Leaves (shape, size, color, autumn color)	Broadleaf; gray-green above, white and sticky below; reddish fall color
Type of Shade?	Good
Type of Foliage?	Irregular, open, wide-spreading
HEIGHT:	90 feet
GROWTH RATE:	Fast
FRUIT & FLOWERS:	Females produce cluster of small pods filled with cottonlike fluffy material
SOIL:	Tolerates a variety of soil conditions. pH range 6.5–7.5
PROPAGATION:	Sow seed as soon as ripe; roots near the surface; suckers freely
MISCELLANEOUS:	Presently recommended as a tough tree for urban needs. Fast growing, but weak wooded, they form excellent windbreaks in most areas, except the Great Plains

BOLLEANA POPULAR

COMMON NAME:	**REDBUD, EASTERN**	COMMON NAME:	**REDWOOD**
LATIN NAME:	*Cercis canadensis*	LATIN NAME:	*Sequoia sempervirens*
NORTHERNMOST ZONE OF GROWTH:	5	NORTHERNMOST ZONE OF GROWTH:	7
NATIVE TO:	Eastern United States	NATIVE TO:	California and southern Oregon
TYPE OF TREE: Deciduous or Evergreen?	Deciduous	TYPE OF TREE: Deciduous or Evergreen?	Evergreen
Kind of Trunk?	Frequently multiple	Kind of Trunk?	Tall, massive
Leaves (shape, size, color, autumn color)	Heart-shaped, fine-textured leaves turn yellow in fall	Leaves (shape, size, color, autumn color)	Very thick, reddish brown
Type of Foliage?	Irregular, zigzagging branches; irregular tree shape	Type of Foliage?	Flat sprays of foliage
HEIGHT:	36 feet	HEIGHT:	365 feet
LIFE EXPECTANCY:	50 years	LIFE EXPECTANCY:	Hundreds of years, if not thousands!
GROWTH RATE:	Moderate	GROWTH RATE:	Fast
FRUIT & FLOWERS:	Small, pink-purple, pealike flowers produced in clusters (even on trunk) before leaves, in mid-May; followed by short, brown pods	FRUIT & FLOWERS:	Oval cones with scales
SOIL:	Grows best in fertile, well-drained soil; pH range 6.5–7.5	PROPAGATION:	Stratify seeds at 40° F. for 2 months, then sow. Shoots from burls can be grown as cuttings. (Tree has strong survival instincts, often growing again from cut stump)
PROPAGATION:	Soak seeds in hot water before sowing. Sow when soil is warm. Transplant well only when small	MISCELLANEOUS:	A beautiful park tree, with great history in United States. Once spread over nearly 2 million acres, in belt 500 miles long and 30 miles wide, along Pacific Coast, these big old trees are now limited to few reservations. Official state tree of California
MISCELLANEOUS:	French-Canadians use flowers in salads and pickles. Pods remain on tree in winter, common in woods of eastern states. A desirable, ornamental for small property		

REDWOOD

REDWOOD

COMMON NAME:	**ROYAL POINCIANA**	COMMON NAME:	**SASSAFRAS**
LATIN NAME:	*Delonix regia*	LATIN NAME:	*Sassafras albidum*
NORTHERNMOST ZONE OF GROWTH:	9	NORTHERNMOST ZONE OF GROWTH:	5
NATIVE TO:	Malagasy Republic	NATIVE TO:	Eastern and northeastern United States
TYPE OF TREE: Deciduous or Evergreen?	Evergreen	TYPE OF TREE: Deciduous or Evergreen?	Deciduous
Kind of Trunk?	Gnarled	Kind of Trunk?	Long
Bark (color & texture)	Smooth, light gray	Bark (color & texture)	Dark cinnamon-gray, deeply furrowed
Leaves (shape, size, color, autumn color)	Needleleaf; fernlike, 1–2 feet long	Leaves (shape, size, color, autumn color)	Lustrous, mitten-shaped leaves; brilliant orange to scarlet autumn color; aromatic
Type of Foliage?	Dense, wide-branching	Type of Shade?	Good
HEIGHT:	50 feet	Type of Foliage?	Irregular, twisting branches
GROWTH RATE:	Fast	HEIGHT:	60 feet
FRUIT & FLOWERS:	Produces bright red and yellow flowers in summer, followed by 2-foot-long pods, green at first, then brownish black	LIFE EXPECTANCY:	75 years
SOIL:	Grows rapidly under many soil conditions	GROWTH RATE:	Moderate
PROPAGATION:	Sow ripe seeds in spring	FRUIT & FLOWERS:	Flowers inconspicuous; fruits small; bluish black berries with a red stalk
MISCELLANEOUS:	A beautiful street and lawn tree noted for brilliant flowers; tolerates salty spray of coastal environments	SOIL:	Grows best on sandy loam; tolerates dry, stony, and sandy soil as well as fertile lawn
		PROPAGATION:	Sow seeds when ripe or stratify for 3 months at 40° F. Suckers easily. Difficult to transplant wild trees
		MISCELLANEOUS:	Birds eat berries. Roots are used for aromatic stimulant and to flavor candy and scent soap. Fine tree for rural or suburban property; is particularly noted for upright shape, aromatic odor, and orange-scarlet fall coloring

COMMON NAME:	SILVERBELL	COMMON NAME:	SOURGUM (Black Tupelo)
LATIN NAME:	*Halesia carolina*	LATIN NAME:	*Nyssa sylvatica*
NORTHERNMOST ZONE OF GROWTH:	6	NORTHERNMOST ZONE OF GROWTH:	5
NATIVE TO:	West Virginia to Florida and Texas	NATIVE TO:	Eastern United States
TYPE OF TREE: Deciduous or Evergreen?	Deciduous	TYPE OF TREE: Deciduous or Evergreen?	Deciduous
Bark (color & texture)	Peeling	Bark (color & texture)	Thick, light brown-red
Leaves (shape, size, color, autumn color)	Broadleaf; 2–4 inches long, elliptic; yellow in fall	Leaves (shape, size, color, autumn color)	Dark green, lustrous, leathery 2–5 inches long; brilliant scarlet to orange autumn color
Type of Foliage?	Coarse, open	Type of Foliage?	Dense; pyramidal shape
HEIGHT:	30 feet	HEIGHT:	90 feet
LIFE EXPECTANCY:	50 years	LIFE EXPECTANCY:	100 years
GROWTH RATE:	Fast	GROWTH RATE:	Moderate
FRUIT & FLOWERS:	Produces white, bell-shaped flowers in clusters of 2–5 flowers in spring, followed by 2- or 4-winged pods, 2 inches long in fall	FRUIT & FLOWERS:	Sexes are separate; small blue berries borne in drupes in mid-summer
SOIL:	Grows best in well-drained soil; pH range 4.0–6.0	SOIL:	Grows best in moist, well-drained soil; tolerates swampy places. Prefers pH range 5.0–6.0
PROPAGATION:	Grows well from seed; stratify at 40° F. for 3 months, then sow	PROPAGATION:	Seeds may be sown when ripe. Takes 12 months to germinate. Self-sown in wild. Small trees can be transplanted successfully if balled and burlapped
MISCELLANEOUS:	Very hardy and useful for urban needs. Also mountain silverbell (*Halesia monticola*), 90 feet. Tennessee and North Carolina to Georgia. No serious insects or pests; flowers longer than *H. carolina*; foliage larger; all other facts the same	MISCELLANEOUS:	A fine ornamental tree

COMMON NAME:	**SPRUCE, COLORADO**	COMMON NAME:	**SPRUCE, WHITE**
LATIN NAME:	*Picea pungens*	LATIN NAME:	*Picea glauca*
NORTHERNMOST ZONE OF GROWTH:	2	NORTHERNMOST ZONE OF GROWTH:	2
NATIVE TO:	Rocky Mountains, Utah to New Mexico	NATIVE TO:	Canada and northern United States
TYPE OF TREE: Deciduous or Evergreen?	Evergreen	TYPE OF TREE: Deciduous or Evergreen?	Evergreen
Bark (color & texture)	Wrinkled, light ash-brown	Bark (color & texture)	Grayish, scaly
Leaves (shape, size, color, autumn color)	Needleleaf; stiff, green-blue, 1 inch long	Leaves (shape, size, color, autumn color)	Needleleaf; bluish green, ¾ inches long, sharp
Type of Foliage?	Dense; loses lower branches as it matures; pyramidal shape	HEIGHT:	90 feet
HEIGHT:	100 feet	LIFE EXPECTANCY:	50–60 years
LIFE EXPECTANCY:	50–75 years	GROWTH RATE:	Slow
GROWTH RATE:	Slow	FRUIT & FLOWERS:	Produces cones 1½–2 inches long
FRUIT & FLOWERS:	Produces cones 3–4 inches long (pale red-brown)	SOIL:	Prefers cool, moist, well-drained soil; tolerates slightly acid soil
SOIL:	Grows best on sandy loam; will tolerate slightly alkaline soil: pH range 4.0–6.5	PROPAGATION:	Stratify at 40° F. for 30–60 days; sow seed in spring
PROPAGATION:	Grows quickly from seed; does *not* tolerate severe heat and drought conditions. May be planted as far south as Missouri and Georgia. Tolerates saltwater spray and wind	MISCELLANEOUS:	Variety *albertina* recommended for city plantings. White spruce is very effective windbreak tree and forms strong shelter-belts when planted in all areas including windy Great Plains
MISCELLANEOUS:	Susceptible to spruce gall aphids and red spider, yet recommended as hardy tree for urban areas in recent survey of American Horticultural Society. Variety *glauca* (*blue* Colorado spruce) does well in seashore plantings and is official state tree of Utah and Colorado		

COMMON NAME:	SWEETGUM
LATIN NAME:	*Liquidambar styraciflua*
NORTHERNMOST ZONE OF GROWTH:	6
NATIVE TO:	Eastern United States
TYPE OF TREE: Deciduous or Evergreen?	Deciduous
Kind of Trunk?	Central, tapering
Bark (color & texture)	Red-brown; corky
Leaves (shape, size, color, autumn color)	Broadleaf; star-shaped, 4–7 inches long; autumn color is brilliant scarlet, orange and purple
Type of Foliage?	Dense; pyramidal shape
HEIGHT:	125 feet
LIFE EXPECTANCY:	75 years
GROWTH RATE:	Fast
FRUIT & FLOWERS:	Produces round, horned balls of fruit, 1-inch diameter in fall; may persist through winter
SOIL:	Grows well on moist, well-drained soil; does not tolerate alkaline soil well; frost resistant; pH range 6.0–6.5
PROPAGATION:	Sow seed in spring; 2 years to germinate; transplants easily
MISCELLANEOUS:	Resin used in chewing gum, wood for making boxes, crates and furniture. Often chosen as street tree for hardiness, interesting leaves and bark, and brilliant autumn color. Also good parkway and highway planting

COMMON NAME:	TANOAK
LATIN NAME:	*Lithocarpus densiflorus*
NORTHERNMOST ZONE OF GROWTH:	7B
NATIVE TO:	Southern Oregon, California
TYPE OF TREE: Deciduous or Evergreen?	Evergreen
Kind of Trunk?	Short
Bark (color & texture)	Ridged
Leaves (shape, size, color, autumn color)	Broadleaf; leathery, 1½–4 inches long, smooth, dark green above, rusty blue-gray, hairy beneath
Type of Shade?	Good
Type of Foliage?	Open, dense; narrowly pyramidal shape
HEIGHT:	75 feet
LIFE EXPECTANCY:	100 years or more
GROWTH RATE:	Slow
FRUIT & FLOWERS:	Light green, 2–4-inch-long catkins of flowers, followed by acorn 1 inch long (acorns take 2 years to mature)
SOIL:	Prefers rich, moist, well-drained soil
PROPAGATION:	Sow seed in spring
MISCELLANEOUS:	Bark of this tree at one time used in tanning process—hence the name. Useful only in native habitat

SWEETGUM

SWEETGUM

COMMON NAME:	**TULIP TREE**
LATIN NAME:	*Liriodendron tulipifera*
NORTHERNMOST ZONE OF GROWTH:	5
NATIVE TO:	Eastern United States
TYPE OF TREE: Deciduous or Evergreen?	Deciduous
Kind of Trunk?	Straight
Bark (color & texture)	Gray-brown, furrowed
Leaves (shape, size, color, autumn color)	Broadleaf; long-stemmed, 4-lobed, bright green; autumn color yellow
Type of Shade?	Great
Type of Foliage?	Dense, massive branching; pyramidal shape in forests; broad in open areas
HEIGHT:	150 feet
LIFE EXPECTANCY:	100 years or more
GROWTH RATE:	Fast
FRUIT & FLOWERS:	Green-yellow-orange tuliplike flowers produced in mid-June, followed by conelike aggregate that falls apart when mature
SOIL:	Has narrow pH range, 6.0–6.5
PROPAGATION:	Stratify seed at 40° F. for 3 months, then sow. Give it plenty of room to grow in (75 feet). Easily transplanted
MISCELLANEOUS:	A huge, ornamental tree, good choice for parks and very large gardens. The more narrow variety 'Fastigiatum' may be considered for street planting. Official state tree of Tennessee and Indiana and "unofficial" (by popular concensus) tree of North Carolina and Kentucky

COMMON NAME:	**WAX-MYRTLE**
LATIN NAME:	*Myrica cerifera*
NORTHERNMOST ZONE OF GROWTH:	9
NATIVE TO:	New Jersey to Florida and Texas
TYPE OF TREE: Deciduous or Evergreen?	Evergreen
Bark (color & texture)	Thin, smooth, gray-green
Leaves (shape, size, color, autumn color)	Broadleaf; yellow-green, 1½–4 inches long, serrated; aromatic when crushed
Type of Foliage?	Open and irregular
HEIGHT:	36 feet
GROWTH RATE:	Fast
FRUIT & FLOWERS:	Sexes are separate; small, inconspicuous flowers, followed by small, gray, waxy berries in fall and winter (in drupes)
SOIL:	Able to grow in dry, sterile soils; tolerates salt spray
PROPAGATION:	Remove wax from seed by soaking in warm water; stratify for 3 months at 40° F. and sow
MISCELLANEOUS:	A good small tree for garden. Twigs, leaves and fruit intensely aromatic

TULIP TREE

COMMON NAME:	**WILLOW, GOLDEN**
LATIN NAME:	*Salix alba* 'vitellina'
NORTHERNMOST ZONE OF GROWTH:	2
NATIVE TO:	Northern Africa and western Asia
TYPE OF TREE: Deciduous or Evergreen?	Deciduous
Leaves (shape, size, color, autumn color)	Broadleaf; yellow twig color
Type of Foliage?	Loose, open, graceful
HEIGHT:	75 feet
FRUIT & FLOWERS:	Sexes separate; fruits are capsules, containing cottony masses of seeds
SOIL:	Prefers moist soil
PROPAGATION:	Sow seed as soon as ripe
MISCELLANEOUS:	An extremely hardy tree for urban conditions, according to recent survey by American Horticultural Society. Excellent tree for landscape effects, with its yellowish gold twig color

COMMON NAME:	**WILLOW, WEEPING**
LATIN NAME:	*Salix babylonica*
NORTHERNMOST ZONE OF GROWTH:	6
NATIVE TO:	China
TYPE OF TREE: Deciduous or Evergreen?	Deciduous
Kind of Trunk?	Bulky
Bark (color & texture)	Heavily ridged, furrowed, dark brown to black
Leaves (shape, size, color, autumn color)	Broadleaf; narrow, lanceolate, 3–6 inches long, smooth, glossy, grayish
Type of Shade?	Good
Type of Foliage?	Fine textured, long pendulous branches
HEIGHT:	30–50 feet
GROWTH RATE:	Fast
FRUIT & FLOWERS:	Sexes separate; fruit capsules that break open to release cottony masses of tiny seeds in early spring
SOIL:	Grows best in moist soil. Grows almost prostrate on ground in its first year
PROPAGATION:	Sow seed immediately when ripe, as vitality is quickly lost. Cuttings root very easily
MISCELLANEOUS:	Like all willows, is fast-growing and weak-wooded, often damaged by snow, ice, and windstorms. The roots invade sewers. Nevertheless, popular for its graceful shape

WEEPING WILLOW

COMMON NAME:	**YELLOWWOOD**
LATIN NAME:	*Cladrastis lutea*
NORTHERNMOST ZONE OF GROWTH:	3B
NATIVE TO:	North Carolina, Kentucky, Tennessee
TYPE OF TREE: Deciduous or Evergreen?	Deciduous
Kind of Trunk?	Short
Bark (color & texture)	Smooth, yellowish light gray
Leaves (shape, size, color, autumn color)	Broadleaf; 5–11 leaflets to a stem; autumn color yellow-orange
Type of Shade?	Good
Type of Foliage?	Dense; rounded shape
HEIGHT:	50 feet
LIFE EXPECTANCY:	Short
GROWTH RATE:	Fast
FRUIT & FLOWERS:	Pendulous clusters of yellow-white fragrant flowers produced in early June, followed by thin pods containing 4–6 seeds
SOIL:	Grows well on rich, well-drained soil; deep root makes it drought-resistant
PROPAGATION:	Soak seed in 190° F. water overnight, stratify for 3 months at 40° F., then sow. Deep-rooted at maturity. Prune only in fall to prevent "bleeding"
MISCELLANEOUS:	Yellow dye may be obtained from wood. Is desirable ornamental because of rounded shape, fragrant summer blossoms, and lovely autumn color

COMMON NAME:	**YEW, JAPANESE**
LATIN NAME:	*Taxus cuspidata*
NORTHERNMOST ZONE OF GROWTH:	5
NATIVE TO:	Japan and Korea
TYPE OF TREE: Deciduous or Evergreen?	Evergreen
Kind of Trunk?	Spreading, upright, single
Bark (color & texture)	Reddish brown
Leaves (shape, size, color, autumn color)	Needleleaf; 1-inch long, dark leaves; branching from bottom of trunk
Type of Foliage?	Dense; irregular shape
HEIGHT:	50 feet
FRUIT & FLOWERS:	Small flowers, followed by red, fleshy berries containing one seed
SOIL:	Grows in wide range of soil conditions; pH range 6.0–6.5
PROPAGATION:	Stratify 5 months at room temperature, 3 months at 40° F., sow
MISCELLANEOUS:	Very hardy, even in trying city conditions. Excellent narrow-leaved evergreen for ornamental purposes

YELLOWWOOD

JAPANESE YEW

JAPANESE YEW

COMMON NAME: **ZELKOVA**

LATIN NAME: *Zelkova serrata*

NATIVE TO: Japan

TYPE OF TREE:
Deciduous or
Evergreen?   Deciduous

Kind of Trunk?   Short

Bark (color &   Smooth, gray bark, orange-
texture)   yellow when mature

Leaves (shape, size,   Broadleaf; 2–5 inches long;
color, autumn color)   yellow to russet fall color

Type of Foliage? Dense; broad round-head

HEIGHT: 90 feet

LIFE
EXPECTANCY: 50–75 years

GROWTH RATE: Fast

SOIL: Grows best on well-drained to
                  dry soil

PROPAGATION: Sow seed as soon as ripe

MISCELLANEOUS: Wood used in Japan for ex-
                  pensive furniture, lacquerware,
                  etc. Similar in habit to the
                  American elm, and frequent
                  substitute for it. This hardy tree
                  should be planted more fre-
                  quently on streets and lawns

ZELKOVA